Wrong Face in the Mirror

Lolo Houbein migrated to Australia in 1958 from Holland and settled in South Australia. She studied Arts at Adelaide University, graduating with a BA in Classics, Australian Literature and Anthropology. She also spent a year doing postgraduate work in Papua New Guinea. She has had a variety of jobs, ranging from cleaner, secretary, and research assistant to ESL teacher, herb farmer and importer of Tibetan handicrafts. Lolo Houbein has published a collection of short fiction, *Everything is Real*, and her novel, *Walk a Barefoot Road*, won the ABC-Bicentennial Fiction Award.

An earlier version of this work was awarded the Dirk Hartog Literary Award in 1988 and was published in a Dutch translation by Balans, Amsterdam in 1988 under the title *Vreemdeling in de Spiegel: Autobiografie van een Nederlandse Emigrante*.

Wrong Face
in the Mirror

AN AUTOBIOGRAPHY OF RACE AND IDENTITY

Lolo Houbein

University of Queensland Press

First published in English 1990 by University of Queensland Press
Box 42, St Lucia, Queensland 4067 Australia

Typeset by University of Queensland Press
Printed in Australia by The Book Printer, Melbourne

Distributed in the USA and Canada by
International Specialized Book Services, Inc.,
5602 N.E. Hassalo Street, Portland, Oregon 97213-3640

Creative writing program assisted
by the Literature Board of the
Australia Council, the Federal Government's
arts funding and advisory body

Cataloguing in Publication Data

National Library of Australia

Houbein, Lolo, 1934– .
 Wrong face in the mirror.

 1. Houbein, Lolo, 1934– . — Biography. 2. Authors,
 Australian — 20th century — Biography. 3. Immigrants —
 Australia — Biography. 4. Dutch — Australia — Biography.
 I. Title.

A823.3

ISBN 0 7022 2248 8

Contents

1
One of nine lives

When it comes down to basics, I haven't got much personality. When I am by myself I never feel irritated, annoyed or frustrated, depressed or happy. In fact, I hardly notice I'm there. I am only really aware of what I am doing — writing, weaving, gardening, making sounds — or what I am doing things with — plants, earth, wool, paper, colours . . . and other people.

What people call personality only rears its personable countenance when in the company of other personalities, and then mainly in an adjusting capacity. When I'm with a meek person, I adjust the situation by being firmly assertive, to compensate and get things moving; when with aggressive characters I counteract them by being calm and peaceful and tolerant. In the company of intellectuals I often revert to my rural, philosophical self and when with rural, philosophical individuals I prefer to listen mostly and contribute just the occasional intellectual observation when we get bogged down. When amongst the stingy types I tend to be moderately generous, but when with spendthrifts I change to temperate habits.

In all such situations and their endless variations, I

am. I do not act. I play no roles. I merely try to adjust the situation, the atmosphere, the conversation, to a golden mean of harmonious proportions by being, for the duration of the event or encounter, the opposite of whatever the counterparts offer too much of in my perception.

Hence, if a scoresheet were kept by the hundreds of people who think they know or knew me well enough to give a thumbnail character sketch, not one account would tally with another. I know from rumours, loose-lipped references and intuition that the profile stretches from one extreme to the other: from saint to sinner, from guru to goofer, from peace personified to provocative pugnacity, from sublime honesty to ridiculous caginess, from killing kindness to cold callousness. Whereas some people feel the need to be reintroduced to me every time we meet, others find me so memorable they recommend me for the *Who's Who*.

None of all this has anything to do with any personality of mine, but only with the adjustments I made — in words, deeds or attitudes — to their own state of mind at the time we met.

This lack of personality on my behalf threatens to defeat the purpose of writing an autobiography. It wouldn't really be about me, but about everyone who knew me. The other complication is that I'm the cat with nine lives. No matter how I push and pull and pummel my material, I see no hope of fitting all my adjustment experiences into one book that would simultaneously show me as a product of my times "in the round".

But perhaps herein lies the solution. Having already spent eight of my nine lives, why not spend the ninth writing eight autobiographies? Not eight accounts of chronological periods up till now though. That would not sufficiently reveal the undercurrents at work, the karmic links, the flights of imagination which landed me on solid ground. Nor would it do justice to the crazy patchwork created by history in the making, which cross-stitched erratically all over the nice regular pattern I was working on.

Instead of eight chapters called "Childhood", "Adolescence", "Migration" and the like, I am planning to write eight accounts of my half of this century, each with its own "leitmotiv" to show that, depending from what standpoint you look back over your shoulder, you see a different landscape — or should I say "lifescape" — every time.

Although I do not want to appear elusive, neither do I want to stand by my opinions of yesteryear until death do us part and no one can quote me on what I say today in 1999 without a sound knowledge of my life and times. A sage — or a wit — once said that to be perfect is to have changed often and I have been aware enough of my imperfections not to hold on to all my cherished illusions.

People live at least two lives, an inner and an outer one, because society dictates that whatever it is that moves us remains largely hidden so as not to complicate "reality". But many find their lives so inextricably rooted in the inner life that it colours all aspects of daily existence. I realise that after living eight lives in just half a century, I have become tired of hiding my sources, or what I imagine my sources to be. I want to reveal what it is that stirs me into action and not hide behind a fictional character.

Instead of chapter headings I now have a list of titles to cover my lifescape from the points of view of my varied career: my hop-skip, never-ending education; health, and how to proceed despite the lack of it; the carnival of people who moved through my life and their influence on it; and the countries through which I've travelled and the cultures I've absorbed.

One day I will write my life purely from the aspect of religion and my life philosophy; of how an animistic child followed drums that no one else could hear and came to discoveries that every mystic understands, but which still stand outside the experience of society as we have made it, because we have made it so.

And then there is love. I may never write about that. To me it is still the greatest secret in the universe. Not a mystery. A secret. That's different. No one knows love in its entirety, yet everyone speaks of it. We just keep trying because we've had a glimpse here or there. Mind you, the trying can be very rewarding. But our earth does not seem to be the sort of stage for love in all its magnitude. Not yet, anyway.

Lastly, there is the life to be written up from the muddy feeding ground of race and culture, or race and identity. I will take that approach in this, the first of my eight autobiographies. It is right that it should be the first one, for the peoples of the world joined forces to make me. Not only genetically, as I arose like a pale vapour from the human soup stirred by invasions, persecutions and migrations, but also culturally, as I tenaciously reached out to forever-receding ideals, instilled in me by my ancestors from Abraham to Genghis Khan, to a sixteen-century court painter and a string of musicians. Wending my way through culture after culture, either *in situ* or by association with their representatives, also on the road to other horizons.

This autobiography pivots on the great 1958 migration, when I convinced husband, children and authorities with my reasons for leaving the land of my birth to go to the other side of the world in order to get closer to where I sensed my origins lay. I am less certain about their location now, thirty years later. The question is, do I need certainty? And the answer to that may well be a resounding "No!"

2

Gathering the pieces of the puzzle

It is time to report my auspicious birth on 7 January 1934 in a street in Hilversum, Holland, named after that scoundrel of a stargazer, Galileo. Scoundrel, because he stole ideas from others without acknowledgment, especially from the shy Johann Kepler, to blow his own trumpet. But at least he lifted his gaze above mundane things and, as such, his street was a proper place for me to see the light of day. Although I did not *see* until 8 January, because my birth took place at children's bed-time, seven o'clock in the evening. This habit, of often doing the opposite from the expected and appearing in places at the most unexpected times, has been a feature of my life. It accounts for much of my sense of dis-location.

When the curious-minded with eager fingers rip open the much blemished skin of Mother Earth to seek a con-nection with a past they do not feel unless they have tangible evidence before them, the earth sometimes reveals remains of peoples and events in the place where they lived and happened, instead of somewhere else where trade, war, famine, the plague or the sheer lust for adventure had transported them. Such remains, in the places where they belong, are said to be *in situ*.

People get excited by things which prove to be in place. People's aim in life is to remain in place, or, if they weren't born so lucky, to find the mystical place where they might perhaps belong and stay.

For a human being to be born in place, to be born *in situ*, it is not just necessary that the conjunctions of the heavenly bodies are of the most auspicious kind, but that trade, war, famine, the plague and the sheer lust for adventure have in no way affected those destined to be the caretakers of the new being for at least a full cycle of seasons. For such is the minimum period for a being that has died to shed the attachments to the old life and seek rebirth, albeit within the matrix of its potentialities, or, if you like, its karma.

Nor should the displacements of trade, war, famine, the plague and the sheer lust for adventure afflict them for the duration of a decade and a half after that event. And even then . . . even then . . .

There are now on the face of the earth too many children who peer into crowds, hoping to spot the features of an unknown ancestor, or a gesture giving away a secret code of behaviour they remember across the gulf of death and reappearance, or a skin which bears a hue not wholly the same or altogether different from the one they have been given in the redistribution of physical attributes.

There are black children who feel white and white children who feel black and brown children who feel yellow and yellow children who feel bronze. They react passionately to strange music in their early years before the sense impressions of the new environment, in which they sense they do not wholly belong, clog up their perceptions.

They sing haunting melodies when left to their own devices, in attempts to call up the spirits of lives lost but still remembered in the magical hour of dusk or before the new day breaks into memory-shattering light. They dance exotic patterns, draped in sheets and curtains, knowing that there are gods who are pleased by such displays. They worship the sun or the trees or the full moon in places where they are expected to worship the red star, the cross or the crescent moon. They embrace the rain as though it were a sibling and secretly kiss the earth while a storm rages. They hear prophecies in the ordinary phrases of plain messages.

They become aware, by the age at which they are made to attend places of scholarship, that they are not *in situ*. They soon nurture a private dream that there *is* a place where they *could* be *in situ* and *will* be so if they search diligently and never lose the dreaming. They cannot wait to grow up and they will do anything to prove that in fact they have; no matter their numerical age, height or the lack of ripeness in their voice, or any such purely physical ploy to keep them from exploring.

One who never lost the dreaming was Jopie, the child I then was. In the echo of my name I heard another one on the wind in a cacophony of ordinary noises, mixed with the strains of supple strings which nobody else could hear.

When the first dream ever dreamed — and ever since retained — intimated that there were links between death and rebirth, companions who got lost in the fog but whom I did not altogether lose sight of with my third eye, crudely sealed though it was by the wax of mother's womb . . . when this first dream was persistently shattered by the impact of new apparitions and appearances, called mama, grandpa, aunt and teddy-bear, then the lifelong search had begun.

So what is my race? What my culture? Which begs the question: "What is race?" and "What is culture?" Not that definitions have not been forged for these concepts, but do they fit my situation? I constantly have to draw my attention back to beginnings, of a sort.

There was my mother. Small, with chestnut hair. The second child in a family of four. Her parents, a petite, straight-nosed, eagle-eyed, pretty dressmaker, small of stature, deft of finger, possessing the gift of humour, and a statuesque, hawk-nosed, handsome man with magnificent bone structure and dark curly hair, who dealt in antiques and second-hand wares, but spent his energies in pursuing philosophies that were to save humankind from itself. He espoused everything in turn, from theosophism to revolutionism, to communist socialism when it was still new, fresh and untested.

The other siblings, in order of appearance, were my Uncle Wim, Uncle Frits and Aunt Truus, and they all had dark hair, though their eyes ranged from grey-green to blue-grey. Uncle Wim became a printer and what is now called a hobby farmer. I think the first paid the bills, but the second definitely fed the family. Uncle Frits was a musician, playing the violin, saxophone, clarinet and trombone. Aunt Truus also became a musician, playing violin, percussion and singing. And my mother became a typist and bookkeeper who played the violin in her spare time. None of them, as far as I can see over my shoulder, took up the political struggle for justice to the poor and for peace instead of war that their father had pursued. That consciousness skipped one generation to lodge in my unprejudiced mind, and, following this pattern, my children are doubly shy and my hope for the continuation of grandfather's line lies in my grandsons.

I don't know when these maternal grandparents of mine got their divorce, but I think it was before my birth. Grandma, or Opoe, as she was called in Dutch, then married the widowed father of Uncle Frits's fiancé, another Jopie, but blond as a Renaissance angel and also a violinist and saxophone player. Thus, Opoe became her own son's mother-in-law as well as her daughter-in-law's stepmother. My stepgrandfather, or Opa as I knew him, was a man of short stature and hence became "little Opa" as against "tall Opa", who, after a spell in a nursing home for a heart complaint, set up house with a red-headed nurse twenty years his junior. She was a widow of a defrocked priest, who had died of the Spanish flu after World War I, together with their only child, a little girl. In retrospect, I can just see how people's verdict of the wrath of God on her marriage turned her to support my grandfather's atheistic ideologies.

Aunt Bep, as I called her, brought a discriminatory quality to my placement in the family, as she often treated me as a small adult, something I responded to very well. She was also the only one in the family who told me straight-out when I behaved insensitively or carelessly towards others, especially her beloved defacto husband Frederik, my "tall Opa", whom she nursed for years through his heart's weak spells and whose political ideas she fervently shared. She had red hair and fierce blue eyes and a sister who coached opera singers in Italian. Thanks to her I sat, as a shy toddler, on a mute opera singer's lap, looking through tall Opa's window at the life in the street, while the family argued in noisy Dutch over Sunday afternoon politics. Being a guest of Bep's sister, over from Italy for an engagement with the Dutch opera, he couldn't understand the language, and I couldn't understand the content. His name sounded something like Resquel Yun and he ate preserved ginger every day to help his voice and never smoked at all.

The other in-law was Aunt Saar, Uncle Wim's third

wife, who gave him his three children. On Aunt Truus's side there was her first husband Uncle Henk, an Amsterdam breadbaker, then Uncle Fred, a pianist, and lastly Uncle Jo, who worked in the public service. I'm sorry to say that none of them lasted. I liked them all. I liked all our in-laws and they had a great bearing on my sense of identity, because for several years I was the only child in my generation in our family. The in-laws padded out the small family of two grandparents plus four offspring into a sprawling extended family, in which I floated rather like a small wildflower in a bowl of heady punch.

Opoe's marriage to "little Opa" brought his other children into the family as well. There was Uncle Jan, also a baker, who had been engaged for ten years to a wonderfully large, warm, generous and exuberant woman called Stien, who lived with her parents on a farm. There was Aunt Trees, a filmstar-like beauty with platinum hair and the sweetest of smiles, who had married another Uncle Frits, who was tall, dark and handsome, had a harelip and owned a shoestore in a small provincial town. They were visibly and eternally in love. They usually held hands and brought me milk chocolate when they visited. The one I saw least of was Aunt Rini, who'd married above her station and hence lived in a villa in our hometown of Hilversum. She too, like Jopie and Trees, was blond, beautiful and elegant. None seemed to be daughters of my comfortable, pipe-smoking, ash-dropping little step-opa and later I wondered what their mother must have been like.

Little Opa became, in many ways, the centre of my life. He and Opoe lived next door, only a thin wall dividing our first-storey flats. He always had time for me, saved up riddles and stories, took me shopping and let me play with his gilded watch chain, presented to him on his twenty-fifth anniversary as a master cigarmaker. He never showed impatience with me and once, when he took me fishing, he merely decided not to repeat the exercise, but never blamed me for talking and chasing the fish away.

He and tall Opa were the main male figures in my childhood years, living two streets apart, referring to each other as "him over there", with a scornful toss of the head, or as "that man" by tall Opa and "your mother's papa" by little Opa. Little Opa was a bright red socialist and tall Opa was a hammer-and-sickle communist, but to whoever thinks they might have had more in common than a wife, I can only say that nothing could be more erroneous.

These four dark siblings, they were talented. They not only played music but sang together, did sketches, embroideries and read books, and Uncle Wim became quietly skilful with plants and small animals.

It is time to admit I did have a father. It was he who was responsible for my blondness, my long legs, my pale eyes and my Mongolian eyelids. But as he didn't enter my imagination until I was thirteen, let's leave him till later. At this early stage he is no influence beyond his genetic input and that only becomes interesting in the light of my later development.

I was not content to sit in the playpen. Behind the French doors was a tiny patio surrounded by a moss-covered, damp stone wall, above which a strip of sky was just visible. That strip of sky was full of movement. I wanted to know what was behind the wall that caused the movement of the colours and the occasional winged creature. At barely one year of age, I was frustrated. I remember looking with utter boredom at the half dozen (not that I could count then) wooden balls on a rod, stuck in the playpen bars, painted red, blue and yellow. I remember thinking what else I could do with them that I hadn't done already. I gnawed them until my jaws hurt, then fell back on my bottom on the yellow checkered blanket with the thin black and brown lines and proceeded to throw all my toys out of the playpen. No doubt I thought I was doing something original that I had personally invented. Then there was nothing but the blanket and to this day I can see its weave in my mind's eye. It was a twill. Maybe it stimulated my interest in weaving and one day I may warp my loom to reproduce its comforting pattern again.

The first faintly familiar face I beheld in the crowd, as I toddled on Mama's hand through the village main street, was expressionless and wrinkled in its entirety, like expensive tissue paper. Slant eyes like wounds that would not heal, not yet devoid of the glowing embers of a once steady fire. The blackness of hair perched over a wooden box containing pins and buttons, razor blades and peanuts, sticks of liquorice . . . And apart from all those, the very smells and textures of a cruelly mislaid memory store.

Unable to speak my mother's language as yet, I cried silently inside my head, where my newly acquired agonies lodged themselves as a chain of linked concepts.

"Oh mother, my heart broke in splintered recognition. The colour scheme is out of place in this wintry bleakness. I must break the leash. My small fingers rip out of your constraining palm to touch in the flesh this first fragment of the lost companions from the lost world, out of which I was catapulted not only by my own death but who knows, through a journey by a pregnant woman many lives removed from you!

"Give me! Give me a cent, high mother, your face so

white above me, yet your hair almost as dark as his. Slim genetic remnant linking you with my losses. One cent to buy peanuts from the Chinaman to forge a speechless message where my borrowed language does not match his wondrous tongue which he withholds from foreigners like us.

"His smile turns on! A quickening of the settled glow in those slit scars and he is mine! First pulsating piece of the prenatal puzzle — from the middle or the edge is not important yet."

Later I learned that the Chinaman sold his wares in our "cold frog land" (as the Dutch called their country of birth when the weather got the better of them) because he wanted to earn enough money to be buried in China. This infinitely sad goal filled me with puzzlement: why hadn't he stayed in China then? But, since he was here, I was also filled with compassion and insisted on contributing to his funeral fund every time we passed by, buying liquorice or peanuts from his tray. His mute smile and bony hands reminded me of unspeakable things that my growing awareness of the past told me had not happened to me, yet I knew of them.

One day he was gone. No doubt to be buried in China. No Chinaman would die on foreign soil, Opoe told me. It seemed a good recipe for eternal life. My fascination with the Chinamen remained until all of them suddenly disappeared from the streets, together with the Gypsies and eventually the Jews. Holland was invaded and soldiers of pure Germanic blood took over the school building where I had hoped to spend the next six years with the same schoolmaster who had taught my mother what she knew of the world during that other war from 1914 to 1918.

Thus, the concept of race and the existence of differing cultures were part of the life in the streets until the idea of a super-race obliterated all that was colourful, virile and capable of producing a society that was tolerant and at peace with diversity.

Before tall Opa met Aunt Bep, he was living with me and Mama in the little house in Sun-and-Moon Street in the ancient heart of the town. It is still there.

Here I first became aware of the technical wonders of the twentieth century and to me they were like growling demons ready to crush me, devour me. I recall tall Opa shaking his fist at the strip of sky outside the window as it trembled ready to burst and shouting: "Go away, naughty aeroplane, you frighten little Jopie."

Jopie, diminutive for Johanna, was almost the family's synonym for womanhood. Opoe, Mama and I were Johannas, as was Uncle Frits's wife. I didn't like the name and made a few attempts at a name change before my real name came to me at age twelve. But that is running ahead of time.

At an early age I was initiated into the rituals of mid-winter-month December and learned this famous children's jingle:

There is a saint
who lives in Spain
Saint Nikolaas is his name . . .

Through the weeks before the good saint's birthday he is said to ride a dappled horse over the rooftops of houses where the good children live. Furthermore, he resides in shoe shops, department stores and corner bakeries. He is a saint of miraculous multiple appearances. His image graces the window of luxury boutiques and buildings devoted to the cult of money alike.

It was the unwanted purchase of blister-producing

shoes for hated winter weather which led me to his holiness. He sat on a platform against a wall of shoeboxes in one thousand sizes. In picture books of real worlds, children wear no shoes.

"Why can't I be real, oh mother! Set my feet free at least . . .''

The saint might not be real either. His beard was made of cotton wool, golden staff pocked with torn paper, his holy mitre hollow and his scarlet cloak too faded to instil confidence. Behind him, like a shadow, stood his helper Black Pieter, realness manifest in the whites of eyes which stared at me through the crowd of children born *in situ*, children who knew how to behave in situations like this.

I bypassed the saint for the black man-child. I walked past the saint to the sinner.

Stopped once more by language I turned around. "Why is he black, mother?'' The child's translation of the situation confronts a long-suffering parent with the latest unspoken accusation: "Why am I not black like my brother?''

Someone from the crowd answered: "Because he doesn't wash!'' Fungous clusters of people let their senseless laughter ripple tenderly around the alien white child who had asked the wrong question. But rising above it sounded the full throttle black laughter from behind the mock saint's cassock.

I stood lost. Lost in first love — renewed love, recovered love. I declared I would not wash until the saint's birthday had been celebrated and he had taken his black sinner back to Spain. However this act of identification with a new ideal did not turn me dark overnight, but instead left me grubby pink and white as usual.

By the time the saint and the sinner returned the next

year, I had been made aware of the deceit of their costumes and makeup. Only the love lingered, but it had no object to fasten itself on.

Apart from aeroplanes I turned out to be scared of vacuum cleaners and electric hairclippers. I was delighted by radio however, eager to meet the little people inside the box. Once left alone, I crept behind the corner table to look into the open back of the radio and saw nothing but coloured wires and silver fittings. At another opportunity a children's choir was singing and I repeated the exercise, convinced that there had to be a race of little children who ran along these coloured wires inside the box as they sang old Dutch nursery rhymes. My mother's explanation of voices coming through the air I dismissed out of hand as the usual adult fantasy, without any logic or credibility.

Newspapers began to intrigue me for the spell they were able to cast on adults. What was there in those pages smelling of printing ink that kept Mama, Opoe and both Opas glued to the things they called words, mumbling: "Not now, child . . . let me read the paper first, then I will play with you."

Yet, the next day these same papers were burnt in the stove, wrapped around vegetable peelings, used to polish dusty windows or wipe the floor, line drawers and shelves, stuffed in shoes during wet weather, sewn in cotton covers for the beds in winter, given away to the ragman, or simply put in the rubbish bin.

Unable to read, I could only study the newspaper's photographs, fuzzy black and white pictures of unrelated subjects, and badger Mama with queries. Whatever was learned that way about the country, the world, the universe, was melted down to that instinctive body of knowledge and common sense most people seem to gather before and during their formal education and on which they build their adult predilections and prejudices.

Only one photograph is remembered after half a century. It showed an impish, yet serious, face of a child of my own age wearing a pointed pixie hat, wrapped in a voluminous garment and seated on a pile of square cushions upon what appeared to be a throne.

"Who is this child, Mama?"

Mama read the caption, then interpreted it for me.

"He is a god-king."

"What is that?"

"The people in his country, which is called Tibet, think he is a god and he is also their king." Mama, although tolerant of other people's beliefs, was not given to propping up what she deemed to be superstitions.

"Where is Tibet?"

"In Asia. In the high mountains. It's very far away."

"What else does it say?"

"It says he is four years old."

That did it. It lodged the face under the cap, above the robe and cushion, upon the throne, forever in my mind.

"Just as old as I am . . ." The inner question was: "Why is he a god and a king and I am Jopie, if we're both four years old?" I felt I had failed myself. I resolved also to be a god and a king, or a queen, if not at four then at some later date. How to achieve this was at present a mystery, but my conviction was so instant and resolute that I trusted that time and growing up would reveal the mechanics by which this ambition could be fulfilled.

The four-year-old, fourteenth Dalai Lama was lodged

for future reference in the "growing up" compartment of my memory. Growing up, I knew, would solve a lot of riddles. Waiting for it was at times frustrating, but I was gathering the pieces of the puzzle of grown-up life in the meantime.

About this time I was introduced to a race of little people through a storybook called *Pikkie Duimelot* by M.A. van Oven-van Doorn, with lots of wonderful little drawings by Freddie Langeler (published by G.B. van Goor-Zonen, Den Haag). Not that either author or illustrator was important to me then, but their creations certainly were. The pixie family in the forest at last presented to me life as I knew it really was. They regarded humans as destructive intruders, led a life of rustic simplicity in burrows and moss huts, using the products of the forest for their sustenance, clothing, utensils and dwellings. They had few duties and many adventures and operated with a code of behaviour I innately understood: mutually caring, inquisitive of other species but tolerant and endlessly resourceful and fun-loving.

Soon there was a second volume on the market, and then a third, and my family obtained these for me, no doubt under pressure. But, as I had to have stories read to me every night and part of the books was paid for by coupons from the cooperative grocery store, they probably didn't put up much resistance.

The stories in the pixie books sank in deeply. I walked through the days looking for places where pixies, and fairies too, might live. In the cavities of Mr Steen's brick garden wall? Under the veronica bush? In the hollows of the old trees in Oaktree Lane? And why not under the carved wooden gables of the little houses in Meteor

Street? I knew they were about, even if they kept themselves invisible.

One rainy Sunday Mama gave me some good white paper and a new packet of coloured pencils. Rainy days sometimes moved Mama to dip into a box of treasures she harboured on the top shelf of the linen press.

I could hardly have chosen to draw anything other than what I did, my mind was so constantly occupied with it.

I drew red toadstools with white dots and fat trunks in which windows and doors were cut out. Pixies pushed wheelbarrows made of acorns. Bluebells nodded high above their peaked red caps. Fairies were hanging garlands in a tree and pixie children were playing ball with a horse chestnut, its pale patch left blank in my depiction of its deep brown skin.

"Finished!" I shouted, face glowing with creative zest, eyes shining with satisfaction for something that had turned out the way I had seen it in my mind's eyes.

"But that is wonderful!" cried Mama and this time I knew she spoke the truth.

Mama sent the drawing away to a competition run by the cooperative grocery's children's club. Weeks later a parcel addressed to me arrived in the mail. It contained a thousand-piece puzzle of a sailing ship on the high seas, an element for which I had not the slightest liking, never having seen the Big Puddle. I had won second prize in my category of the drawing competition. My delight about the unexpected honour and receiving my first mail was surpassed by the amazing insight that adults evidently believed in pixies too. I had assumed that they didn't because my adults were so non-committal about pixies and spoke of them, when prodded, with such obvious lack of knowledge. But to give my drawing a prize, adults too must have been aware of the existence of that other world. To me, adults were one solid block of homogeneous opinion, just as, to some adults, children are a multitude of spoilsports, devoid of individuality.

Adults had at last confirmed my world. I knew then that I had begun to doubt it myself. But no longer . . .

As I grew into the stories of Pikkie Duimelot, his relatives and friends, I resolved to join the pixies in the forest one day.

Late summer sun extracts fragrances of nectar from the heather, just about to turn deep purple for its autumn display. Even hot sand has its own scent and to lie in a sandpan, nose pressed flat against the ground, was my idea of an afternoon in the heath. Not that I'd lie there for long. Only minutes. Then I am up, collecting twigs and stones and pinecones from the edge of the forest, to build little dwellings with miniature gardens for the pixies and fairies that inhabit these wild places. My whole time in the heather is activity. Yet, when away from it, I remember the heather fields by the smell of hot sand, the press of my body against it, the warm sun on my back and the sonorous hum of a solitary bumblebee.

When I was very small, Mama would put me in the cane seat on the back of her bicycle and pedal to the heather, where, with the aid of a small picnic basket, I could be kept busy with my own play while Mama read a book. But I outgrew the cane seat and Mama found it too far to walk, carrying picnic and book in the hot sun . . .

So I had permission to go with the children of the street and neighbourhood. I didn't really belong to the group, although I knew them all. They sought me out when there were not enough children for a game, but they seldom came to stand at my garden gate to entice me to come out by calling in chorus "Jo-o-o-pie! Jo-o-o-pie!", as much as a dozen times, as they did in front of other children's houses. But when it came to going to the heather fields, we were thrown together by a rule of safety in numbers, made by all parents alike. No children were allowed to go off alone, or even in pairs, beyond the last row of houses in Oaktree Lane, to play in the heather or amongst the clumps of oaks and pines which were the vanguards of the dark, distant forest.

On sunny afternoons in school holidays, groups of children, aware of the lurking presence of bad wolves, as the little ones are told, and evil men, as the big ones know, trek into the heather with balls and sticks and waterbottles, to get their pale skins sunburnt crayfish-red and collect more freckles on their noses until the patches join.

When ball games ended in disagreement or, as they did this afternoon, because one side kept winning, someone suggested hide and seek. Tired of their pushy voices, I ran off, past convenient bushes, ignoring clumps of trees, running deep into the heather to find a sandpan to lie in until it would be time to go home. Despite my ineptness at the ball game, I felt exhilarated by the physical tussle, the shouting, the sweating, the roars of victory, the gulps of lukewarm water after the game, the dirt on my clothes and in the creases of my body, the whole sense of abandonment and the lack of restraint in this thin, honey-filled air, fresh with ozone.

I found something better than a sandpan. A deeply eroded trench, invisible from the centre of play, opened up at my feet. Quickly I slid down behind a bush and into the trench and all the human noises suddenly became just pinpricks in the air, like the plosives of breaking icicles in the distance or the sounds the milkman made on a foggy morning. Farther than real. Unreal. I heard the human noises the way the pixies would hear them in their burrows when human children invaded their forest.

The sand was warm and spicy. The wall of the trench was full of pebbles and hair roots sticking out between black woody roots. The heather bushes sat on top like a flower hat on an old woman's warty face, ready to burst into bloom any moment.

In the wall there was a burrow, or a rabbit warren, half obscured by a dead tree root. I knelt down to look inside. There stood the pixie, his figure just outlined against the pitch dark of the burrow's interior.

My heart seemed to stop. When I caught my next breath, it came out as a shriek of sheer fright and that very instant the pixie disappeared into nothingness.

I clambered out of the trench, scratching my legs on roots and rocks, running blindly away from the burrow in the trench wall. My socks were falling down. I knew I'd lost my waterbottle. The world of my Inner Life had collapsed and I was worried about a waterbottle as I ran away from what I had dreamed of seeing for as long as I could remember. I ran, not understanding why I ran. My breath was going in and out as rasping whistles, my heart pounded as if it would break the thin chest wall. I fell down in a heap where the other children were, gathering for one last game of hide and seek before going home.

"Where were you?" a girl from Oaktree Lane asked, looking a little worried at my dishevelled face.

Why I told I'll never know. But I didn't know what else to say from my shattered world.

"I saw a pixie," I said, trying to stop panting.

The girl's expression of concern changed instantly.

"Hey, listen," she shouted, her face breaking into a large grin as she gestured with her arms for the others to come forward. "Listen to Jopie! She's just seen a pixie!"

A howl of derisive laughter rose up from those who cared at all. The rest remained indifferent. That brought tears. Heaving and blubbering I scrambled up and ran again, this time in the direction of the houses and the streets. My brain was working now. What should I tell Mama? I had no hope of hiding my distress, nor did I want to. Would Mama think me a coward for running away from a pixie, a being I claimed to be so familiar with?

"What did he wear?" Mama asked kindly instead.

I had to think. It was an aspect of the pixie I had not paid attention to. I had reacted to the pixie's very existence, his being in the flesh instead of in the pages of a book or in a prize-winning drawing.

"Green . . ." I said at last. "But it was dark inside the burrow . . . but I think it was green."

"It must have been," Mama helped me along. "Maybe one day you will meet it again and then you won't get a fright and you can tell me more of how a pixie looks, because I have never had the luck to see one."

That Mama should call it luck, put yet another perspective on my experience with the pixie, but try as I might that evening in bed, with the sheet and blankets drawn around my head, I could not enter that dreamland where pixies live in red toadstools and fairies flutter up to rest on crooked boughs or inside bowers of creeper vines with tiny fragrant flowers. That world just wasn't there any more when I closed my eyes. It was gone. Gone for good. It hadn't stood up to that after-noon's reality of the little being, possibly in green, but, in any case, drab clothing, standing sideways as if ready to flee to the inner bowels of the earth, but as yet staring defiantly at me. One inviting gesture from that tiny hand, one smile to recognise me as a familiar being, and my next breath would have issued as a sigh of exhilaration instead of a shriek of fear. The pixie was in no way like the pixies in the stories by Pikkie Duimelot and Co. Yet, he had destroyed their world by materialising as he did.

I would have to do with him to live my Inner Life after nightfall. But I didn't want him. Partly because I had run away from him, at the same time regretting my faint-heartedness, partly because he wasn't a tribe. I didn't want to play with just one pixie. I started to wonder whether he'd have relatives, deep inside the burrow. But even if he had, they wouldn't shape up in my mind's eye. My imagination didn't work any more.

For lack of company, for the first time as far as I could remember, I cried myself to sleep, moaning into the blankets for the loss of my world. A world of hot, scented sand, of little stick dwellings and pebble gardens (for I would never build them again), a realm in which I was creator and spectator of a gentle, private world, almost to the point of being a participant.

In the days that followed, I poured over the pages of my pixie books and made drawings in an effort to recapture. But by the end of the week I packed it all away, closed my cupboard and asked Mum for safety pins so I could play with the heap of old clothes and curtains Mama had brought home from one of her workhouses. Dutch mothers always want their children to play outside when the sun shines because they are always underfoot in that rainy climate. But she didn't object that time.

"I want to play theatre in the attic," I said. But I

really wanted to become a fairy. And if I couldn't have wings, then I would at least learn how to flutter about in wide silky sleeves, until other fairies were attracted by my fairy songs.

Safety pins in hand, I climbed the attic stairs with new hope in my heart. Renewed hope has been a feature of my life. I have never yet failed to come up with an idea of how to build up on the ruins of my latest life experience, often with no more to aid me than a bunch of safety pins or a touch of financial genius with amounts under one hundred of the going currency.

The attic was dim and dusty and my world. Outside the sun shone warmly and the voices of many children at play could be heard through the window.

3
Sustaining the Inner Life

Untenable, ancestral pulls from Spain or maybe Hungary, from the near and far East and the whole sun-splashed Mediterranean, re-enter at age five, at the hour of five, when mystique runs wild even amongst brick and concrete dwelling places in the last autumn before all hell breaks open in the holocaust of one madman's war.

Gypsies! *Zigeunerinnen!* I had my first sighting of non-white womanhood, close-up, and lo! they looked not unlike an already beloved grandmother. Same black plaits, beaked nose, fierce eyes. What do they know, these fierce-eyed women, of the future recorded in Mrs Daniel's workworn left hand? And will they be compassionate enough to withhold the truth from her, or even ask her to join them in their flight south, away from the grasp of the approaching monsters?

They wore their long black skirts swinging over bare brown feet, these splendid leathery women. Golden earrings dangle from their lobes, silver bangles cover their strong wrists, jewellery is planted in their thick black hair. But nothing could match the glitter of their fierce black eyes and some good people closed the door on them as quickly as they'd opened it, so as not to have a spell put upon them.

But I . . . I was ready to be bewitched as I sat on the front doorstep, watching little groups of the street's women standing at each other's gate in the falling light of dusk, peering into their calloused palms after their consultations with the Gypsies.

And what could the Gypsies say about that small child's past as it rose behind her, shimmering in the limiting door-frame? Who would blame the mother of such a past-ridden child for refusing to know the future for ten copper cents? Fear and agony come free for such a parent.

As for the child . . . Even Gypsies sometimes turn their gaze in wonder as they stride away with stolen soul shards hidden in the folds of black skirts swinging over strong bare feet . . .

"Those Gypsies!" chuckled my beak-nosed old grandmother with relief: "They steal anything that has no roots!"

And she closed the door on possessions *in situ*.

After the loss of the pixie world I did not find another tribe until I could well and truly read. If one does not retain a memory of stories one has read, it means that one knew already what they had to say and the point they were trying to make. I was endlessly fascinated by how a book told a story, but very few are remembered for having given me something special during that early childhood.

There was a book about a cave boy that left a deep impression and that same sense of loss of when the pixie ran out on me. But this time it was caused by knowledge. School had taught me that cave people were largely a race of the past and that I could not expect to find them anywhere in the world, waiting for me to join them.

But at eight my birthday present was a *Bos Illustrated Atlas*. Geography was one of my passions. An understanding of national borders had come early and brutally, when German soldiers invaded Holland on 10 May 1940. By 1942 the education system had to heel to Nazi orders concerning instruction of the young and our tuition was lopsided in many ways. School books were censored, but in the Bos atlas the island archipelago, now known as Indonesia, was still recorded as the Dutch East Indies.

I poured over maps for hours, reading exotic place names, travelling with my finger up mighty rivers or along rocky coasts, figuring out routes to travel the world on foot, as I certainly didn't expect ever to have the money to pay for transport. Besides, travelling was out of the question during the war, but from year to year the expectation used to be that it would all be over by Christmas. So I didn't worry about the present restrictions, knowing that by the time I'd grown up, all would be back to normal. I would be ready to walk over the border the day I reached maturity or gained parental approval.

I spent much of that birthday with my nose in the Bos atlas. After having taken in the outlines of all the continents, I began to turn the pages of the second half of the volume, the pictorial section. Starting close to home, the photographs became more and more exotic, until my eyes were arrested on a page depicting scenes from the Dutch East Indies.

Spread over the top of the page was a photograph of the Borodubur, the greatest Buddhist stupa in the world, in its full width. It was as if my eyes became magnifying lenses. I was sucked into the galleries of grey volcanic stone, came eye to eye with the Buddha in all his manifestations, while I rolled the name on my tongue like an incantation . . . Borobudur . . . Bo-ro-bu-dur . . . Its magnetic pull was irresistible. I had to go there!

I tore my eyes away with difficulty. I can't remember the second picture in the left-hand lower part of the page. But the third, in the right-hand lower corner, was of a girl and boy posing against a stone temple gate.

The girl's body was tightly wrapped in a fine sarong, her hair oiled and coiled, a jewel over one ear. She stood seemingly at ease, one arm folded across her body, the fingers lightly resting on the other arm which trailed over the stone wall. Her feet were bare. In a strange sense she wore my face. Less pale, the eyes somewhat rounder, but unmistakably my face.

Fragments came floating, refusing to yield their context. Dreams of places never seen, swaying palm trees known only two-dimensionally from grey pictures in magazines, their royal gestures connected to pre-birth memories too strong to have been wiped by the issue of a new brain, or perhaps retained in hidden chromosomes recording the dance of the wind as it sings through humid air in lands hugging the equator, and the mingling smells of living fish, damp rot of dugout canoes and the poignant spice of smoking cooking fires.

Such scenes were gliding into the confined reality of childhood's outer structure, barely able to contain — even at this early stage — the swollen kernel of one child's centuries or aeons old heritage of accumulated essences and multiple other, and further-reaching, realities.

Behind her . . . me . . . stood the boy. His high headdress with the fan of pleats on one side like the outspread wing of a bird, framed a soft, dark face, the eyes jewels, or pools of still water.

What was his name? I searched my memory as if I should know.

What the Chinaman and the Gypsies had started to awaken in me now rose powerfully to my lips. Why, oh why, was I so pale, if I could have been, should have been, otherwise . . . different? I had discovered the diversity of the human race and with it came the knowledge that I was born into the wrong tribe. My shape was alright, the form of my eyes too, my hands and narrow long feet did not disturb me, but the colour of my hair, my eyes, my skin were wrong! My hair should have been raven black, my skin mahogany and my eyes two pools of brown liquid.

I looked in the mirror and faced a stranger. From that day dates my alienation from my outer appearance, which does not match who I am inside. I resolved to change the stranger by every means within my power.

The most ready means was my Inner Life. That evening, before going to sleep, I transformed into a sleek brown girl with oiled and coiled hair. Hitching my sarong over my bare feet, I climbed a sandy path to a grove of palm trees where my friend was waiting. His name was Kunan, it turned out. I'd made it up. I liked the sound. And he answered to it.

Loneliness was banished once more. Kunan took me by the hand and we walked to the village where the tribe lived. We went out to have adventures every night and did many good deeds to help people and animals in distress. Kunan was a hero and as I shared his deeds I quietly, almost without being aware of it myself, became a heroine.

*   *   *

From the time of my awakening, pain entered my life. There had been physical pain already — I was not robust and rather accident-prone, but the growing sense of grief over my displacement and a perceived loss of a beloved country and a tribe developed into a dull, gnawing pain, which was only relieved temporarily when something came close enough to my present life to infuse it with a grain of that magic the other life held for me.

Usually this sort of comfort came from books. The small neighbourhood lending library had shelves full of girls' books set in the Dutch East Indies. I not only devoured the stories, which were mainly written from the colonial point of view, but gleaned from them information about the life of the Indies people in their palm-shaded villages, information I used for the nightly adventures with Kunan. I also recorded every word of Malay, as the trading language of the archipelago was then called, making a small dictionary by cutting tabs into the edges of a notebook and turning it into an alphabetical index. There was a plethora of phrases to utter to servants, but I collected enough words to be able to say to Kunan: *"Saya tidah sejok"* (I'm not cold), when we climbed an active volcano one night to rescue a stranded foreign sailor, or *"Ada tanah harimau"* (This is tiger country), when we crossed a dark jungle forest looking for a lost child.

Before the war was over I had worked my way through the entire children's books section and had started on light thrillers and other adult fiction which the library lady deemed not too unsuitable for a fast-growing girl with a searchlight in her eyes. I remember one book from that period. It was *The Blue Tiger* and the only part of the story my memory retained was set in Tibet, where monks called lamas brought the corpse of an important person back to life by means of religious rites and some esoteric exercises.

Living in the midst of death and destruction, as World War II wound its tortuous way to a bitter, bitter end, this could not fail to impress me. It also brought back from the memory bank the god-king-boy who was my age and I wondered whether there was war in his country also. I resolved to find out one day, but due to the lack of further books on Tibet in the library, I filed Tibet and the Dalai Lama for future reference.

To this day I am uncertain what oils the mechanism by which our mind selects and our brain stores information from the vast masses we wade through, even in childhood. Of all the newspapers seen and read, only one picture was stored and remembered. Of a thousand books read with deep fervour, only two bits remain: the cave boy's image and the lama's rites in *The Blue Tiger*. Did I select these items of information on the basis of an inborn predilection and, if so, was that determined by lives lived before my birth? Or do we store information at random, whereupon it becomes natural to add to it because one piece is already in place? Is this how we become specialists in prehistory or mystics or metaphysicists of Tantric rites?

I didn't become any of these. My interest in cave dwellers was transferred to living tribes who still roam forests and deserts in this age as hunter gatherers and I will speak up for their rights to go on doing so and not join the modern world even though it seems a lost cause. I even lived briefly amongst them, aided by some western trappings and they already possessed by wristwatches and wireless. I yearned to stay longer, but short of throwing myself on their mercy, I had no means of support in that environment.

Certain it is that childhood ended prematurely

because the war caused a famine where we lived. Even Uncle Wim couldn't save us from starvation.

Uncle Wim's farm is a treasured memory. When, as an adult, I discovered the concept of the peasant, I immediately welded it to the image of Uncle Wim and Aunt Saar's farm, put on a long brown skirt in my daydreaming and became a peasant farmer. One day I knew I would have a farm and grow my own food and wool and fruit trees.

Uncle Wim kept chickens in large, airy chook-houses, the smell of which I remember to this day. It was a healthy smell of grain, manure and warm bird bodies in ceaseless activity. Nothing like the smell of chemical death and dried blood that exudes from the battery hen farm down the road from where I now live.

Aunt Saar's parents, who had farmed there before, were dead, but had left a healthy black soil behind, in which Uncle Wim grew bountiful vegetables. In the family photo album there is a picture of his two elder children, younger than me, and myself, posing on the steps of a ladder against a backdrop of climbing beans, the lushness of which I haven't seen in South Australia.

There were also gooseberry and red currant bushes, which formed a dividing hedge between the vegetable plots and the lawn with the giant walnut tree in the middle. In summer we kids sat there with plates of red currants, sprinkled with sugar, stripping them off their thin stems with a fork, or impatiently between our teeth.

Agriculture, I was sure, was to be part of my future life. Despite my city upbringing, I felt it was not strange to me. In the absence of a garden I contented myself with pot-plants and jam-jars full of rooting cuttings.

After the famine and a four month spell in rural Drente, an eastern province on the border of Germany, during which time the war ended, I entered adulthood with three secret wishes and one very unsecret, very realistic wish. The latter was to get away from cities, from gardens so small they didn't deserve the name, and to find a way of life where self-sufficiency, to a large degree, would be possible, so that no war or famine could ever catch me out again. Frail and sick as I often was, I longed for the physical activities that such a life entails.

Although I achieved a measure of self-sufficiency fairly early in my Australian years, I know full well that come war and famine, my vegetable garden, my chickens, and my spinning-wheel and loom will not protect me from the fate that befalls the nation in which I live. My self-sufficiency means I do not have to rely on shops for half my food, can turn out a meal from the garden at any time no matter what season, and am able to make all our woollen clothing and furnishings. I also have a tendency to use what I find in the bush. For years I gathered stones and logs to build garden beds, before I came upon a supply of old red bricks. My idea of a rainy day at home is sitting behind my spinning-wheel near a pot of homegrown vegetables simmering on the stove. For years I lived on an amount of money so small that people around me believed I had a secret source of income, such as a sugar daddy or the like. I, on the other hand, living on an income too small for taxation, could never understand why they complained of not being able to pay their taxes. The more taxes the more income, I figured.

I have an inner need to do things primitively, to live close to the earth. I didn't agree to having a washing machine in the house until I was fifty-two! I also have a need to live surrounded by things I have made with my own hands. I need to sweat in the sun, get tired to the point of collapse, sleep like only a peasant sleeps (I most probably snore heartily), eat food picked fresh off tree, bush and vine and have the daily drudgery of feeding animals, cleaning their quarters and watching their little society evolve, not so very differently from our own as it turns out.

Only when these basic conditions are part of my life do I experience a real sense of well-being. When I walk out of the door on early dew-wet mornings into the wonderland of colour and fragrances my gardens have become, I experience the only perfection possible in this life. Tears of sheer gratitude come to my eyes when a fruit tree I raised from seed produces its first blossoms, followed by fruit sweeter than any bought fruit could taste. I helped to bring it into being and the tree and I have a relationship where I, the caretaker, bow with respect for the tree's ability to produce the sustenance without which I cannot live. To rest on a stump in the shade of plants I raised and nurtured satisfies my creative urges. To tend to a flock of bantam chickens, already eight years old, who are assured of enjoying a ripe old age amongst the trees, even though they only lay a few eggs in spring, gives me a view in miniature of the tribe I have always searched for. These bantam grand-mothers, one blind in an eye and lame in a foot, still raise chicks each year, while the old rooster reigns like a benevolent patriarch over a tribe of seven generations.

It is these simple things which I have found in Australia that give a deep meaning to my daily life. Yet none of these things were offered to me as a prospective migrant. The picture Australia painted of itself was of a country of opportunities to earn vast amounts of money, live in big houses, drive fast cars, bake on crowded beaches, walk through wide city streets, shop in modern department stores and have barbecues and picnics in well laid out public parks. Success, it was called, and still is. The aspirations of consecutive Australian governments seem to change little over the years, though greater numbers of its young people long for what the country has in abundance: space, nature, a chance to live simply and honestly in harmony with the environment. Their needs are not acknowledged and their ambitions not supported. Just as I could not simply go and live in a hunter-gatherers' village without upsetting the local economy, so these young Australians can't simply walk out of the cities and squat on the land without upsetting established interests in rural areas. Because I worked fruitlessly for several years to bring about a change of attitude in government and community leaders to accommodate alternative ways of living, a bitterness has grown in me about the copy-cat urban society Australia has become, with all the ills such a society entails: juvenile criminality, drug addiction, drunkenness, family breakdowns, domestic violence, massive road fatalities, mental institutions, degenerative diseases and a general lack of idealism and hope. Seventy-five per cent of the Australian population lives in seven coastal cities, imitating life in New York, San Francisco or Singapore, not out of necessity, but out of fear for the wide open spaces at their backs.

Despite the tremendous pressure to conform to this infrastructure, I have led a rural life for twenty-six of the thirty years I have lived in this country, even though I often had to travel to the city to earn a small livelihood.

My three secret wishes have also been fulfilled over the years. In order to have a good reason to go on living I have made a new wish, one which, at the moment, appears almost impossible to fulfil.

The three secret wishes that emerged with me from the war were:

- to sit under a palm tree in a tropical country,
- to meet the Dalai Lama of Tibet,
- to be found by a partner with whom I could live life the way I need to live it.

After the isolation of war time, there was a sudden influx of food for the imagination with which I set to work to materialise the conditions that would turn these three wishes into reality. Much of what I selected was still tied to my perception of myself as a displaced person, a pale version of my true Inner Self which had roots in more exotic realms.

American movies replaced German films and the English began to export their celluloid products again. These brought me two new companions.

During my stay in the province of Drente, where I saw the end of the war as an evacuée from the famine in the western provinces of Holland, I had lost contact with Kunan. The displacement, homesickness, worry about my relatives (there was no mail, no radio, no newspapers to tell me how things were in my hometown), and the sheer lack of any input, had killed my Inner Life as far as it was shared with Kunan. What was left was a budding adult perception, increasingly besieged by the opinions of real adults, who tried to steer it into known and tried directions.

Such inborn, compulsive searching, as had moved me until then, creates concepts and ideals about life and love and living which, in the rarefied atmosphere of childhood, rise to tremendous heights of expectation, before meeting with the cold touch of the spoiler our betters call reality.

These concepts and ideals may let themselves be temporarily reduced and harnessed and will descend to so-called reality level for the brief span of adolescence, when biological urges take the upper hand. Afterwards they fly high as kites again, while we swing precariously at the end of a tangled rope, cutting our fingers in punishment for grasping so much and so high, feet dangling helplessly just off the ground, sometimes landing provisionally with a resounding bump and always ending in a headlong nosedive to the ground . . .

The famine, perhaps more than anything, sharpened my imagination into a weapon ready to defeat all objections or arguments by elders. As I was fed on our daily-diminishing porridge, freed from the burden of learning since schools had been closed for lack of fuel, I spent my days sitting haunched on my heels, my knees supporting my outstretched arms, rocking to and fro beside the little tin stove, feeding it with chips of wood and strips of cardboard to keep us from freezing to death in that last harsh winter of the war.

I always took up my position imagining I lived in a dense jungle and the tiny stove was my cooking fire.

As I sat there rocking, day after day, too limp to hold a book, too far gone to care about the pains in the centre of my body, my mind explored the unchartered wastelands of the human psyche, my psyche — the places and spaces from which our consciousness seems to be barred in "normal" times, when there is food and work and social activity. In these explorations I had insights which are still, decades later, tortuously forming themselves into words, those straitjackets of communication which trim and cut and reduce until the original insight fits a traditional pattern and in the process has lost its lustre. My mind soared high to realms so nebulous that thought becomes pure bliss and the arrow of enquiry goes straight for its goal each time it is released.

I was brought back to those times in 1975 and 1976, when I befriended a man called Kali in a longhouse in Balimo on the Aramia River in Papua New Guinea. Kali was about my age, father of ten children and a self-taught woodcarver, who was helping to restore his tribe's culture — he belonged to the twelve thousand strong Gogodala tribe — with the assistance of Adelaide friends of mine, Tony and Jenny Crawford. While staying with them I daily walked the sandy path to the longhouse, which drew me like a magnet. Sometimes I sat on the veranda, learning to make string and fingerweave it; my teachers were two marvellous old women with whom I communicated in signs. Almost daily I spent some time at Kali's firepit inside the great hall of the longhouse, where he sat carving dance shields and masks. I put no particular queries to him, as I was not on an academic quest nor inclined to be nosey. He sensed I came because I liked being there and his English was good enough for us to have slow conversations. Although no local news or gossip was neglected, Kali often ended up telling me about Gogodala spiritual beliefs and their world view. It was very evolved, sophisticated, abstract and not easy to put into a prosaic language such as English, which, let's face it, is still culture-bound to British ground and doesn't accommodate many a metaphysical principle that is meant to be taken deadly seriously in daily life, rather than be grist to the mills of the Sunday papers.

Sitting around Kali's firepit in the Balimo longhouse it became clear to me that we shared a similar world view and philosophy of life which I had tapped into during that famine in 1944–45, and which had made me an alien in the worlds I have had to live in ever since. I started to fear for Kali, his children and all the Gogodala, for the time of first contact was already over and their march into a modern, technological society, albeit in their own independent country, had already started. All I can hope is that Kali's children and grandchildren will feel strong enough to hold on to their world view, not from a sense of tradition, but because their confrontation with the new world will make it clear to them that they *need* that world view to stay in touch with realities the modern world — and Christianity for that matter — does not recognise, to its and everybody's peril.

There's little doubt that diet has something to do with the contemplative life. The Gogodalas traditionally live on sago, fish, coconut, green vegetables and lotus seeds, with some pineapple and eggs. The latter may have been introduced. Meat is scarce and comes in the form of small birds or the odd pig or cassowary. They live in a land of plenty and I hope put the lie to western beliefs that one must necessarily fast in order to reach higher levels of thought.

Nevertheless, I have to admit that a drastic change in diet put an end to my life of contemplation, which would have ended in certain though blissful death. The input of good farm eggs, potatoes and bacon pancakes, products of Drente's soil, brought me back to earth and the worries and agonies of war and separation.

Even though the noumenal realms seemed barred to me as postwar life geared up to recreate the old world that was remembered with fondness and to build a new order on the ruins of the old, the experience was mine to keep. Forever after, each experience, no matter how trite or limited, was cast against the backdrop of my sojourns in those realms beyond mundane perception. With that comes an awareness that the world so many

41

people think they live in is unreal, no matter how easy it is to touch, measure and record.

But during my teenage years I indulged in new fantasies to feed my craving for a companion with whom to share my views of the future, my future. There were no suitable candidates in my environment, so I brought home Sabu from the movie theatre. He was a young Indian who acted Mowgli in Sir Alexander Korda's rendering of Kipling's *Jungle Book*. I still enjoy seeing that film, even in black and white on an old television set. I would still like to live in that jungle, although I am less keen to live with wolves or converse with black panthers.

With Kunan lost in the shadows of childhood, Mowgli became my partner in the adventurous nightlife I needed to offset the compulsory drudgery of my days. I went to see Sabu's other films, *Elephant Boy* and one set in South America, but it was as Mowgli that he captured my adventurous heart and gained for his sanitised, glossy Hollywood photo a place of honour in a metal frame on my bedside shelf.

Sabu could not sing, only howl like a wolf. In time he lost to Paul Robeson, whose wonderful bass voice sang songs of spiritual nostalgia on radio, whose films cast a warmth of humanity on the human condition. These qualities I felt were missing in postwar Holland, where the restoration of buildings and economic life set a pace unsuited to compassion, tenderness and simple generosity. When *Bosambo of the River* was released I was ecstatic with excitement. There was violence in that world too, but a noble spirit won the day. My daydreams took on bolder form, the mighty rivers of Africa replaced babbling brooks in steamy jungles; vigorous dancing around a smoking fire and the singing of compelling tribal chants became the stock-in-trade of my nightly adventures. I would be a chieftain's wife, no less, if not a female chief myself . . . one day.

But as the outcome of the war had taken away the Dutch East Indies from Holland, so too had the colonial empires in Asia and Africa became arenas of bloodshed and ideological turmoil as the tribes I so hankered for struggled to gain independence from foreign domination and exploitation.

At thirteen I still had a hope of getting to the Indies. Dutch ships were still plying the Batavia route and, being short of staff, they took on young volunteers, who made the return trip for little more than their keep and pocket money. A girlfriend's brother had seen the East this way and I saw my chance. I applied on behalf of myself and the girlfriend and one other girl. Both were older than I. The shipping company's reply indicated that the other two could apply for an interview, but I had to wait a few years for the maturity of age fifteen! The girls did not go. I gnashed my teeth as time was grinding on too slowly for my purpose; by the time I reached the required age the situation had altered and adventurous volunteers were no longer required. Beneficiaries of this failed migration exercise were my relatives, for whom I peeled potatoes and cooked sandy soup (I wasn't too good at washing the vegetables) in preparation for a career as cook's assistant in a ship's galley. They were grateful when the mail brought the rejection of my services and Mama took full control of the kitchen again!

I returned to the Bos atlas for consolation. The world I wanted to see was still there. Photographs of my favourite countries were by now indelibly engraved on my mind, but the maps became new hunting grounds. I charted journeys on foot across Europe to Asia, travels by boat to Africa, even trails for a well-packed bicycle to carry me into the direction of my dreams.

About this time, my father decided to find out whether I had survived the war. The event of our first meeting is a story in itself; it resulted in a holiday in Friesland where he lived. Although the Friesians are indeed still a tribe and have their own culture and language, they were not my tribe, much as I loved the land. But this new father had sent me a plane ticket to soar on a clear summer's day over the patchwork blanket that is Holland, in the year 1947 when the skies were still unpolluted enough to see it. This experience saw the birth of a new idea to get me launched in directions I wanted to go. I would become a pilot!

An application to the pilot school in Wassenaar brought a polite reply that girls were not admitted to the course. Enquiries about stewardess training netted me a formidable list of conditions. I would have to do high school for the full five years, learn English, French and German, get first aid or nursing experience and childcare qualifications, wear no glasses, and grow no taller than a certain height convenient for the aircraft of the day. No one in our family had undergone so much education. No one in our family was as tall as I promised to be. No one in our family started to wear reading glasses at thirteen.

Nevertheless I set about achieving my goals by pestering my new father for financial support to enter the HBS (Higher Burgher School) instead of wasting my time in extended primary education (MULO).

Although this was forthcoming, elements unique to my own life nearly spoiled it all, as seems to happen so often to opportunities that offer themselves to me. Two days before the entrance exam, for which I had swotted up all the capital cities and countries in the world, I broke my right arm in a bravado attempt to jump down a "tank wall" in the heather fields. These were dug out defence hiding places for German tanks, left over from the war.

What moved me to thus show off my physical prowess to a girlfriend is hard to explain, but in times of waiting, while being in limbo, I have often done things which have completely blocked the way for my next projected course.

However, luck was still with me. I was allowed to be examined six weeks later, a week before the new school year was about to start. I passed all four subjects with ease and felt that the world lay open for me now.

Eight years down the track, at twenty-one, I would be able to apply for a post as stewardess with KLM, passport to the world.

At twenty-one, I found myself sitting across a heap of black coal, a candle burning on an upturned crate, my two children in a foster home, telling my sorry story to a policeman sent to protect me from the violent intentions of the landlord, who had evicted me from the draughty attic I rented from him. Amsterdam, winter 1954–55 was the pit of destitution for me and, but for the grace of the first-floor neighbours, I wouldn't even have had the shelter of their attic with coalheap — I would have been out in the streets. In those days, my Inner Life revolved around where the next meal was to come from, my mind's eye was blocked with money arithmetic, my imagination's wings had been cut by a malnutrition of another kind.

To go hungry and cold in a society which is beginning to aspire to affluence is very different from dying of starvation together with everyone else. Bitterness entered my mind and was slowly poisoning me.

Where did things go wrong? Did the seed of failure germinate at that imposing new school, or was it ready to erupt anyway? If the school did not help, the memories of my short life there are still mainly pleasant.

Grand arches in conservative red brick, stained glass windows, two towers where doves built their nests, lawns, flowers and vines. Across the road the mysterious, secret world of an ancient oak forest. To add spice, a circus spent the winters on the opposite street corner, for this was the very edge of suburbia.

My years at primary school had been one happy pursuit of knowledge. The MULO had been utter boredom. But at the HBS I had an inkling of the pleasures of life apart from study, pleasures which hadn't reached my working class home. Burghers were people who lived in smart houses, who neither ran errands on foot, nor wore patched clothes, nor ate leftovers and wormy fruit. Burghers were lucky people and their children were happy-go-lucky creatures who got taught interesting things and had libraries from which to borrow beautiful books.

Had the word been coined then, it would have been called a multicultural school. The student population was made up of three distinct groups. There were those who were born and bred in the pleasant small and large villas cluttering the leafy suburbs on the school's north, east and south, the oak forest being in the path of the setting sun. They were healthy, carefree children, who had survived the war and the famine rather better than I, who came from across the railway line.

Secondly, there were the Jewish children, who had personally survived, but whose families had not. They were orphans who lived in a large Jewish orphanage in Laren, where Uncle Wim and Aunt Saar had their farm. They travelled a long way on buses to come to this very good school to gain qualifications, new tools for their parentless survival in the postwar world. In the life of the diaspora, the only portable possession that cannot be taken away from one is the intellect. The Jews at HBS were energetic, inspired by their group life to great exuberance in play as well as in study, and they had a penchant for moral and social justice in the classroom. I would have liked to belong to them and sometimes dreamt of living in an orphanage and eating porridge for breakfast at a long table full of porridge bowls for exuberant orphans. I would be trouping onto a bus in a bunch of legs and elbows, rather than pedalling my solitary way to school on a bicycle.

But most of all I wanted to belong to the third group, the Indies kids. Access to it did not demand leaving home or changing status, nor the adoption of a religion. The Indies kids had been repatriated, with what was left of their families, after the Japanese army in the Dutch East Indies surrendered. They were mostly white, of Dutch stock. Some were half-castes, such as Wim, with his enormous brown eyes and peach and almond skin. All the Indies kids had an accent, used Malay expressions like *"Adu!"* or *"Adu-la!"* in any circumstance needing exclamation, walked with their hips and jerked their left shoulders backwards at every step. They also laughed a lot with a tendency to roll on the ground to let the laugh run its full course. They liked parties, were sexually more advanced than the Dutch kids and were habitual gossipers of the light-hearted kind.

Class 1B only had two girls, Lisa and myself. Lisa was blond, buxom, green-eyed, older than everybody, sophisticated and bilingual! Born in Hong Kong of a Dutch father in the merchant navy and an English mother, she had spent the war with her mother in Ambarawa, a notorious Japanese prisoner-of-war camp

47

for women and children on the island of Java. Her father had died and the widow came to Holland with Lisa and her older brother, where the Dutch grandparents lived in a rambling old three-storey villa, hidden in clumps of gnarled trees and covered in wisteria.

It was inevitable that Lisa and I became friends. We shared a school bench.

"My mother says she'll make an exception for you," Lisa had confided. "Normally I'm not supposed to go around with kids from the lower classes."

I was confused, as we were in the same class, namely 1B, but when Lisa's mother made it clear that I could play at Lisa's house but Lisa could not come to mine, I became aware of the lady's prejudices. I thought them quaint and was amused by her mannerisms. I liked her, inspite of these. Having English tea and biscuits, and being engaged in polite conversation while sitting straight on a sofa, became part of being Lisa's schoolfriend.

Lisa introduced me to the concept of reincarnation. Some people in the Indies, she said, held to a belief in rebirth. I found this easy to incorporate in my worldview, as if I had known it all my life. I even started to disagree with Lisa within minutes of being introduced to the idea.

"What do you want to come back as?" Lisa asked. "A dog or a donkey? Or a lion, or what?"

"I want to come back as a human being," I replied.

Lisa explained that as far as she knew that was not in the rules. I decided I would change the rules for my own purposes.

"But if you had to come back as an animal, what sort would you choose?" she persisted.

"An elephant," I offered at last, but unconvinced. I resolved that the system should logically include human rebirth and that of course implied that people now walking around might have walked around here before. Or somewhere else on earth.

"Where did you live in your previous life?" I asked Lisa. But she'd lost interest after choosing some elegant animal I have forgotten for her future existence.

Over the years I have met people who had knowledge, so they said, of their past lives. Those that claimed to have been princes and princesses of the blood, or priestesses of esoteric cults, or other persons of note in exotic places, I disbelieved.

"What a comedown," I wanted to say, "to be a housewife or plumber now. What happened that made you come down to these lowly levels?" Of course, my reactions contained the hubris of a person born at the lowest levels herself; one who could only go up.

For a person lowly born, I had some uncomfortable traits. I gave orders to the people around me with the greatest of ease and as a matter of fact, without being bullying about it and despite my characteristic shyness. I also had a tendency to organise other people and their energy in order to achieve what I perceived as a common goal, but which was usually my brainchild. Furthermore, I had an ability to get on with people from all walks of life and all classes. Indeed, I was unimpressed by displays of wealth and felt untroubled by moving in rich houses, such as my mother's work houses. I had an aversion to rough language, rude jokes and the earthy discussions of blood, gore and sensational events some of our neighbours and acquaintances liked to engage in. But the latter was characteristic of my whole family and may well have been a result of my upbringing. But the other early character traits were not stimulated by my present life, nor conducive to it. In fact, they were a hindrance and I had to learn to ask politely for people's cooperation and suppress my desire to force others into my schemes and projects.

Not that I had any sway over Lisa. She was wilful and older and bigger than I. Her house lay between mine and the school and by letting her have the lead, I had company half the way and a running mate at school.

Into this snug and unavoidable arrangement came Fransje, midway through the school year. Fransje was from the Minahasa, a name music to my ear and attached to that spiderly tongue of land in the north of Sulawesi, the old island of Celebes in the Indies.

Fransje was the real thing. Small, quick, brown as a chestnut, she had never seen snow, had grown up among palm trees, and spoke fluent Malay, not just a few phrases for servants or the market place. And Lisa didn't care for her. Lisa's nose went snooty. I don't recall how it was arranged that I should henceforth sit next to Fransje, but it was done and I'd never been so close to the land of my dreams as in that wooden, scratched and ink-stained school bench, helping Fransje to catch on to the way our lessons were run and our learning was done. She lent me her Malay textbook from her old school in Indonesia and helped me with pronunciation. Finally, Fransje took me home to introduce me to her parents. By this time I was thirteen and touching on 180 centimetres in height. I shall never forget the pain my appearance caused during that visit.

Fransje, her brother and parents lived in the renovated attic of an old villa. The housing shortage was severe and newcomers from Indonesia were packed into all the nooks and crannies of dwellings too big for their owners. This attic was miniscule. So were Fransje's parents, their rattan furniture, their delicate teacups. So was Fransje herself, but our friendship had not been bothered by the fact that there was twice as much of me as there was of her.

The decor was brown and batik and beautiful. We sat, took tea, and conversed. I had difficulty understanding their heavily accented Dutch and I had to be careful not to speak in my cultivated Malay accent, which impressed a few Dutch friends in the street, but would have been a travesty in the presence of real speakers of that tropical lilt.

I suspect that Fransje's parents were as embarrassed about my giant appearance as I was. I even suspect that they too had a class consciousness which was not enamoured of having their daughter cavort around with the Dutch plebs. The visit was never repeated.

Fransje and I parted company when the second school year started. Shortly after I was hit by a car. My injuries resulted in chronic headache and I left midyear, unable to carry on studies or even read books to sustain my Inner Life.

4
Love and reality

During those few years at high school, several incidents and developments added fuel to my conviction that I was something other than I appeared to be. In all cases it was my spontaneous and unpremeditated choice to pay attention to a certain detail, unprompted by any outside influences. Again, I wonder about the mechanism that controls such choices and what came first: a predilection for, or a fascination with, the detail observed?

It seems a pity to me now that I paid so little attention during my life in Holland to the many expressions of separate identity that are so evident in the rich heritage of regional costume and furniture in the eleven provinces.

I grew up seeing men and women from Huizen, on the Ijssel Lake, selling their fish in the market. The women in their stiff white caps like the wings of a seabird sailing on the wind; the men in baggy black trousers, striped shirts and suspenders, with a silver-domed button somewhere on their costume.

Later, when I worked in Amsterdam and commuted

by train, other trains brought in the young women from Volendam and Marken, the first in their stylish, elegant long skirts with aprons and tight, embroidered bodices, and the latter in a blaze of striped skirting in red, green, white and yellow, with multicoloured embroidery covering everything above the waist.

In Drente, where I spent the end of the war, costume wasn't worn any more, except for wooden clogs. But in Friesland it could still be seen. The one that attracted me out of hundreds of styles was that of the Friesian town of Hindeloopen. The women's costume is rich in a tonal rather than a colourful way, the skirts chic rather than voluminous, the head dress of refined design and execution. When I found out that Hindeloopen folk had their own style of wooden furniture, painted bright red and decorated with tiny flowers and linework, I became excited to the point of nostalgia. The Hindeloopen culture, different from all that surrounds it, somehow reminded me of a lost world. I never went there during the holidays with my new father. Never went there on return visits to Holland. I only saw Hindeloopen culture in a museum and was settled with a craving to wear dark, long skirts and rock a red wooden cradle . . .

The great renaming of Jopie, the discovery of my true name, took place when I was twelve! My mother had remarried in 1944 and at last I had a real sibling, a red-headed little brother. I had, on my insistence, been upgraded to Jo, but I still didn't like the name.

Brother began to talk and tried to say my name. He could not manage the ''J'', so changed it to an ''L'' with the flexibility of the very young. Then he doubled the sound, to prolong his own creation of this new word. Thus, out came ''Lolo''.

"D'you hear that?" I shouted at my mother, pointing at the delighted toddler. "That's my name! That is my name! From now on that is what I want to be called by! My name is Lolo!"

I had recognised something, though what it might be I only got a glimpse of in later life. Intriguing glimpses, pointing to a heritage of a most unusual kind in an ancient culture of wild beauty . . . if it were true . . .

The family complied, relieved to be rid of one Jo, the calling out of which brought all feet running or no response at all, when each thought it had to be another that was wanted.

The rest of the world took a bit of convincing that Jo or Jopie was no more and that a strange being called Lolo had taken her place. It wasn't Dutch. Where did it hail from?

"Never mind," I said, "It *is* my name." I made it legal in Adelaide, Australia in 1975.

The world still takes a bit of convincing. People who think I have trouble writing my own name change it kindly to Lola. Others, never having met me, assume I must be a male. Most think it must be a funny Dutch name.

I was perhaps in my late twenties when, in my search for books on the country of that little god-king whose photographic image was still imprinted on my mind, I came across a book on the Lolo Tribe. Later, a friend presented me with another. The Lolo live in the borderlands of Eastern Tibet and Yunnan. They are mountain people. Lolo women are tall, independent and pursue small business ventures. All descriptions of Lolo women tally with what I was and have become. And no, I haven't been there either yet . . .

*　　*　　*

54

The relationship with my new-found father was not an unadulterated joy. It petered out after two holidays. But I had gained some interesting facts about my origins from his side of the family.

The Houbeins came from Austria-Hungary. They had gradually worked their way north-westwards, which accounts for the name appearing in three spellings at least: Houbein, Houbijn and Holbein. I also remember my father saying that the name used to be Houbeinich in the past, but that could have been an obscure joke I missed, alluding to *"habe nicht"* or "have not". I once received a free ice-cream from an ice-cream vendor called Houbijn, who acknowledged my father as a remote relative. Since the publication of this autobiography in Holland, long-lost relatives have made contact with me and it turns out that my paternal grandfather — whom I never met — was a Polish half-Jew who migrated to Holland as a young man with his brother.

As far as the Holbein connection was concerned, there were still painters in the family some four hundred years after the heydays of Hans Holbein Junior and Hans Holbein Senior, the famous painters from Switzerland. My uncle Gep Houbein painted sombre seascapes and sketched people in trains and buses from behind his sunglasses. He later migrated to New Zealand where the sea is a good deal sunnier! My elder half-sister Lien, who changed her name to Nina, was a talented artist with charcoal and modelled beautiful little figures of clay. For some time she studied with Henry Boot in Haarlem, which was also Uncle Gep's base. She started clay modelling because of me. On a visit to my rented rooms in Amsterdam, she saw the little heads I had modelled from a lump of wet clay on a board under a teatowel. I heard later from her distraught husband that she went home and used her last housekeeping money to buy clay instead of bread. It broke up the marriage, but I console myself that it must have been the last straw and that she uncovered a talent that hopefully sustained her through her life, which she made none the easier for herself, in proper Houbein tradition! (Nina heard me on the radio in 1988, made contact, and subsequently sent me a collection of her evocative Dutch watercolour miniatures of Amsterdam and surrounding polders.)

I didn't take much interest in the Holbein connection until I studied Elizabethan history at Adelaide University in 1974. There I learned that Hans Holbein Junior painted Ann of Cleeve's portrait for Henry VIII, who was contemplating marriage with this lady he had never met. His right hand, Cromwell, instructed Holbein to "doctor" the portrait as he had heard the lady was no beauty. Holbein made her look considerably better than she did in real life. When Henry met her, he not only cancelled the wedding plans — lucky lady, it probably saved her life! — but assigned Cromwell to the block, where he lost his head. Holbein evidently did a quick-smart disappearing act.

The only self-portrait of Hans Holbein Junior shows features very similar to those in a photo of me, taken at age sixteen, an age when one's face carries its truest appearance, before life obscures the potential one was born with by etching strange new lines across the juvenile countenance. When I showed the self-portrait to Ronald, my son, and asked what he saw, he simply said "You."

Alas, I did not inherit the talent. I draw for pleasure sometimes, but am merely a tolerable copyist.

It is the other heritage which he brought that I treasure. The origins, as far back as we know, in the Hungarian steppes, or woods, or meadows. These not only explain why the Gypsy stole a piece of me, but also why I have Mongolian eyelids. Genghis Khan and his men left a legacy in flesh and blood in Eastern Europe, which worked its way westwards. I've since met other Friesians who have this eyefold and don't need to wear sunglasses! And no, I haven't been to Mongolia yet . . . nor have I roamed across the world's free spaces with the last of the mobile Gypsies . . .

My room — chaos! My room fitted snugly under the sloping roof at the back of the house my mother still inhabits, at the top of the staircase. The small windows jutted out in a wooden alcove just above the gutter. Inside, wooden panelling provided me with a loose plank behind which I kept my diary — it's been renovated since and has no room for secrets, I think.

My slothfulness was proverbial and my mother at last declared she would not clean my room any longer, only change the bed once a week. I lived without remorse amidst the mess of my clothes and belongings, pre-occupied with thoughts of love, the future, my diary. What more can a thirteen-year-old get worked up about?

Yet this lack of concern about my personal material surroundings changed on the day the statue, that had sat on the mantelpiece in the living room, fell and broke in a dusting accident. It was unceremoniously dumped in the rubbish bin. The statue had been given to Mama by Aunt Jopie, some years before . . . it was a pity, but no one thought much of it.

I roared! The rubbish bin! How could you, Mama! I groped between the smelly refuse and came up with the three main pieces. I washed them, dried them, glued them together again. The statue was a marbled moss-green plaster cast. I carried it upstairs cradled in my arm. In my room I found there was no place suitable to receive it.

First I made the bed, to rest the statue on it. Next I collected a bucket and sponge, dustpan and brush. I worked all that Saturday and transformed my pig sty into an abode fit for the gods.

In the corner under the sloping roof I placed an upturned crate, draped with an imitation batik sarong, and placed the statue in a central position upon it. I found candles and candleholders, small bowls and flowers. I didn't know about incense at that stage, although in the 1960s I became the first importer of incense in South Australia. But I had made the corner into a shrine and I called the statue Buddha.

When all was ready I lit the candles, sat crosslegged on the floor in front of the shrine and meditated for the first time since the famine.

I knew full well that the statue represented a Serimpi dancer from Bali, but the headdress, in the shape of a round leaf ending in a long, well-defined point, the eyes closed serenely and the expression of incomparable peace on its face, justified my sudden renaming of the statue.

In front of its all-knowing, closed eyes, I often sat in contemplation when troubled by the decrees of adults or frustrated at the slow pace of my growing up. My room, now a temple, never reverted to the chaos from before my awakening.

Although I had acquired a Buddha statue and made a shrine, I knew nothing about Buddhism as a religion and it is a source of wonder to me that I did what I did out of some hitherto dormant instinct. In this incident it seems impossible that there was only an unfounded fascination with an eastern deity. The renaming of the statue was as determined and decisive as the renaming of Jopie had been.

Of course, as a teenager I participated more in the conversations of adults than I had been permitted to do as a child. On one occasion, when the visitor was my mother's woman friend of many years, I was given an insight into how primitively, even crudely, adults judge the preoccupations of young children.

During the war there were cultural films on Sunday morning in the Rex movie theatre. Mama enjoyed these films and took me along for the educational value they had. Here I saw such unforgettable gems as Sven Hedin's crossing of the Gobi desert and many a film of jungle tribes dining on python flesh while carrying supplies for intrepid western explorers. One such film was also viewed by Mama's woman friend. To my eternal surprise, when the Sunday morning films popped up in the conversation, this "auntie" queried what I, as a mere child, could possibly have gotten out of films like that and jokingly remarked that it must have been the bouncing naked breasts of the tribal women that had kept my eyes glued to the screen!

My love for hot, humid climes was born in that dark cinema and with it the first of my three life wishes — to sit one day under a real palm tree. Auntie's remark came back thirty years later when I flew out of Mount Hagen in the Papua New Guinea highlands, after a ten-day stay, my first visit to that fascinating country. Next to me on the plane sat an Australian woolclasser, who had paid a three-week visit to his brother, a patrol officer in the then Australian administration. As I looked out of the window to that grandiose world below — where ten days had seemed half a lifetime and friends for life had been made, where smells and textures had reawakened my senses, where I had sung songs with tribal girls in misty hills, "talked" with old women without a language between us — I knew life had gained a new dimension through what I had learned there from a vigorous, generous people, still in touch with nature for their daily sustenance.

"Incredible place, isn't it?" said the woolclasser. As I nodded confirmation, unwilling to discuss my discoveries so soon with a stranger, he went on: "I still can't get over all those naked women and those men with their arsegrass."

That's how far he'd come in three weeks. He was returning home after a spell on another planet. I was tearing myself away from a place where life was warm, vivid, violent sometimes, but truthfully naked and in tune with something deeply buried in my psyche.

Mama's cultural Sunday mornings became flesh and bone in Mount Hagen in 1971.

My longing for warmth, moisture and colour, cherished in childhood adventure dreams, fostered by reading and finally experienced in Papua New Guinea, has never left me. I enjoy the changing seasons at Middle Hill, where I now live, and know my tropical years in Papua New Guinea and Darwin sapped some of my energies, not to mention the dreaded malaria. But every two years I try to have a short sojourn in some tropical place, be it the fabulous twenty-first century city of Singapore, the rural peace of Malaysia, or a Pacific island. It revives that starved nostalgia inside me, lodged in a still undiscovered gene that caters for the memories of past lives.

The old queen of the Netherlands, Wilhelmina, was

handing over the sceptre to Princess Juliana and the country feasted for a week. With my girlfriends I went to street-dances and fireworks and we joined company with the Indies boys. Some were from my school, but others we had never met. One I had an infatuation for, which was principally fed by getting the odd glimpse of him in the school playground and that was enough to keep the little flame burning and feed my teenage daydreams.

One of the Indies boys who was new to us walked me home one evening, explaining why he couldn't come to the next day's street-dance.

Billy Graham, the American evangelist, was in town and would speak in the big church, accompanied by a man with a trumpet and another who played the marimba. Would I come? Yes, I would. A trumpeter in a church was unusual enough, but there was the Indies boy asking me! A man really, he was twenty-one already. I was more than thrilled. It all happened so unexpectedly and at the same time there was something so familiar about him, that only in my room did I discover that he was not unlike the revered Sabu, but endowed with an engaging smile and an irresistible gregariousness.

Love at first sight is really not a very pleasant experience at all. My dreamlife was suddenly over. I now yearned for reality. But although I went to the church, listened to Billy, the trumpet and the marimba and was walked home again by Jan, I realised he felt nothing but pure, evangelistic friendship for me. We talked about reading, books and life, but above all of his new-found religion which had changed his life, but I was not to know from what. He recommended it to me.

Of course I joined the Youth for Christ movement of which Jan was already a treasured member. Of course I became a convert to Christianity. I was the right age to take a spiritual leap, all other kind of leaps having to wait till maturity was reached.

After the car accident I lay in hospital with Sabu's photograph on the bedside table. I wished so fervently for someone to tell Jan where I was, that I made my wish into a shamanistic exercise which I would practise whenever the nurses left me alone. Although Jan had often walked me home after YFC meetings, he hadn't attended for more than a month and no one knew where he was.

By the end of the week, just before I was to return home, he walked into the ward dressed in a navy sailor's uniform. He had been drafted and had not been given any leave during the first six weeks of training. He lent me a set of radio earphones to use during my recovery at home. It was typical of him. He always thought of other people's needs and comforts and felt a personal responsibility to alleviate any suffering he saw.

Of course he regarded me as a child still. I was seven-and-a-half years younger and, on account of my Inner Life, more than usually naive. One evening, walking home after a prayer meeting, he said he felt for me like a brother did for a younger sister. Would I be his sister? Of course I would. I was indeed extremely fortunate that his requests were so decent and modest, for at that stage I would have conceded to whatever he might have asked of me. Such is love.

It wasn't entirely blind love though. With all his genuine nobility of character, I realised I wasn't quite up to living alongside his ideals. Intellectually he was my better (I had quit high school by then) and often I had to stand on my toes to keep up with the conversations he started. After his years of conscription he became a social work student in Amsterdam. As I belonged to a class of people who usually have social work practised upon them, I had a somewhat different view, from the ground up, so to speak, of why people got into the troubles they did. I also had probably less moral but more practical opinions about the most sensible way to get out of them. But Jan's cup of compassion was forever flowing over for other people and he didn't see that I too did my quiet share of suffering.

On another walk home, he was somewhat less lively than usual. Finally he asked whether I knew Annie, a girl with long, very blond hair, who also came to the meetings. As I was his sister, would I do him a favour and sound Annie out on how she felt about him? He felt he wanted to get to know her better.

The blow was devastating. Unable to express my feelings in any way, I lamely promised to do what he asked. But after a fitful night I knew I couldn't bring myself to actually do it. My sense of self-preservation had come into operation.

I started to avoid the girl Annie, whom I'd liked from a distance up till then. Jan never mentioned it again and I don't know whether he made his own advances. If he did I wasn't aware of it. But some of the joy went out of keeping company with young Christians who, after all, made the same mess of their personal relationships as the pagan and the heathen kids. There was no guided coming together in the name of Jesus for the purpose of a love holier than what the women's magazines alluded to. I knew already that praying had little effect if it was somehow not meant to happen, which is what all the signals indicated. Neither did I see any value in shamanistic contemplation to bring him to my side if he did not want to be there. This became a principle throughout my life and I left many a situation where only a small proportion of what was me was wanted and appreciated. I have always found it hard to play half-dead and only live with that part of me that is required, as I did then in my immaturity.

And so life dragged on, with me carrying my chronic headache — a hangover from the car accident — and unrequited, unexpressed love. After leaving school I had several domestic jobs and a failed attempt at being an apprentice hairdresser. During that time I also learnt typing and shorthand.

Then, at fifteen, a wonderful event took place that shows what real faith is able to do. That real faith didn't belong to me. It belonged to an elderly spinster called Corrie ten Boom and I was one of the many beneficiaries of her faith in her God. Properly speaking, this story belongs in my autobiography that deals with the aspect of religion in my life. But the event was so decisive for my further progress at the time that I cannot leave it out.

I had enrolled for a Christian weekend at an old estate near Haarlem. A teacher who was a YFC member told me that a woman evangelist, famous for laying on hands, would attend. "Go and see her," he said, "and tell her about your headache." I did and Corrie ten Boom allowed her God to heal me through her hands.

This is not the place to analyse this miracle. I will do that in the autobiography of my religious experiences. But it needs to be recorded here because I started to take charge of my life again when the space above my eyes became available once more for plain thinking and registering emotions. My gratitude to Corrie ten Boom, though she wanted none, is for more than relieving me of a chronic headache. All thanks are due to God in her opinion. I, believing in a measure of free will and choice, know that Corrie need not have chosen to live her life in dedication not only to all those in need and those who suffer or are persecuted, but also to the salvation of the murderers of her father and sister, who died in German captivity during the war. Corrie survived the prisons and camps. Not Jews themselves, Corrie, her sister Betsy and her father were imprisoned for hiding and helping Jews to escape the death camps. To be, even for five minutes, in the presence of a person capable of such compassion as Corrie ten Boom displayed during her long life, has an ennobling effect on one's own life and aspirations. The experience did not save me for Christianity, but it indelibly printed on my mind the need for saints and saint apprenticeships. I know now that they emerge from all races.

Ideas of flying, travel and adventure had given way to the need to earn a wage and save money towards some sort of independence. I'd lowered my ideals to finding an office job. I was clearly not the "Domestic of the Year", nor did I like it much. Not being very strong made me feel inadequate at many tasks and I hoped office work would be less demanding physically.

At last I found a job as an office junior with a small import company in Amsterdam, with a Jewish boss who did make us work on the Sabbath, but sent me for sausage rolls from the best baker in town for all his employees.

Working in the capital meant commuting by train. Several YFC members took the 7.30 to Amsterdam. One was Elly, a laboratory assistant; another Kees, a press photographer. And there was Jan, my adoptive brother, who was a social work student now.

These were happy days at last and the four of us became close friends. But there were even happier times to come.

Elly wanted to find board in Amsterdam, but her parents didn't want her to live alone. Things were coming to a head at my home because my stepfather and I didn't get on too well. Parental approval was strenuously canvassed and at last given on both sides, together with some surplus furniture, linen and household wares. Elly and I started room hunting and, when we found the right place for us, moved to the top floor of an apartment house on the Leidsekade, facing the canal just behind the hotel American. It was a stone's throw from Leidseplein, the opera house, the heart of the city.

Our move did not please Jan and Kees. During their first visit to our attic of independence, plans were laid to find them rooms nearby so that our foursome should not be broken up. After a fortnight's search, two rooms came up for rent a few doors away from us. The canal curved in such a way that the backs of the houses "bent in" towards each other and so it was possible to call from their bathroom window on the second floor to our kitchen higher up and have a conversation!

This call system was used every Wednesday evening, when Elly and I cooked our favourite meal for four and Jan and Kees would check through the window whether it was ready. Then we tucked into a mountain of macaroni with ham and lashings of cheese. Afterwards we drank coffee and talked until midnight.

Once a month, after payday, we ate at Si-Si's Chinese restaurant on the Weteringschans, went to a movie and, late in the evening, ate breadrolls at Kootje in the square, tucked to one side of the opera house.

It was like having a family of one's own choice. We lived like that for nine months and it was the best time of my life between the ages of six and thirty-two. It was the smallest possible tribe and the only man I'd so far fallen in love with was part of it.

It was Jan who broke it up. One evening he came up the three stairs alone, told me to put on a coat and come for a walk with him. He had something serious to discuss. As usual, I was only too willing to comply, although a little nervous at seeing the expression on his face, too heavy and almost angry, not promising much good. But I was still naive and obediently trundled beside him in the biting evening cold.

We walked over the bridge to the Rijksmuseum then turned right, skirting Vondelpark, to enter the begrimed Overtoom, a long, dull street that happens to feature delightfully in a nursery rhyme Opoe used to sing for me. Something about rowing a little boat and drinking sweet milk with cream. There also used to be a "poffertjes" establishment on the corner of the Overtoom, where one could indulge in these miniscule pancakes dusted with icing sugar and mugs of hot chocolate with malt.

This outing with Jan didn't take in any such delights. He told me gravely, after an introduction about life and people which thoroughly confused me, that he could no longer watch his friend and room-mate, Kees, go to pieces on account of being in love with me and I so cold, so unforthcoming and remaining at my chosen distance. It was true that Kees came third in my affections as far as our little tribe was concerned. But love? It had never occurred to me.

Jan told me what a good and generous person his friend was and how much he deserved to be happy and what was I going to do about it? No doubt, Jan was doing his bit to tidy up the world around him and he didn't mind doing such unpleasant duties as taking a cold female for a walk through freezing streets and laying it on the line!

Once more I was stunned. Clearly Jan had no idea what went on in my mind and never had. Neither had I had any forewarning of what was building up in his. It was one of the most miserable days in my life. If love was as impossible as this, what did anything matter? If the man I loved wanted me to marry his best friend, then why not give in and solve the problem?

I was almost seventeen and chilled to the bone before adult life had even started.

Jan arranged the first date for Kees to be alone with me and do his own bidding. Never having been kissed before, this new experience elicited a response which was somewhat positive. Later I understood it to be purely biological, but at sweet sixteen I thought perhaps it meant that my body understood love better than my mind.

To make a long story short, Kees and I became engaged and I concentrated on my future as a married woman. As Kees didn't ever appear to have any money left over from his pay, I decided to return home to Hilversum to be able to save up for the necessities to set up house. I resigned from my job as a junior secretary at Wiener's steel factory and told Elly I was moving south again. So ended the most carefree and happy period of my formative years.

Not that the four-sided friendship dissolved so easily. We met whenever we could. I also got to know Jan's family during one of our common outings. His father was a tall, red-faced man. He was a white man. All his brothers were white. He also cherished a framed photograph of his beautiful blond mother, who may have been dead, I never asked. Jan looked like his brothers in facial features, the way he smiled, in man-

nerisms. But he was Indonesian and they were Dutch.
Some people in YFC described Jan as black. Over the
years I had seen him get paler and paler in our overcast
climate until he was yellow-skinned, like a Dutch
suntan.

I had never been conscious of the difference in our
appearances, just as I was not conscious of the fact that
I was whiter on the outside than my Inner Life would
have it. Yet, the fact that he was dark and of Eastern
origin had everything to do with my falling in love with
him, though not with continuing to be so afflicted. That
was due to his personal charm, his nobility of character,
his refreshing originality, his loyalty and everything
good that he stood for. How can one explain love?
How, indeed, can people become more skilled at handling love, especially across cultural and racial borders?

I think it is fair to say that from the start I was in love
with an idea. When the age of first discernment arrived,
I fell in love with someone who fitted the idea. It became
a pattern, although I never saw it that way then. Even
now, knowing what I know, at a ripe age, I see that the
idea is always foremost with me and that the men have
had to make their suitability apparent or lose me
altogether.

Jan was not only my "brother". He was Kees's
brother and every child's uncle. When he took a room
with Kees's aunt, she reported on the streams of lovely
girls who rang the doorbell or phoned to speak to Jan
about some aspect of the study of social work. He was
forthcoming to all, even fell in and out of love, but
nothing of permanence seemed to eventuate. After some
five years in Holland he had made so many friends of
both sexes and all ages that a king's court would have
been the right comparison, had he not been the per-
sonification of humility itself.

When Elly married by proxy a helicopter pilot who had already taken up his post in Dutch New Guinea, Jan acted as the stand-in bridegroom. When Kees and I had a son — our first child being a daughter — the boy received Jan's second name and was held by him during baptism. He pledged me assistance for the welfare of this namesake child, no matter how far in the future.

Once, during a light-hearted after-dinner conversation, Jan had exclaimed: "I'd love to have a dozen children, but it is such a pity you have to marry first!" I laughed with the others.

When my marriage broke down and Kees did not pay any maintenance for the children, I eventually called on Jan to mediate on behalf of his namesake. I met him in a tearoom on Leidseplein, close to all our old haunts. His face had the same grave expression as that night we walked the Overtoom. He told me he thought I should have tried harder. It was I who had broken up the marriage. His friend and brother Kees was unhappy again and the onus was on me.

We finished our coffee and parted. That was the last time I saw my black brother who sold me out for friendship. I later heard he'd gone to America to further his studies and research. Even when well into his thirties he was still unattached, living his life for others. If he never produced children of his own to carry on the goodness that was in him, it somewhat explains why the world is not as good a place as it might have been.

Marriage at eighteen, motherhood at nineteen and again at twenty, and divorce at twenty-one led to remarriage at twenty-three to a man who had that way of walking from the hips and the jerking of the left shoulder. I was fascinated by his story. I was still chasing shadows of the old dream. I was still in love with an idea. This time I sold myself out.

Born in Indonesia of Dutch and Polish stock, captured by the Japanese at sixteen and sent to Burma as a prisoner-of-war, evacuated to Holland after the war, my second husband longed for a warmer climate. We married in 1957 and he enquired about going to South America, but there was no job for him there. In 1958, at my instigation, we migrated to Australia, each pursuing different dreams. I never knew this, although I suspected there were things in his life he wanted to follow up, like going to Japan to see the country his captors hailed from and to speak the language again. Perhaps a return to Indonesia, now so close. But like me, he never went to the lands where he had inner connections, but more or less stayed put where fate had deposited him.

We stayed together longer than our first marriages had lasted, but as the gap between our Inner Lives widened, without any material on hand to build a bridge — although I desperately made rafts of straw which all bounced off on the other shore — I once again made an end of it.

This second marriage breakdown didn't just come upon me one fine morning when I woke up. For years I had been trying, remembering Jan's advice, albeit in another arrangement. The knowledge that again I was in the wrong place had come early in the marriage, but I was determined to make it work and migration was to give it the big boost. At twenty-seven, however, I looked back over my shoulder down the last decade and asked myself what had gone wrong. How was it that my Inner Life was so far off the rails?

By this time I lived in a nice house, held my third child in my arms, had good neighbours and friends. But inside me something cried out "Go back! Wrong way!" I traced the notion back to the age of seventeen and heard a chorus of voices gathering strength, chanting: "It is time you faced up to reality."

They had been chanting it for years, but I had successfully ignored them, living my Inner Life without harming anyone. Playing back the memory tape, I heard myself snap out of my cocoon during that walk on a biting, cold winter night along the Overtoom. It was there I first decided to face up to what people called reality, and started to do the things that people do to stop others from asking what's wrong with them, instead of stepping to the drum I heard inside my own head. Back then no one asked whether you knew what you were doing when you announced your engagement, your marriage. No one considered alternatives like living together, or living alone by choice. No one except Jan, for himself. He knew he didn't want to marry then.

At twenty-seven I tried to recall what sort of things made me happy up to the age of seventeen and the admission of reality into my life. Apart from fixtures which had been lost, like the heather fields, Jan, train travel and midnight black-coffee palavers with a bunch of friends, there had always been books.

I had to get back to books. Books had always been the entrance portal to the realms that fed my Inner Life and my Inner Life held my outer life together as my skin kept my flesh on my bones.

If I possessed one thing in those days of motherhood and housekeeping, it was solitude. The two elder children attended school and the youngest slept much, played quietly and was self-possessed, preferring solitude himself.

I discovered the State Library in Adelaide, South Australia, when I lived in a village some seventeen miles from that city. My youngest son's frequent trips to a hospital there, for treatment of a bone disorder in his poor little nose, gave me the opportunity to visit the library and change books. In the cool halls I found solace for my constant fears for his well-being.

Losing myself in books whenever time allowed, I picked up the old trail again. The trail into Tibet. With my newly acquired ability to read English, however imperfectly, I found a treasure trove awaiting me. In a short time I became something of an expert on Tibetan history, culture and society. Not that it was difficult to become an expert on Tibet in the early 1960s in South Australia! The limelight that briefly played on that country and its fleeing ruler in 1959 had stirred little lasting interest in a world used to injustices. On the other hand, I truly understood what I was reading and I was reading nothing else. I also began to comb second-hand bookstores and bought paperbacks remotely relating to my chosen subject. I now have a collection that covers not only Tibet, but most of Central Asia and China, including two volumes of Sven Hedin's famous Gobi crossings and treks into northern Tibet, as well as a best-seller written in 1865, when British soldiers on leave made it a habit to disguise themselves and dash around Central Asia in troikas and on horseback in order to check up on what the Russians were doing. Nothing much has changed except the modes of transport!

One paperback sat on my shelf for over a year without being read. It was entitled *Buddhism* by Christmas Humphreys and the back cover declared that it contained an outline of the religion of a number of Asian countries of which Tibet was one.

Now it needs to be told that I had left religion well and truly behind me. It had not stood by me in my darkest hours, although some religious people did, bless their souls. I had learnt that my suffering was my own, that no one could share it and that only I could change the tenure of my life, if not all the ingredients that were already cluttering it up. I had over the years evolved my own philosophy and, with my resolve to turn my back upon other people's reality and live my own, that personal philosophy was growing strong and proving much more useful than bible and prayer ever had.

I'd only bought the little book on Buddhism because, as an expert on Tibet, I felt I had to set aside my aversion to religion in general and not remain ignorant of what my favourite civilisation used to oil its spiritual mechanicsm.

One day, for want of anything better to read, I took it off the shelf and settled down with it. To my unending surprise I discovered on page one that I had been a Buddhist virtually all my life! This was both dampening and exhilarating: the first because I had deemed myself quite unique and my philosophy an original piece of metaphysical thinking, and the latter because after all one third of the world was Buddhist, so I couldn't be wrong, could I?

Within one hundred seconds of starting on the book, I had plunged into a spiritual fraternity that was spread over a quarter of the world's landmass.

Of course, Buddhism too has its schools and schisms and new ones forever arise. But the Buddha had foreseen all that and forewarned his followers to rely on their own observations during their quest for enlightenment. Just what I had been doing!

My reading switched to books on Buddhism and soon I found that no matter how attractive it all was, my non-existing soul came naturally to rest in Tibetan Buddhism, despite the often elegant reasonings of Theravada Buddhism, the aesthetics of Zen and the pragmatic approach of the Chinese Buddhists. My reading included a liberal intake of Indian philosophies to break up the ritualism and in later years I adopted Kwan Yin — or Kwan Yin adopted me, who shall say? — the Goddess of Mercy, for the sheer love of life.

But all this belongs to my autobiography of religion. Wish I could write it here and now, for it has sustained a life that was at death's door eight times and yet never ran into spiritual bankruptcy. Not that it is going to be easy to separate these influences on my life so clinically from here on. They become more and more interwoven like warp and weft, as the cloth of life unrolls.

Yet I must resume the trail of race and identity and try to express what living in Australia added to my understanding of these first denominators of our fate.

5

Ancient land, ancient people

Despite being fatherless, I had grown up with as many men as women looking after my welfare. But during my working life I found myself more often than not in places where men were in the majority and so I became used to having them around.

I developed many friendships with men over the years which were founded on common interest or plain liking, not love. When I left Holland I had no idea how important a part male friendships had played in my outlook on life, my sense of adventure and my notion that everything is possible if you wish for it hard enough. When it came to men I felt myself to be a partner, not a subject of projections of an emotional kind.

Australia is of course a different society from Holland. But Australia is also very young as a society and the influence of Victorian England is still palpably felt. It was a joke among migrants that when you were invited to an Australian party, if you were a man you would end up in the kitchen with the boys and the beer, and if you were a woman you would spend the evening in the lounge talking about babies and operations with the other females!

Basically, that was what male-female relations were like in the Australia of the sixties. Much has changed since then, but mainly on the surface. It takes longer for people to change inside. I have been upset and hurt many times in Australia because men I felt a liking for have either dismissed me as a mere woman, or mistaken a proposition of friendship for an opportunity to add to their sexual scoringboard! It is quite unbelievable how blind Australian men are to the variety of possibilities for relationships with women.

Not that I have been a fast learner! It is so natural for me to take an interest in people, no matter what their sex might be, that even in my fifties I find myself biting off the tip of my tongue, as I discover another sex maniac disguised as a really nice person I might have wanted to get to know!

Relations with women have almost been as uneasy. Is this the result of a life without siblings? That seems to be the answer, but I don't believe it is. I still have dreams left, which have not been tested. Dreams built up from incidents and clues that promise better traffic between two or more minds, if only circumstance would one day allow for a more than fleeting meeting.

Many women are so enclosed in a world of women and women's business that it repulses me. They have no understanding of men as human beings and their friendships with other women rest on that lack of understanding. I see nothing wrong with expressing emotions but not at the cost of the life of the mind and humanity's attempt at reaching degrees of spirituality.

Unfortunately, these experiences have been restricted to women of European stock. Although I have had countless women friends, only a handful are left since I stopped spending energy that I no longer had on relationships which mattered less as my purpose in life became more clear to me. As I grow older and better able to express my motivations, it may well be possible that this trend will reverse itself and I shall find more people of like mind who want to spend their later years on the contemplation of peace, truth, compassion and the striking of balances.

In Asian women from various countries I have found an extra dimension that enabled them to invite me to be who I was, instead of switching on just that aspect of me demanded for the occasion. No doubt I am being terribly biased here. Had I grown up in Asia, I would probably complain that my female companions were incredibly emotional and would praise the liberating nature of my friendships with western women! I have that streak of contrariness in me.

However, the fact remains that non-European women have figured more prominently in my friendships than European women — again, with the exception of that precious handful — and I share an understanding with them that has to do with an intrinsic understanding of the vulnerability of human life, its beauties and its cruelties. This is opposed to the general western belief that one must be in control of life and if one is not then something rational and technical can be done to put it right. The Asian women, on the whole, understand the policy of lying low and when to lie low. They intuitively understand forces at work which western women, if they want to acknowledge them at all, need to explain scientifically or fit into a complex system, such as astrology.

Meta was my friend for many years, from when we were teenagers right into middle age, when, through sheer distance in time and space, we lost touch at last.

We only met once. Meta was a penfriend. When we began to exchange letters I still lived in Holland and she lived in a sanatorium near Bandung on the island of

Java in Indonesia. She was of mixed Dutch and Indonesian background, a Catholic and suffering from weak lungs. I loved Meta's letters full of little stories of tropical outings, parties and visits. Despite her limitations due to lack of good health and money, Meta had a great sense of how to enjoy life. At least, that is how she came across in her letters.

She recovered and emigrated to Holland, where she went to live with an aunt and uncle in a northern province. Such was our poverty, that we had to remain penfriends, even though the distance between us had been reduced from half a world to a little over one hundred kilometres.

At Easter, it must have been 1958, her aunt and uncle were going away for the holiday. They feared that Meta was not yet familiar enough with the gas stove and oil heater, so they offered her a trainfare to the southern town where I lived with my Indonesian-born second husband, if we could put her up.

I was so excited! I hoped that somehow that first meeting would herald an even closer friendship than we had built up in our letters. I was sure we would get on well. And so we did. Meta was like an older sister I had never had. She was about five years older than I, and had a mature outlook on life and a quiet wisdom which were like a balm on my own heavily scratched and torn adulthood.

I remember that long weekend being filled with easy companionship and gently undulating conversations. Meta cooked a wonderful Indonesian banquet for us and played with the children. I still have a snapshot of the four of us walking in the park, rugged up against the cold.

In October 1958 we migrated to Australia and I never saw Meta again. We kept corresponding for many years.

She had another spell in a sanatorium, but took up life with courage and eagerness when she was once more released. Staying single, she spent holidays in sunny Italy, for she missed the sun badly. Later she spent vacations in the United States, where her brother had settled.

When I finally returned to Holland, we had lost touch. I rang the phone number I had kept, but there was never any answer. It was holiday time and maybe she was away. During my next visit the same happened.

As if rekindling my memories and writing about her stirred her into action, Meta wrote me a letter in March 1988. She still lives in Holland and still longs for sunshine, but now looks forward to early retirement from her job in social administration to do the things she postponed so long because frail health left her too little time to develop her own talents.

I was sure we'd meet at last in May 1988 when I visited Holland for my mother's eighty-third birthday. But the news of my win of the Dirk Hartog award broke that week and when I flew off after six hectic days I'd seen more journalists than relatives. With Meta I only had a telephone conversation, saying "better luck next time".

Meta is the only person I seriously encouraged to come to Australia. I knew she would appreciate the warmer climate, but don't know how she would have taken the racist undertones in Australia in the 1960s. During that decade a young Perth couple of Indonesian birth told me how one of them had had to "prove" to the Australian Immigration authorities that the Indonesian genes accounted for less than twenty-five percent in the family's racial make-up. Nazi Germany demanded the same "proof" from part-Jews in World War II before selecting who was to be sent to extermination camps, who had to wear the Star of David and who could, for the time being, go on living.

No doubt there was a good deal of selfishness in my attempts to talk Meta into migration on her own and she settled in the cold northern regions of Holland where fate had landed her.

Meta and Fransje were the first of a long line of non-European women with whom I've had relationships amounting to sisterhood, no matter how brief or beset by circumstance. In fact, I have learned that friendship must be savoured on the wing, so to speak, because my own and other people's mobility often prevents longstanding bonds.

My meeting with a young, dark-eyed woman from Alice Springs in Central Australia was beset by circumstance. She had driven, with husband and baby, for a day and a night in an old rattling car to find their old friends, our neighbours.

The neighbours weren't home. It was one of those blistering, dust-laden, hot days during the Australian summer that drives people to the seaside. The husband had come to our door to enquire. I said I was sure the neighbours would be back later that day, but how late was hard to guess. Would they like to come out of the heat and have a cup of tea inside?

The husband thanked me, but said the wife was too shy. He went back to the car with the mattress bound on top, bundles and boxes on the backseat. Even from a distance I could sense that they carried all their possessions and were hoping to bed down for the night at the neighbour's place, before looking for a house to start a new life.

I found that my thoughts were so occupied with them that I broke out in a sweat of discomfort. Having a baby myself, I simply could no longer stand the fact that the other woman sweltered in the heat of the day with no space to even change a nappy.

I took my courage in my hands, rehearsed my halting English sentences in my head and walked up to the car on the gravel road, dust rising at every step, my breath sheer cut off by gusts of searing hot wind coming from the north.

Coming closer, I realised why the wife was too shy to come in. She was an Aborigine. I knew enough by then of the short history of race relations in Australia to realise she could not risk accepting an invitation from someone who had not yet seen the colour of her skin.

Overcome with a mixture of anger and compassion, I pleaded with her to please come out of the heat and into my cool house. I did not need to plead long now that I had seen for myself. She gathered baby, bottles and bag and, followed by her husband, came with me to the house.

I was not only excited to have her in the house, but very, very aware of how breakable this connection was, of what a slim thread we had between us to sound each other out. But being mothers together helped considerably; showing her where things were in the kitchen so that she could prepare the child's bottle. Later we sat and drank coffee, or tea, or cordial, and talked.

I have only a vague memory of her husband, who was white, and I suppose my husband talked with him over drinks and cigarettes. But the real communication was going on between her and me as I was given a first-hand education on how Aborigines felt about their treatment as second-class citizens in Australia. She must have known I wanted to know, for to talk as she did about humiliations and lack of rights was almost a subversive activity in the early 1960s! In the end I was allowed to hold her baby and when the neighbours drove into the street, we parted with a sense of regret, knowing that their road did not finish here and they would be gone by morning.

If more of my encounters with Aboriginal people could have been as open and direct as that meeting with a woman my own age, I might have found an Australia in which I did not have to live as an alien, but could have come to a resting point in my journey towards a balance of race and identity within myself. Yet, again, this may be no more than wishful thinking . . .

In coming to Australia, meeting with Aboriginal people had been high on my list of expectations.

Before then, I had travelled no further than Paris, which was full of Algerians as Holland was with people from its former colonies, albeit more segregated, less part of the French image of France.

Australia, I presumed, would have a mixed black and white population, seeing that the races had coexisted for some one-hundred-and-seventy years. And when I saw my first beach full of bathers, that's what I saw: I mistook suntans of a depth of brown unknown in Holland for Aboriginality.

I was surprised we saw no Aborigines in Melbourne streets and parks. Adelaide, too, appeared to be an all-white community in 1958. Nearly thirty years later the people in the streets of Adelaide have all the skin colours the world can produce and just for once I'd come too early. Aboriginal people are also to be seen in Adelaide, but their story is not such a happy one as those of the majority of the immigrants.

It was 1962 before I had another meeting with a representative of the ancient race. I noticed an old, dark man walking towards me in an Adelaide thoroughfare. I have since learned that my immediate attention to an Aborigine in the crowd is picked up by them and often results in a footpath conversation. Unfortunately, all Aborigines who have been thus drawn to me, were under the influence of alcohol, which loosened their normal inhibitions in dealing with white people.

This old man asked me for ninepence. Knowing that besides my busfare home I had two shillings on me, I asked him why. He wanted to make a phone call. Phone calls cost sixpence in those days. He then asked where the ''Abo'' department was. I had no idea, but suggested the policeman at the intersection would be able to help him with that.

He looked me straight in the eye and said: ''You no Australian lady. You migrant?'' I said I was.

''Aboriginal people in this country don't go see policemen,'' he explained. In those days they were forbidden to take alcohol; only whites were allowed to get drunk. I understood.

''You very good lady,'' he said and was about to wander off. But we hadn't solved his problem, so I counted half my fortune into his lined, pink palm. One shilling and we were equals.

During the 1960s I made friends with an Australian woman who had lived in the country and told me wonderful tales about the Aborigines in that area, with whom she'd had much contact on a basis of mutual liking and trust. She invited me to come to a meeting of an association which fostered friendship between Aborigines and other Australians. It had been in existence for more than a quarter of a century, I believe. I accepted eagerly.

When we arrived at the meeting place, the large room had two blocks of seats with a path in the middle. All the Aborigines sat on one side, the whites on the other.

At suppertime, over a cup of tea, there was some hesitant mixing in which I, a shy stranger, had no part.

I can see now, after thirty years of getting to know the historical evolution of this country's problems, that the people who ran that organisation were laying the groundwork for the slow advancement that is indeed being experienced by some sections of the Australian Aboriginal population. But to me, having come from a society where people were not then judged by their race (this had changed by 1977, when I made my first return visit to Holland), I felt absolutely desolate about the possibility of bridging the gap of the path between the chairs of the blacks and the whites. I resolved to leave the Aboriginal problem to the Anglo-Australians whose ancestors had created it and whose national guilt I was not prepared to shoulder.

Even though Walter, a handsome young Aboriginal man, was somewhat drunk when he met me and a companion on the same thoroughfare one rainy night, he was lucid enough to speak up for his race.

"We understand things you whitefellas know nothing about and never will," he said with a cunning smile, because that sort of statement is hard to refute and he knew it. "We understand the spirit of the land. You whitefellas only know 'bout money and things like that."

Walter was a product of Aboriginal advancement, white man's style. He'd had a western education and no doubt paid the price for that by losing some of his tribal skills. In fact, I suspect that the more Aborigines speak about their special knowledge, the less they have of it. The white men's alcohol, by this stage freely available to all, was completing the scrambling up of Walter's values. By the way, in view of the all too frequent reports of drunkenness in Aborigines, it is interesting to note that half the alcohol in this country is consumed by fifteen per cent of the population and the Aborigines would hardly figure in that as they only make up one per cent of the total population.

I did not tell Walter what I knew of the Aborigines and their land. I don't argue with drunks, white or black; it's useless. But I think we might have gotten along fine, had he been sober. But then he wouldn't have talked to me . . .

In the late sixties I was studying for matriculation, one of my subjects being geology. I studied on my own, without the benefit of school or night classes, so I was at a loss how to get the necessary field experience.

A friend put me in touch with a group of volunteers, who worked on an archeological site on the River Murray for a local museum. The curator badly needed more "diggers". This misleading word may be a hangover from nineteenth-century archeology, which was more concerned with intact artifacts than with the recording of the historical progress of a group of people. Digging is strictly out these days. I was to learn that toothpicks and pastry brushes were the tools of the responsible archeologist. The curator of this project was caught between his desire to keep the site a secret to prevent vandalism and his need to attract more unpaid workers. From time to time someone leaked news about it and so, on this day, the curator was deeply disturbed at the sudden appearance of two new faces, one of which was mine. The other new girl and I had to promise not to speak to the press, or tell relatives and friends where we went, or reveal the location of the site in loose-lipped conversations. We were sworn to secrecy for the term of our natural lives.

I joined and was allowed to bring my nine-year-old son, who was also sworn to secrecy. I planned to go for three consecutive weekends to study the earth layers, conglomerates, limestone cliffs and oxbow lakes that occur in that locality.

I admit I was green. I had no idea then of the sacredness of Aboriginal burial sites. Neither, I suspect, had archeologists. The first night I spent there I was nearly killed. I slept in a museum tent with a centre pole. It had rained the evening of our arrival and during the night a storm and all hell broke loose. The tentpole snapped and the top half came to rest like a giant spear in the ground, inches from where my head poked out of my sleeping-bag.

It may well have been a good omen. After all, I was completely unhurt, as if I had been protected from harm.

By morning the sky was clear. Son Ronald woke up, opened the tent flap and looked out. I can still see the back of his blond head as he sat on his knees, immobile, silhouetted against the morning light. Then my Australian-born son gasped: "Land! Land everywhere! Come and look, Mum!" He turned around and I saw the ecstasy in his eyes. Children often know intuitively what adults have to learn from books. I knew I would come back for Ronald's sake, earth layers and geology exams or not.

The storm and the tentpole which had nearly speared me were discussed. Maureen and I were newcomers. In the two years the site had been worked, bad weather had usually accompanied the arrival of newcomers.

Maureen, Ronald and I returned for the next dig a fortnight later. This time we were flooded out. We returned again a fortnight later and the sun shone all the time. We had been accepted.

Ronald sometimes strenuously objected to having to accompany me to adult gatherings, since his elder sister and brother had moved away from home. I was a supporting mother then and although I tried to make the most of weekend home life, I sometimes insisted that he fall in with my needs. But the Roonka visit — for the name of the now protected site is a secret no longer — was such a revelation to him, and the people who worked there were so unusually sensitive and generous of heart, that for two-and-a-half years my son accompanied me every fortnight, winter and summer, to this sacred piece of land.

I made one valiant effort to get in touch with living Aboriginal people myself and offer friendship and assistance. In the dentist's waiting room I had found an obscure publication in which someone claimed that the Aboriginal women and girls of Point McCleay Reserve could do with a volunteer to teach knitting and similar crafts. That happened to be within my capabilities. The publication was over a year old, but I decided to visit the community and offer my services. Although penniless — I was by then a full-time student, so the year may have been 1973 — I had access to wool remnants, enough to start a class off with small projects. Enthusiasm would do the rest.

Weather and studies delayed good intentions, but a few months later on a cool Saturday morning young Ronald and I headed south down the Fleurieu Peninsula to visit Point McCleay, a drive of several hours from the Adelaide Hills. My head buzzed with opening sentences and ideas for craft classes on weekends. When we drove into the grounds of Point McCleay there was some activity around a small community building, so I made straight for it.

Inside an elderly man was doing something with sheets of paper while Aboriginal people queued up with familiar reluctance. He took one look at me in my jeans and jacket and snapped, "What d'you want here," or words to that effect. All my marvellous planned introductions dissolved in the face of this "welcome" and I could only give a garbled account of my intentions.

"That's nothing to do with us now," he said. "But you can go and see the chairman of the council. They make all the decisions now. He lives over there." He pointed towards a weatherboard house on the far side of the lawn.

Ronald and I walked across the grass, climbed the veranda steps and knocked on the door. A woman opened it and when I reiterated the reasons for my coming she called her husband. Together they faced me with unsmiling eyes as I explained for the third time how keen I was to drive two hours once a fortnight to share my skills in knitting, crocheting and other fibre crafts. There was no immediate response to my proposition and by now I felt thoroughly deflated. The conversation progressed painstakingly, like the proverbial pulling of teeth. Ronald got bored and went to watch a football game in progress on the grass. Soon he was playing with the Aboriginal children.

At last the chairman said he would put my proposal to the council and let me know. It was obviously time to leave. I turned to the ball-playing children and mumbled something about having to tear Ronald away from the game.

"That's my son," said the chairman, indicating the tallest boy, who played skilfully and with joyful verve.

"Children have no problem," added his wife, and for a few moments the three of us wordlessly contemplated the ball-kicking youngsters; a black head and a blond mop bobbing up and down according to the rules of a commonly understood game.

On parting the woman asked me whether my reason for coming had been the report in the paper. What report? I didn't understand what she was talking about. She went inside and came back with the newspaper. On the front page a headline announced that Point McCleay was going it alone, becoming independent, would run its own affairs and hold elections that very morning.

"Oh my God," I moaned. "I had no idea." How like me to pick the moment of transition and put my foot right in it. Now I understood why the white man had bitten my head off. He must have thought I was a journalist or stirrer. Now I understood the reluctance of the couple to take another do-gooder on board.

I protested my innocence, explained how long ago I'd intended to make the visit. They believed me. We laughed a bit about the coincidence. Thank heavens we laughed a bit, together.

We parted with the atmosphere less charged between us, but Ronald didn't want to go. I told him we might be back soon if the council accepted my idea and then he could play football with the Point McCleay boys to his heart's content.

But we never heard again and I didn't have the heart to ask them why. I was too much like them, once bitten, twice shy.

In 1977 I met the Aboriginal poet and activist Kath Walker — now Oodgeroo Noonuccal — at a literary conference. In tearoom conversation she criticised me for having engaged in "digging up our bones".

"Who gave you the right?" she shouted. I had no idea, as I had always accepted that my bones could be dug up a thousand years from now if someone deemed them important enough.

"Nobody," I admitted. "But no living Aborigine ever wanted to associate with me because I have the wrong skin, so the dead have been kinder and I have come to know them very intimately. Besides, coming from a landless people, I had to learn about the land, but I did have respect and love for it."

She calmed down somewhat, although she stuck to her main argument that I had no right to engage in what she regarded as disturbing her ancestors' graves. If she was related to the Ngaiawang, the recent inhabitants of Roonka, or to the different people we found at lower levels going back as much as twenty-two thousand years, it would probably be in the way I am related to the Gypsies and Genghis Khan. Like me, she also pays scant acknowledgment to her part-European ancestry. I promised her that I would do no more archeology. It was 1977 and, as it turned out, my days in the field were behind me.

I could have told Kath, had she been prepared to listen, of "my people", the remains I worked on during those years, with trowel, toothpick and pastry brush.

The skeleton I remember with great tenderness was that of a premature or just-born baby. So fragile were its little ribs that they had to be steeped many times in a toughening solution before they were strong enough to be taken up. There was also the old woman who had arthritis of the spine, which I suffered from myself. Across the centuries a wave of sympathy joined me to her, as I imagined how she stumbled and limped across the plain, looking for roots and small game, turning in her sleep to relieve the pressure and hugging the fire and the sunlight to lessen the pain.

The man I excavated with Johnny, the potter, had died from a bone-point stuck into his abdomen from midriff to well below the navel. The set of his jaws told of his death struggle. One can only guess at the conflict that earned him his cruel demise.

I worked as an extra hand on many other skeletons. Once I was given one of my own, the top of the skull just showing. With a deep sense of responsibility I worked away all day, but had to conclude by sunset that there was only a skull and nothing more.

However, it was my trowel that removed the last layer of sand covering a skull which was given the number 108 in the scheme of things. This happens to be the Buddhist sacred number and I cried out: "This will be the most important skeleton on this site!" As the excavation proceeded this turned out to be true and 108 is now very famous indeed. The sand I removed had covered him for about eighteen thousand years. He was a man, cradling a small child in his left arm. On a burial site where no burial goods or decorations had been found, this burial was astounding: 108 was adorned with a crown and necklaces of wallaby teeth and there were other artifacts. The entire burial pointed to him as having been a person of great importance in the tribe. Although I didn't continue on his excavation after the crown of teeth appeared, I felt and still feel that 108 connects me with that land. He may have been the shaman, or in any case a man of wisdom. Recently I saw him again in a set of slides at an anthropological lecture. He has a lot to tell and has only told a little.

The argument for archeology in Australia is that it puts on record the long habitation of this continent by Aboriginal peoples. Although *they* knew they'd "always" been here, the white settlers saw them mostly as an itinerant problem that prevented profitable exploitation of what they regarded as an "empty" land!

The Aborigines have had to fight for landrights and cultural survival with weapons the white population understands. One of these is an archeological record that shows antiquity. Their struggle has been greatly helped in recent years by findings that prove they have been around for at least forty thousand years and this date is expected to be pushed further back as older remains are carbondated. More and more, Aboriginal leaders are quoting this figure, which is gaining them respect for their tenacity to live in a land as harsh as Australia has been for many centuries and for their right to run their own lives instead of being patronised and "protected" by the fledgling white "civilisation" of barely two hundred years.

Their struggle is only just beginning, but results augur well for their survival as a distinctive race with a wonderfully sane culture. In the thirty years I have lived here, I have seen racial prejudice change from being the acceptable point of view — "They're no good for anything, the Abos, they'll probably just die out" — to something you have to be careful about how, and to whom, you express it. This means of course that the diehards either have gone underground, bursting out occasionally in nasty fascist rashes, or are clinging to organisations which traditionally saw Australia as a white man's land given to them by the Christian God.

Whereas early contact resulted in a small half-caste population whose descendants had much reason for bitterness, later immigrants, such as the Chinese, Afghans and Kanaks also intermarried with the Aborigines. When I settled in Australia, all these people were still more or less expected to die out quietly and leave Australia to the Australians, who were not only white, but specifically Anglo-Saxon, Scottish and Irish. But, with the continuing accumulation of other races by means of postwar immigration, the balance has shifted. Over a hundred distinct ethnic groups are recognisable in Australia and intermarriage is the order of the day rather than the exception. I now have a more than fifty per cent chance of getting daughters-in-law with ancestries other than British and children born around the coming turn of the century will be able to point to a multicultural ancestry. Any who then want to claim "pure" blood will be small enough in number to form a social club and meet in the neighbourhood clubhouse once a month to lament the takeover by the people of the world!

The danger that always lurks is, of course, that people are inclined to pick out of their ancestry the particular strand they favour, be that exotic or lacklustre, depending on whom they want to impress. If they then start to dress, eat and live accordingly, they have a chance to pass as "pure" this or that. However, because of the great number of ethnic groups now here, there is a greater possibility that a new — or renewed — Australian type of people is evolving. As long as these new Australians manage to maintain all the skin colours of the world and keep up a sample collection of all the traditions that were imported here, including the indigenous Aboriginal culture, there is little danger that they will present themselves to the world as something elitist. But then again, they may claim to inhabit the first truly pluralist continent in the world and become patriotic about that . . . And patriotism is no respecter of differences . . .

One hot summer's day, Ronald and I were driving back to Adelaide in our little open Mini Moke, having spent the weekend in the Flinders Ranges, the fabulous wild land on the way to the west.

As we came over a rise, we saw a woman standing on

the road, waving us down. We stopped and saw their family car parked by the side of the road with a flat tyre. An elderly man and a young one were changing the wheel. A grey-haired woman, two young ones and a boy sat waiting on the brown grass.

The woman asked whether I had a jack. I did and gave it to the man. Then I tried to start a conversation with the woman. They were an Aboriginal family on their way to Port Augusta to bring a son back to his place of work. They lived not far from us in an Adelaide suburb. These details emerged with much prying on my part, as she was reluctant to talk. To fill in the time, I decided we should have drinks all round, since the heat was stifling.

Getting out the container of cordial and two plastic cups, I instructed Ronald to bring drinks first to the men, who were sweating in the dust under the car. The grey-haired auntie had walked off with one of the girls. Next, Ronald brought drinks to the young woman and boy and then filled up for me and the woman who had stopped us. I'd invited her to sit in the car with me, out of the sun, but she had refused. But when she realised that we were all drinking out of the same two cups, she seemed suddenly to change her mind about sharing such close proximity with me and accepted. So we sat in the car, talking as two women do when they don't know each other.

Suddenly she turned and said: "We were just lucky it was you who came past."

"Why?" I asked surprised. "Anyone would lend you a jack if they carried one."

"The others didn't even stop," she said grimly.

Then I realised that in the five or so minutes before we reached this spot, at least three cars had come from the opposite direction. None had stopped. This has been the life of Aboriginal people for most of the two hundred years since white people came here. They've been left standing in the dust of their own land, with a hand raised to draw attention, while the intruders flash past in their cars on the roads they built for themselves, too callous to stop, or too frightened.

Yes, frightened. Some Anglo-Australians have a deep-seated fear of people vastly different in lifestyle from themselves. They theorise loudly about the Aborigines' transient way of life, drunkenness and unemployment and how they would solve all that, but run when they meet a real Aborigine on a lonely country road.

It will be the truest sign that we are part of a civilisation when this land accommodates the lifestyles of the encapsuled city dweller and the roaming hunter-gatherer with equal fairness and grace.

There is now a new generation of Aborigines growing up who avail themselves of a western education and enter white society on a par with all immigrants and descendants of immigrants of the last two hundred years. At what cost they do this will be hard to assess now, but the choice can't be easy.

When I worked at the university again during 1977–78, one of the departmental secretaries was a young Aboriginal woman. Gail appeared shy, reluctant to talk. However, we felt an emptiness after she left to take up music studies and do some travelling. A set of suitcases seemed a fitting farewell present from the staff. During the 1980s I saw her in a film entitled *The Wrong Side of the Road*, with the band "No Fixed Address". The film was made and acted by Aboriginal people and Gail had a prominent role in it. She was not shy after all and not a bit reluctant to speak up in scenes which depicted the shabby treatment Aborigines still receive in many areas of South Australia. I heard later that she was working in an Aboriginal medical clinic in Sydney.

Gail also miraculously materialised soon after I wrote about her. It had been ten years since she had left when we met in an Adelaide Street, near a noisy building site. We shouted at the top of our voices to exchange news while her friend, an Aboriginal woman from Sydney, stood waiting silently. Gail had become the mother of a little boy and had also just enrolled to do her Bachelor of Arts. Knowing how well prepared she was through her work at the department, I expressed my delight and referred to a mutual colleague who had entered the diplomatic service. "Perhaps one day you will represent Australia overseas." "Aaah, not me," she laughed. But her silent friend suddenly came to life with a vigorous nodding of her head in agreement.

Whereas New Zealand has had Maori people as representatives for many years, Australia tardily keeps seeing Aboriginal people as a "problem" and a "burden" rather than an asset. But Aboriginal people can only work in the public services if they can do so without having to compromise their culture and heritage. The question is when will Australia come of age and allow this to occur?

My neighbour, Jen, who is a historical researcher with an Aboriginal community and Australian-born herself, passionately believes that the Aboriginal heritage will have to become the heritage of all Australians, for it is tied to the land in which they were all born and that is all they have to identify with. It should be more than enough . . .

I know more about the ancient land of Australia than

about its ancient people. Yet it is the land that links them and me, whereas it still separates the settlers and the Aborigines. The land has a sacredness about it that comes from being imbued for over tens of thousands of years with energies of the living and the dying, the suffering and the worshipping of people who saw a significance in all that surrounded them. The animals, plants, rocks and all that lived — and isn't that everything — absorbed these energies, passed them on and kept them alive.

Travelling through the outback I can feel free and alone with the sun and the wind, or suddenly surrounded by presences unseen, either accommodating or repelling me. Contrary to what some Aborigines would believe, the Roonka site was friendly. It accommodated us, despite initiation storm and floods, and provided healing experiences for many a bruised personality.

It was somewhat different in Koonalda Cave, in the Nullarbor Desert in South Australia, near the Western Australia border. It had taken me two years, with the help of John and Maureen Hodges from the Roonka tribe, to organise the 1973 Koonalda expedition, which released Aboriginal history from its "final" ten thousand years BP (before the present) label, to thirty thousand BP, since extended to forty thousand BP.

I met Dr Alexander Gallus, the Hungarian archeologist who had discovered Koonalda's importance as a prehistoric site, during the twenty-eighth International Congress of Orientalists in Canberra in 1971. Roonka archeologist, Graeme Pretty, introduced me to him and I soon realised that here sat a deeply embittered man. His two degrees, in Law and in Classical Archeology, were not recognised in Australia. Neither had his archeological work in Europe made him acceptable in academic circles. Coming to Australia as a displaced person, he was set to work shovelling sand at Port Phillip Bay near Melbourne with a crew of contract migrants. During lunchbreaks he would dive into the nearby bush, turning over chips of stone, hoping to find secondary workings on their surfaces, evidence of a stone-age human civilisation. When the two years' government work were up, I believe he earned his living teaching French, spending his holidays in the outback looking for prehistoric remains.

His one-sided conversation was fascinating and intriguing. Here was a man not afraid of attempting to connect wildly disparate human mythologies like those of Carl Jung and the Australian Aborigines and to draw conclusions from them which, aided by his quite amazing intuition, led him to the sites he had excavated with the help of voluntary workers.

He told me of his promising finds in Koonalda Cave, bemoaning the fact that he was getting too old to return to unearth the revelations he knew to be waiting there. Besides, there were not enough people willing to commit themselves to a month of voluntary labour in a remote desert.

I protested. I said I knew people in Adelaide who would gladly go. So would I, if it could be done in the holiday month of January, also the hottest month of the year. Before I realised it, I had become the organiser of the 1973 Koonalda Archeological Expedition.

Since then I've known that if ever I want to start a new career I could go into catering for expeditions. From that point alone the expedition was a great success. Whereas people had returned from earlier expeditions with all sorts of complaints just short of scurvy, the 1973 members returned healthy and well-fed and remembering mealtimes in the sinkhole with good feelings.

The expedition also brought back decisive carbon samples that proved Aborigines had used the cave as far back as thirty thousand years ago. Present-day Aborigines are reported to be shy of getting near it, let alone entering the cave. To me personally, Koonalda has become forbidden territory also. It's a place where I would like to return, but I don't think my experiences there will ever let me.

We were twelve in the end. The six-week desert expedition with a four-week "dig", which Dr Gallus had planned in his renewed optimism, had been cut down to a three-week dig on account of his indifferent health and other people's commitments. Five helpers had come with him from Melbourne after all and the others were Roonka people.

Camp was set up on level ground, but the kitchen was installed on Dr Gallus's advice under the sinkhole's overhang, some thirty-three metres below ground level. We planned to take kitchen duties in turn, so that everyone could have a part in the archeological work.

During the first day's exploration it turned out I could not climb up to the "gallery" and tunnel which connect Koonalda Cave with subsequent caves and an underground lake. The first night's sleep on the ground had exacerbated the arthritis in my spine and I was unsure on my feet.

Knowing my limitations, I said I would wait in the cave while the others did their exploring. How long I sat there I did not know, but later it was said to be more than two hours. The cave is timeless. I sat on a limestone "bench" against a powdery limestone wall. My hands stroked through the moist powder and formed a small white egg. I scooped a "nest" to put my egg in and continued until I had made eight eggs and my mind had gone entirely blank. There was a splotch of light high up at the entrance. The rest of the cave, the size of a cathedral, was dim and dank. It was a very good place to be in.

When I heard human voices coming back through the tunnel, I perceived a barrier between them and me. Their laughing voices raised echoes that did not belong here and broke a silence that had enveloped me like a membrane. That silence had a substance, a content and a meaning, which they scattered in their relentless coming.

"I wonder where Lolo is," someone shouted as they clambered down to where I sat at the foot of the scree slope.

"Probably gone back up," someone replied.

I found I had no voice to say: "I'm here." My throat was closed. My mind wanted to block out other beings forever. I wanted to stay by myself in the cave.

John almost fell over my feet before he saw me, still sitting exactly as they'd left me, my hands held protectively over my nest of eggs.

"Oh look, you've made some eggs!" John exclaimed.

I found my voice then. I used it to clear up a strange contradiction I had perceived in his words and which had to be corrected.

"They aren't chicken eggs," I said. "They are snake eggs!"

Several people now stood around the nest of eight snake eggs, looking down, puzzled no doubt.

Suddenly I got up, stiffly, and joined them to climb out of the cave towards the light. I did not look around. My snake eggs may still be there, waiting for a future archeologist's interpretation.

I was unable to climb out of the cave by myself. My back was now so stiff and painful that I couldn't plant my feet on the narrow rocky ledges, even though there was a pipe railing to hold on to. Sweat broke out all over me as one by one my team mates disappeared over the edge into the daylight. In the end, realising my real distress, John and Michael hauled me up. It was a hair-raising ascent for me, although the others did it as nimbly as mountain goats, twice a day for three weeks.

We enjoyed our first hot meal in the kitchen between the many tonnes of rock that had once fallen there from the sinkhole's roof. To get back to camp there was a thirteen metre climb up a rocky slope to reach a twenty metre hanging ladder.

I was petrified. I told the others I could not make it and pleaded to be left in the sinkhole. They promised to haul me up, even bind me to a stretcher, but met with my persistant refusal. From where I sit now, behind a typewriter, telling the story, I know that in my normal frame of mind I would have done anything to get back on level ground with the rest of the group, to spend the evening around a small campfire with campfire conversation.

Finally it was agreed I could sleep in the sinkhole by myself. My bedroll, clothes and torch were brought down and I was given a whistle in case of emergency. I spread my bed in the part of the sinkhole that was open to the sky and was relieved when I saw the last pair of legs disappear over the rim, thirty-three metres above me. I was alone in the largest sinkhole in the world (see *Guinness Book of Records)* with the stars above me as my only protection. Protection from what?

As I lay in my sleeping-bag with dusk rapidly falling, the small cave bats began darting between my face and the stars, always bouncing off just before touching me. I was at peace there and fell asleep. Sometime during the night I woke up as something slithered across the rubberised sheet that covered the sleeping bag. There were of course snakes in the sinkhole. I had found their shed skins near rockholes. Snakes hunt at night, but not for human prey. I am not normally so at ease with reptiles, but I was then, alone in Koonalda's sinkhole with its bats and snakes for company. I fell asleep again.

The next day I proposed that I should be on full-time kitchen duty, thus relieving all other expedition members for work on the archeological sites in the cave. I knew I could not go back in there. My plan was accepted, rather gratefully, and so I prepared breakfast and lunches for eleven people, as they would stay below all day.

Left alone like Snow White as the dwarfs trundled off to work, disappearing down the cave's mouth one by one, I looked around my "home" for the ensuing weeks.

Planning and preparing the next day's lunches and that evening's dinner would take most of the day. The bulk of the food was dehydrated and had to be reconstituted. Water was at a premium. We carried enough for one-and-a-half weeks, after which we would drive fifty miles or so to Eucla in Western Australia to fill up the tanks. Firewood was even more scarce. Every morning I scampered between the snakes' rocky hiding places, where sticks and bunches of dried desert plants had lodged in cracks between the stones. With these I made a tiny fire inside a ring of rocks to precook certain foods and ended up with just enough hot charcoal to fry a giant omelette from eggpowder, one fresh onion and dried herbs. It took intelligence and organisation to know how much to use of the wood, water and foodstuffs to offer twelve people a three-course meal with enough variety to keep them wanting it for three weeks. I don't think I have ever enjoyed housekeeping more than those days at Koonalda.

As the sun warmed my bones, the arthritic pains lessened. By midafternoon the meals were under control and I could take a little rest under one of the two giant fig trees that grew there. It was while lying under that fig tree that a profound thought struck me about Adam and Eve in paradise. Looking at the shape of the fig leaves, like a large hand on a thin stem, I realised the leaves have often been depicted upside down in paintings and pictures. Yet, if Adam and Eve had really wanted to use them to cover up their lower parts, they would have done best by having the leaf fan out with the right side up and the stem fastened to their body hair. From this profound insight I moved to Christian symbolism and decided that most probably the fig leaf always appeared upside down because it was a symbolical hand, covering the parts which Christianity deemed shameful. I communicated these revelations to my team mates that evening in the hope that their lives would be enriched by them.

The owner of Koonalda station, a wizened old pioneer named Cyril, then in his eighties, had planted the two fig trees in the centre of the sinkhole and watered them through a pipeline which connected with the underground lake. Later he added an apricot tree, a plum and a banana palm and maybe one or two others I can't recall. With the protective wall of the sinkhole to cut down the abrasive desert winds, and Cyril's devoted care, they grew well. They must be the only fruit trees, indeed the only trees, in the whole of the Nullarbor (the name means "treeless plain").

As I sunbaked under the fig trees, I truly felt I was in paradise. On the second day I went topless about my kitchen duties, to let the sun caress my still painful back. Suddenly I heard voices from above and to my amazement two men came climbing down the ladder. Hastily I restored my costume to something fit to receive guests in. The two were geologists, "dropping in" with Cyril's permission. Koonalda is a protected site and we were there with a museum permit. Even Dr Gallus, after whom the excavations are named, needs a permit to enter the cave.

As the hostess with the mostest, I offered a wide choice of beverages from my kitchen. They made their choice and sampled our high-protein biscuits before they went down to visit the site.

That afternoon I decided to shift the kitchen out into the open, as I started to have uneasy feelings about the rock overhang. Dr Gallus had casually pointed to a heap of several thousands tonnes of rock with the remark: "That's where we used to sleep last time. It must have come down recently." What was there to stop the kitchen roof falling in just the same manner? Strangely, Dr Gallus disagreed with my move and assured me that nothing would fall down while we were there. His intuition was sure and certain, but it wasn't mine. I preferred the open sky and to leave the rockheaps to the mice that had started to ravage the food supplies. If they came out in the open during the night, the snakes would catch them before they reached those supplies which did not have mouse-proof packaging. The snakes were more interested in mice then bread, I reasoned.

It was during the third night that I had the dream. It was not a visual dream — more an awareness. There was a message, but there was no voice. Just a presence and me becoming aware of the message, which was clear and simple: "You have to go or you will die."

It woke me up. It was early dawn, the desert still, the night life already on the wane. Then, in the distance under the overhang, I heard the low rumble of falling rocks. They couldn't have been large rocks, but they did plunge from on high to the rock-strewn floor of the sinkhole. Even a rock no larger than a human fist can kill a person when it falls from that height. The rockfall confirmed the message.

I rolled up my bedding and packed my few belongings. I prepared breakfast and when the others came down I told them of my decision to leave. I did not give a reason other than my fear that the arthritis would make me a burden to the expedition. I said I felt it was getting worse.

John again assured me I could easily be hauled out on a stretcher, but anyone who would have seen that rockwall against which the hanging ladder bounced would have been far from elated by that prospect.

And how would I make the three-day journey back? I assured them that once I was seated behind the wheel, I would be able to drive and that I would seek out a doctor in Ceduna to obtain anti-inflammation tablets. In passing I mentioned the early morning rockfall. None had heard it, none could see any change in the rock formation on the sinkhole's floor. Then Mike, at seventeen the youngest expedition member, supported me by saying that he too had heard it when he had walked over the overhang before the sun came up, to have a wash and make his toilet. I was glad he said that, because one part of my brain was beginning to query whether the other part was hallucinating. I certainly felt that my experience of Koonalda was different from theirs and that I had to follow the dictates of my mind.

They were of course the dictates of the cave. When years later I discussed the experience with my neighbour Jen, she told me she had had an experience in many ways similar. She and her anthropologist husband, Bruce, had visited the cave with permission and her description of awe and her use of the word "cathedral" led on to a story of awareness of a presence there. A presence of which she was afraid on the one hand, while on the other hand she would have given a great deal to have been able to sleep there just one night. She too felt the sinkhole was paradise, but Bruce was so in awe of the place that he tore her away. Bruce's reaction is similar to that of present-day Aborigines. I heard of an Aboriginal man who came with his grandson and Cyril. The boy was eager to go down, but the man drew him back, saying it was the cave of the big snake. The rainbow snake is part of Aboriginal mythology and my snake eggs took on a deeper meaning when I heard that story much later.

When, after a whole day's driving along the then unsealed road to Ceduna, I arrived in the caravan park, my back seemed to have unwound itself. I vowed that if I was still upright the next morning, I would return to Koonalda. After a night under a pine tree, I was as crippled as before and decided to continue my journey southwards.

At home I spent time recovering, taking my medicine and worrying about the others. I knew again that what I had experienced was real. Was the message only meant for me? Had my decision not to disrupt the expedition and the work by being silent been the right one? If anything happened to any of the others, I would never forgive myself. Yet wasn't it a matter of each individual's own attitude to the land and the cave and the forces that ruled them?

At last the news came that all eleven team members had returned and the Melbournites were on their way home. There had been one accident, but it hadn't happened in the cave. One of the Melbourne girls had injured her head while swimming at Eucla on the day they went to fetch the water. She was quite ill for some time after returning home and had to drop her plans for study that year.

In May, the Adelaide members had a reunion and there it was revealed that all of them had experienced nightmares at Koonalda, but none had spoken to the others so as not to disrupt the work and upset Dr Gallus's dream of finding the evidence he knew was there. I won't tell the dream I remember, which was John's dream. It is his property, although he shared it with us.

Then someone remarked that each of our lives had undergone a significant change since our return from Koonalda. Young Mike had changed his religion, Michael his business plans. John had been promoted at work and his wife Maureen was going to be a mother. I myself had given up my job and was doing full-time university studies. There had been letters from Melbourne with similar changes in the others' lives. One girl went to a dig in Cyprus that year and survived an outburst of war there.

I told them my experience at Koonalda. It fitted in entirely with their feelings, even though everyone had been affected differently. Not all felt that they could not return, and some indeed did. John remarked that my time alone in the cave had intensified my impressions. I am sure that it was to this intensity, as well as the dampness and sleeping on the ground, that I can ascribe my body's reaction in turning on an attack of arthritis.

The Koonalda experience also made me understand a little better why the white settlers on the whole settled in cities on the coast and still have a sort of fear for the inland. Without being able to describe it, they do sense that the land is not empty, even though they speak of the empty land and the dead heart. In the last few decades, with affluence amongst the working classes, it has become fashionable to go around Australia in a caravan after retirement from one's job. Each year more people do it and young couples take a year off from work to make the pilgrimage. Maybe that is what it is after all, a pilgrimage to the sacred places of the land. There has also been a recent exodus from cities to towns and from towns to villages and from villages to the bush. They are called the alternative people; or the grassrooters, after a famous Australian magazine called *Grassroots* that caters for the needs of those who pursue alternative lifestyles. So perhaps the coming together of the land and the people who are born here has developed momentum. If it has, the Aboriginal people will not only benefit from the growing understanding, but will be the teachers of the land's wisdom.

All I remember about Bert — I think that was his name — are his eyes and his great height.

He was travelling in a friend's car to the picnic races in Maree, a tiny railway settlement in the northern desert of South Australia. Ronald was with them and I drove the Moke with my friend Cath, the painter, as passenger. She wasn't a painter then, but a very hard-working, very frustrated schoolteacher.

What I remember of the accident was Cath's voice holding forth on some point of ethics, her hands fluttering to add strength to her argument, when I felt the wheels slipping from under us and the steering wheel not responding to my desperate hands. Then the roll-over and Cath's voice finishing off in mid-sentence with "Oh my God!"

We were hanging upside down in our seatbelts in a car that had only a plastic cloth for a roof. The place was the Hawker to Leigh Creek road in the Flinders Ranges, then an unsealed dirt track. The bus from Leigh Creek had just passed, and to avoid dust and flying stones I had veered to the left, hit a pocket of loose gravel and lost control.

Cath, shocked but miraculously uninjured apart from a shallow cut on her forehead, talked me out of my seatbelt, where I hung like a bat in a cave. We crawled away from the car in case it should burst into flames and lay in the thin shade of a gum tree.

The first car that stopped was full of teachers. The woman teacher took up where Cath had left off. "Oh my God!" she exclaimed, running around, picking up the pieces of our camping gear.

The second car was full of scouts. The scout master was a doctor. In an area where there was but one doctor per one hundred kilometres, that was a bit of a miracle. He examined our limbs, looked into our pupils and gave permission for us to be moved to hospital in Hawker.

The third car was full of friends and Ronald. Ronald asked panic-stricken: "Will you die, mum?" I told him I didn't think I would, but my bloodied face, swollen eye and faint voice made him produce a little Bible from heaven knows where and he sat with me under the gum tree and prayed for my survival.

Then Bert, tall and silent, bent over each of us, Cath and me, and looked deeply and at length into our eyes. I felt something like an injection of strength and instead of losing consciousness, as I kept wanting to do, I had a moment of lucidity that made me gather my wits. I was not to slip away. I would struggle to remain conscious.

I did. And painful it was. Although I left the hospital on foot several days later, my injuries took months to heal and left me with some disturbing disabilities.

Bert also retrieved our handbags from the bush, where the impact of the crash had sent them flying. But it was his eyes in his round Aboriginal face which I remember, because there was an act of will behind his penetrating look at us. There is no saying that he did not save my life from slipping through my fingers on that occasion, because sometimes death is also an act of will and I may have been ready for it subconsciously.

Later, I sometimes heard his name in connection with welfare work in Aboriginal communities. Maybe he was one of those saints who keep popping up through life, just when the lines of creation and destruction meet and either one may merge with your own life's path, depending on what is due to you . . . or who intercedes. Some people, like Bert, not only have the knowledge of how to intercede, but have earned the power to do so, to the benefit of all living things they come in contact with.

Mutual understanding finally came one day when I sat on a grassy knoll with a Pitjantjara woman from Ernabella, in the northern desert of the state. At our back the South Australian Museum, in front the lawn and fountain where the Pitjantjara children, on their ten-day visit to the school where I was a student teacher, were splashing in the water. To the right a dinosaur's skeleton in a huge glass display case, which had made them swallow their questions till later. To the left the roar and fumes of traffic and the din of people marching along in shoes. Turning to the desert woman by my side, my hand automatically went up to cover my left ear. She smiled, pointed at the street, shook her head and covered both ears with her hands. We were of one mind.

That didn't stop me driving my car to work, nor did it stop her enjoying the trip back home in the bus. But we agreed on our preferences. Earlier, in the main shopping street, I'd heard her hum a little melody. She walked in an invisible envelope of simple magic that kept the foreignness of the surroundings just enough at bay to keep her in comfort.

Later that day we took the kids up in the lift at the teachers college, then the highest building in the area with its twelve storeys. Pressing the button, I felt like a sham magician who knows she can't finish the act. I wanted to explain that I didn't know either why we were going up because I pressed a button. As we rose, the desert kids squealed and clutched each other, one quarter delight, three-quarters fear. But they marvelled at the view from the top and I agreed it was a sight better than on the ground. They declined a lift-ride in another tall building and I admired their moderation, which elevated the one experience to a good story when they got home, without the need to risk life and limb again.

Our school had a large proportion of Italian and Greek children and cultural exchange was the purpose of the visit. By the end of the week we had learned a Pitjant-jara woman's dance and how they keep the beat on their thighs and the Ernabella kids were dancing Zorba the Greek. They enjoyed their visit and the wonder of wonders was going to the beach and seeing the sea. But when one boy showed me his drawing of Ernabella and I asked him to describe it, he simply said: "It is the best place in the world."

On Australia Day 1988 fifteen thousand Aboriginal people converged on Sydney to demonstrate their very existence, to make it clear to the nation that they were not dying out, that they were here and meant to live on. Amidst all the celebrations and a harbour full of tall ships, that demonstration was the only truly historical event, not a re-enactment, because never — as far as anyone knows — had so many Aborigines gathered in one place simultaneously. Their statement changed the whole tone of the bicentennial year. The media came on side, printing photographs of Aborigines cooling off in the water of Sydney's famous harbour, tall ships in the heat-hazy background. Any Australians who up until then had not stopped to think what the Bicentennial meant to Aborigines, must have been shocked into recognising the stark fact that Aboriginal people had nothing to celebrate but sheer survival by the skin of their teeth.

One realised then that 1988 was going to be their year of turning the corner. But one also feared that if they didn't manage to bring their plight, their wishes and their hopes to the eyes and ears of the nation during that year, their case was in danger of being superseded again by new calamities which might shift the focus of the public eye. Furthermore, worsening global problems, which appear to have solutions, can detract from issues at home, which seem to escape any solution. Problems must present themselves as being solvable before they attract the right sort of action. Moreover, the related causes of third world debt and the degradation of the global environment will soon present developed nations with bills their short-sighted governments have not budgeted for. In a worldwide context, Aboriginal peoples who find themselves custodians of a rainforest may soon get more money to maintain their traditional lifestyle than Aboriginal peoples who inhabit deserts.

These are nasty, cold facts in a world on the brink of disaster unless nations stop in their accustomed tracks and people choose whether they want life for their children or just for themselves. Specific injustices to minority groups — although they may receive sympathy and support from abroad — must increasingly be solved locally by the larger community of which they form a part.

The only real leverage that Australian Aborigines could have had in the political sphere, from where most of their solutions are now coming, would have been the existence, on traditional tribal land, of substances capable of being mined. But the only leverage they have to obtain rights to those substances is the public conscience, which, if it were just, would not necessitate any need for leverage.

I know I am at a disadvantage looking at these issues as an ordinary person, an immigrant at that, and not as a professional involved with Aboriginal people. Consequently, some of my opinions may seem naive. On the other hand, I am a component of the public conscience and if I do not speak my mind I will not be further educated.

Although the problems that Aboriginal people have are part of the global human rights problem, it must be realised that specific solutions lie embedded in Australian society itself.

With the Aboriginal population standing at approximately one per cent of the total population, it must be possible for every Aboriginal person, who so wishes, to have a non-Aboriginal friend they could call on when harassed. I don't mean patronising friendship. Surely there are one hundred and fifty thousand courageous non-Aboriginal people in Australia?

One wanted to shout to some Aboriginal people in 1988 while the going was good: "Why don't you get all non-Aboriginal people who are on your side, really on your side? Now is the time to harness their energies for Aboriginal advancement. Don't condemn them to merely oozing sympathy or being a willing receptacle for accusations. Use them to regain your dignity and independence." But few were able to remove the barriers that have been put in place from both sides.

There is so much need for dialogue between ordinary people from all walks of life, Aboriginal and non-Aboriginal. There is a need for non-Aboriginal people to be instructed — without accusations about what their ancestors did — in what land means to Aborigines. Non-Aboriginal people ought to be able to explore what ownership means to them and re-examine it in the process. I feel my own "nesting instinct" ties me to a piece of land, but not forever. I can shift and make new ties elsewhere, to trees, rocks, skies of a different land, with a different climate and culture. I can make ties with people vastly different from my own, without necessarily feeling threatened. This makes it difficult for me to see the significance of land for Aboriginal people other than on an intellectual level. On an emotional level, I might be tempted to think that exclusivity about land originated from hostilities between tribes. But I can't discuss these things and develop my thoughts, or be re-educated, if I continue to be seen as part of a repressive, dominant group because I appear to have a white skin.

Wide acknowledgment of injustices, past and present, is part of the healing process. But one can't struggle for a better future by fighting with one's back turned on that very future. There comes a time when one has to turn one's back on an acknowledged past, having extracted enduring values from it, and face the future . . . which is tomorrow.

But to return to the specific issue of harassment of Aboriginal people, by the police, authorities, or members of the public. There must be some other means by which justice can be done, albeit belatedly. Flimsy evidence or handy rules to "move on or else", are still being used against Aborigines whereas other people would merely get a warning. Long police records stop people's advancements. Yet the number of charges bears no relation to the seriousness of the offences. In the case of many Aboriginal people their long police records do not even pertain to anything so serious as petty crime. Surely, such records should now be examined by, yes, another committee or commission, and wiped clean by state governors? The training of special Aboriginal police personnel to deal with Aboriginal offenders seems such an obvious necessity that it is surprising it isn't done more.

Government promises from past years that have not been fulfilled should not be superseded by new policies, but acted upon, so that Aboriginal people are able to choose where and how they want to live, as Gough Whitlam once promised they could. Theory and practice have not as yet been reconciled. More funds for the recording of oral histories among Aboriginal people would benefit the education of all Australians, so that following generations might coexist, understanding each other's social and cultural needs, knowing each other as fellow human beings, no more, no less.

Some Aborigines believe that white people can "work the system", that nothing that befalls a white person can affect him or her as badly as it affects an Aborigine. Although this may be true in specific situations, to adopt this attitude for the whole of life absolves the individual from all personal responsibility, with a resultant loss of dignity and self-esteem. The myth that black is beautiful and white is always warped is no basis for coexistence, let alone for the removal of injustices and inequalities. For any person to be of some little benefit to another person, he or she must be acknowledged to be as human as the other, or there can be no fruitful dialogue. Nobody likes to be judged by the colour of their skin. That fact alone ought to be enough for people to explore different ways of identifying with each other.

But with the bicentennial fervour behind us, we are still, as a society, struggling to escape from the strands of two hundred years of mythmaking on both sides of the issue. Both black and white Australians are inveterate mythmakers, feeding as they do from the same soil.

One person who courageously unravelled her own family's mythmaking is Sally Morgan, whose autobiography *My Place* (Fremantle Arts Centre Press, 1987) will hopefully be followed by other life stories written by Aboriginal people themselves. Her personal history proves clearly that despite the fact that Aboriginal descent was denied even within the family, they lived with all the disadvantages of it.

Now that there are benefits to be claimed by people of Aboriginal descent, a debate has arisen in certain quarters about "where to draw the line". People not widely known to be Aboriginal are coming forward to claim these benefits to advance themselves. Office holders and citizens who want to prevent a person claiming Aboriginal descent on the basis that he or she doesn't have enough Aboriginal blood for it to show, because it is going to cost money from the public purse, are the very reasons why making oneself known as Aboriginal is still a risky business indeed.

It is people like Sally Morgan, who are not afraid to stand up and be counted as Aborigines, who should be claiming no less than any Aborigine, so that the injustices done to their forebears can be redeemed and their children will live in equality with other human beings everywhere.

When one takes into account that the Aborigines

make up only one per cent of the Australian population, and even if hidden Aboriginal descent doubles this percentage, it is pretty disgusting that some people complain about educational grants to Aboriginal people covering more expenses than those for non-Aboriginal people.

You simply can't put historical records straight with words alone.

6
Reaching out to Asia

The contents of my family photo album provided the clue to one strand of my ancestry that I feel was of great importance in my early life.

The photos were spread out on the kitchen table at a Dutch friend's house in Australia, as we swapped memories. Picking up tall Opa's portrait, she said: "What a beautiful Jewish nose!"

I was astounded. I looked. And I saw.

The friend was herself of Jewish extraction and she ought to know.

I wrote to my relatives in Holland. My Aunt Truus replied that tall Opa had had to appear before the occupation authorities during the war in order to establish to what degree he was Jewish. Somehow he managed to maintain that it was less than twenty-five percent, which was the reason our family did not have to wear the yellow star of David.

This information rocked me profoundly. I suddenly realised that many of my grandparents' friends had been Jews. I remember a beautiful brown man in a caramel coloured suit, called Reuben, who had a moustache and very large brown eyes. He used to plan the future of socialism after the war with little Opa, who was a gentile. Opoe was friends with a family of eight children whose father was a tailor. All, except one daughter, were gassed in German concentration camps.

If no other people than this family had ever been exterminated in Germany, I still would never have been able to forget the crime, and regard it as a warning to all political leaders who aim to make history at the expense of races other than their own. That healthy, boisterous, hospitable family which had lived around the corner . . . wiped out. Can anyone tell me WHY?

Mr Blom, a violinist who lived across the street, wore a star of David, but his wife did not. I can't remember whether his daughters, Miep and Anneke, had to wear one. When I was ten I was given a restored violin for my birthday, so I could follow in the family's footsteps. Mr Blom was not allowed to earn his living or teach, so I sneaked across after eight o'clock curfew, violin hidden under my coat, to learn scales and études.

I wasn't brilliant with the bow. I was already suffering from malnutrition and simply holding the instrument in place was a major effort. The lessons came to a cruel end when Mr Blom was picked up by the Nazis and sent to a work camp in an eastern province. Had the war lasted longer, we might never have seen him again, but Mr Blom survived to return and take up a successful career in radio. He did not give lessons any more, except to one star pupil. It was the end of my musical career.

During the war I carried illegal newspapers, the size of a folded business letter, from tall Opa's house to ours. Tall Opa was connected with the underground movement and saw to the distribution of news to the rest of the family, including "that man", and some trusted neighbours. I carried the papers inside my woollen hat, while rehearsing my defence alibis:

No. 1 — I was deaf and dumb.

No. 2 — An old woman had pushed these papers in
my hat; I knew nothing about them.

No. 3 — I had found the papers and they kept my
head warm and the wind out.

Despite my preparedness, I always expected to be shot
dead on the spot if I were searched and the papers found
upon me.

At home, the papers were put flat under the carpet,
from whence they were distributed as visitors called or
Mama visited recipients. Before they all disappeared, I
read the lot. And so I knew about the gas chambers and
mass graves and what would happen to the people who
were pushed into the cattle trains that travelled east. I
knew about the insanity of theories of racial superiority.
I knew about hatred.

I was eight, nine, ten. I was informed about the world
I was growing up in, but I did not know my own origins.
Great as my fear of the Nazis was, I do not know
whether I would have lived with the invincible hope of
survival that kept me alive, had I known I was a Jew
myself.

After the war I had Jewish friends like my relatives
used to have. I even had a hankering to see Israel when it
came into being, and the persecuted flocked to what
they hoped would be safety for them and their descendants. I heard that one had to be a Jew through the
mother's line, or a convert to Judaism, to be acceptable
for immigration. I felt Judaism to be the peculiar
possession of the full blood Jews, something I did not
want to stake a claim in.

But, like the Jews, I felt the need to leave Europe,
where the horrors had been manifested. Although Hitler
was dead, I had lost any belief that the continent could
ever be a safe place in which to raise children or to

attempt to live in peace. As a child I had finger-travelled to isolated places on the maps in the Bos atlas, places where no one would wage war for lack of spoils to be had.

Of course I did not foresee that the stakes of the game would change so soon. Australia and New Zealand seemed to be such places, tucked away at the end of the world, en route to the South Pole.

Sometimes I wish I'd chosen New Zealand, then a small agricultural nation, but now a much more independent country than Australia, which dances to the tune of the United States of America, no matter what party is in power. Also, having met quite a few Maoris (the people who were there before white settlement) I feel I could have slotted more easily into their culture and community than I did with the Aborigines, on account of the historical developments in each country.

But to Australia I came. With husband, two children, four suitcases and one wooden crate of household goods. And there was space. And there was a certain tranquillity. And there was land . . . everywhere. With these three one has no need for war. Or so I thought.

I sometimes wonder whether I would have stumbled on my Jewish identity had I stayed in Holland. Whether it would have dawned on me that some of the expressions we used at home were not Dutch, but Yiddish. But what is the point of such questions? Knowledge, once obtained, willingly or unwillingly, cannot be returned, whether it suits one at the time or not. The loss of Judaism in my family may have taken place a long time ago, but the morality was still there and I grew up with it. I feel I have that much at least of an otherwise lost heritage, a lost tribe.

The acquisition of Buddhism, also facilitated by life

in Australia, has made up for much that was lost in persecutions and migrations, my own and those of my ancestors.

I cannot help but wonder whether the Australian immigration authorities would marvel at the miracles they gave rise to! And whether the Dutch government would lament the loss of the citizen I have become . . .

Governments, by their nature, see people as statistics. The Netherlands had too many people. The Australian government felt their country was under-populated and under-developed. They were afraid of invasions from the north, from Asia. The two governments did a deal. As part of that deal, I ex-Jopie, with a shadowy but ancient past, was shipped as one item in the statistics of the year 1958, to Australia, land of unlimited opportunities.

And what did I do, considering the opportunties the country had to offer? Did I become rich? Did I become successful? Did I contribute great works to Australian society?

I did none of these things. I went into the space and tranquillity which is the other Australia, Australia the ancient one, the Australia of the Aborigines, perhaps. There I discovered the music of silence and heard the earth revolving, so quiet could it sometimes be at night, in the bush, under the stars.

I never thought of myself as a statistic of course, nor as an economic asset or liability. I simply used the space of Australia to "map out" my ancestry in which the bloodstreams of Asia, Europe and the Middle East combined, to give rise to an ordinary human being in all her complexity.

To whom or what should I direct my gratitude for having had that opportunity?

*   *   *

The proximity of Australia to Asia and the Pacific had been a major consideration in my decision to migrate. Now that I had come this far, it would surely only be a matter of time before I would climb the steps of Borobudur, sit in temples, burn incense at shrines long held sacred — . . And while I learned English, raised children and made a home for them, I would quietly prepare for my eventual arrival at an as yet unknown place.

I was not plainly naive. I still feel that way. I am still preparing myself.

I felt cut off in Australia as much for the lack of European news, as for the lack of information on Asian affairs. The news from Britain was always extensive, but it meant nothing to me. A great reversal has taken place over the last three decades, but in the 1960s this was, in essence, still Britain's colony. I used to listen to the radio with a discerning ear and read the papers with a prejudiced eye. Thus, a four-line item of "News in brief" gave me a Chinese son.

When the Chinese cultural revolution got into gear in the 1960s and life there became uncertain enough for many people to flee their homeland, Hong Kong received the brunt of the exodus. Famine followed.

One day I read in the newspaper how a Sydney public servant had decided he was not powerless to help the hungry and homeless. He sent a pound of rice to the Hong Kong Council for Social Services on a weekly basis. I thought that if all the families in Australia who could afford to give that much were to do so, the people of Hong Kong would stop suffering from lack of nutrition.

Touched by the simplicity of the idea, I too sent a pound of rice. I received a letter back from the Council, suggesting I sponsor one of their young charges. He was a ten-year-old boy called Tai Yue Keung, who with his brother Kwok and his mother had fled from the mainland, where the father had died. The mother was in bad health and hawking small wares to try to earn a living. The Council had found a place for Yue in a boarding school and ten Australian pounds (later twenty dollars) a month would keep him there and free the Council to help the next child in line.

My husband agreed that since we now enjoyed shelter, enough food and clothing, and a measure of security, we could extend ourselves in this way. Thus, Yue became our Chinese foster son. He wrote neat letters in Chinese ideograms, sent his photo and told of his scholastic efforts. The Council's social worker translated his letters and added remarks of her own or those of the school matron. If Yue wrote dutifully that he enjoyed his school work, a note would explain that he was often less than interested and would rather play sports! But there was little doubt that Yue was very bright.

Now I did Christmas shopping for five children. We also remembered Yue and Kwok's birthdays and paid for Yue's holiday outings and camp. When it was time for Yue to go to high school, I suggested he come to Australia and attend with our eldest daughter Else, who was about to leave primary school also. Letters flew to and fro, but Kwok did not want his brother to leave. As their mother had died in the meantime, this was understandable. Luckily, they had found an elderly relative in Hong Kong, so they were not entirely deserted orphans.

Yue and Kwok fulfilled a desire in me to be caring for some of the victims of war and hunger in Asia, as well as for my personal need to be in touch with Asian people. I exchanged letters with Yue for six years. Toward the end he had left school and became an apprentice couch-maker, writing very infrequently. Our support was now mainly moral, apart from birthdays and Christmas, which as a good Buddhist I made a lot of!

At last a letter came, translated and with a note from the social worker, saying that Yue had delivered it in her absence, without an address. He wasn't with the couch-maker any more, but was working in more lucrative employ and learning English at night school. He wrote: "One day I hope to visit my Australian mother". That is the last I ever heard of Tai Yue Keung, my Chinese son.

Other children in Asia were sponsored over the years, but often the charity organisations who offered them stood like barriers between sponsor and child. I never came to know any in the way I had come to know Yue, thanks to the sensitive social worker at the Council for Social Services in Hong Kong.

Yue and Kwok should be in their thirties now, perhaps with children of their own, rebuilding their shattered family. In the next decade, Hong Kong will become part of China and all the refugees who still live there will find that if they don't return to the motherland, the motherland will come to claim them. As one becomes older, political patterns are seen to repeat themselves and the ferris wheel of history comes full circle, with people caught in its spokes, hanging on for dear life, or dropping into the chasm each revolution seems to leave behind . . .

I have now, in my middle age, started to learn Chinese and maybe next year I can read those twenty-year-old letters of an orphaned Chinese boy, bright as a button, looking for a direction.

I have always loved languages. The mystery and miracle of learning new sounds and then finding that one is really understood has a never-ending thrill for me.

While Ronald was young and I was fairly house-bound, I gathered enough people together who wanted to learn Malay (the language of Malaysia and Indonesia and one of Singapore's four languages), to get a teacher from Adult Education. This was no mean feat in a village where adult education rarely extended itself beyond such delights as cake-icing and hat-making. The class kept going for three years, thanks largely to the abilities of our teacher, a British ex-police officer. He had been born in Malaysia and entered the colonial service there, later to be transferred to Singapore. He seemed to have had more Malay friends than British and his regard for the Chinese was high. He would have been more than sad at the present developments in the land of his birth, where the two races, each remarkable in their own way, are at loggerheads.

Our teacher revelled in the telling of one story after another from his colourful career and even confessed to having an open mind on the inexplicable mysteries of the east, from spirits in trees to dancing lights in the night. I became aware for the first time of the bond between language and culture and the impossibility of learning the one without the other. The other students also attested that news items from that region, scarce as they were, suddenly took on much more significance and meaning. I think they were all Australian, except me. It is due to people like these, who are able to step outside their own lives for one evening a week and take an interest in the lives of other races, that an awareness of the countries to the north of us grew, so that by the 1970s Asian languages started to appear in schools and are now taught at all levels, although not yet at all schools.

One cultural item that is even more important than

language is cooking. All our class terms ended in an Asian banquet, be it Malay, Chinese or even Japanese. The spouses of the students came as well and these events probably changed some Australian kitchens permanently!

After the class in the village school folded, I continued for a year with Azhar Abbas, a Malay accountant married to a South Australian girl. He taught Malay at a breathless pace at the university's adult evening classes. Azhar also started the Australia-Malaysia Cultural Organisation, which held some wonderful gatherings where we enjoyed Malay food, music and dance, yet somehow always conversed in English with the many Malay students who by then lived in Adelaide. Azhar was tragically killed when a plane flying from Penang to Kuala Lumpur was hijacked, with the loss of all one hundred people aboard. The shock reverberated through the Adelaide community where he had made hundreds of friends since his high school days.

After Malay, I took up Sanskrit during a three month summer course by a classics lecturer at Adelaide University. I felt as though an old wooden door was being opened on a treasure trove of ancient wisdom. Most of the texts to be translated were ancient wisdom scriptures. I soon wrote the Sanskrit script as if I had grown up with it, although I didn't understand what I was writing without looking at the word-list. Sanskrit is the language from which the Tibetan script is derived. So is Prakrit, in which the earliest Buddhist scripts are written, and eventually Pali, the language of much Buddhist literature. Unfortunately, time ran out as the academic year approached. But the course gave me an insight into a past that should not be reserved for a few scholars. Later, when I studied classics myself, I felt that primary schools could teach a subject on "Ancient Wisdom". It would gather the pearls from all the wisdom teachings in the world, from ancient to modern, so that all children could be given something more than purely factual knowledge. Something that makes them stop and think, something they can ponder on while sitting in the branches of a tree, or before they go to sleep in their beds. In my house, wise sayings from my reading end up on little cards, pinned on the inside of the toilet door. My grandson comes out and asks: "Is it true, grandma, that if all the ants of the world got together, they could carry an elephant?" I did not even know he could read such long words, but the African proverb conveyed a meaning that appealed to him, so he sat there until he had deciphered it. I think the key word that got him started must have been "ants", with which he is very familiar.

A shrine had to be recreated in my house and the missing item was again incense. In 1966 there was only one shop which sold it as a sideline and it was smoky rather than soothing. I set up "The House of Incense", got a trading licence, obtained addresses from the Chamber of Commerce and invested $300 of my wages to order incense from India, Hong Kong and Malaysia.

Soon enough fragrant parcels arrived in the mail. Smells have always played havoc with my imagination and here was a riot of inspiration! Suriyakanthi, the first incense I offered for sale, made me feel as if Asia and I had finally made contact. The mail-order business was evening work, after a day of playing secretary. In lunchtimes I carried my fragrant basket around the shops. I made a modest profit and in 1968 — by then separated and living with the three children in Adelaide — I ventured risking some of it to buy crafts from the Tibetan refugees in north India.

I wrote a letter to the Dalai Lama, explaining who I was and what I wanted. People so often asked me afterwards what gave me that idea. But I had always been a letter writer and, in a manner of speaking, had I not known the exiled ruler since childhood? I received a reply from his minister for home affairs with the address of a cooperative in Dharamsala, north India, where Tibetan handicrafts were being made.

The small weavings, inlaid knives and jewellery were so unusual at the time, there was hardly a market for them. But when I imported my first Tibetan rug — it covers the couch in my room to this day — it was a case of love at first sight, from customs officers who stood admiring the back until I flipped it over and they were stunned, to the person who offered financial backing to import a whole bale, to the gallery goers who bought half of the twenty or so rugs during the first seven minutes of the first exhibition.

I realised I was now in a position to do something useful for the Tibetan refugees. In the years that followed I sold two more shipments of their rugs and from each rug sold, a percentage went back to help maintain the carpetweavers' children's nursery.

My contact in the weavers' community was Lobsang Rabgay, their leader and organiser. Lobsang did not speak or write English, his letters came translated by many different interpreters. Yet, amidst a colourful range of styles I learned to recognise his own and felt I came to know him.

When the demand for Tibetan rugs was saturated in Adelaide, I tried an exhibition in Canberra, coinciding with an oriental congress. It was a moderate success but it also made it clear to me that unless I gave up my wage job I could not deal with the vagaries of interstate gallery owners, transport, losses, promotion and the like. That risk was one I could not take, for I had to remain breadwinner for several years to come. But by that time we were in the seventies and the refugees were much more on their feet, so with great regret I stopped importing and sold off what remained of my stock piece by piece. The incense business went the same way as my plans for the future took on another shape. But I'm running ahead of time.

Having worked at the university for three years and a few months with retarded people, I now took on a job with International Handcrafts, the retail division of Community Aid Abroad. My experience with "The House of Tibet" and "The House of Incense", as well as my contacts, gave me a headstart in the shop, which was packed to the rafters with artifacts, weaving and jewellery from India, Pakistan and a few other developing countries. My reading took a new direction and I soon could tell the story of origin of almost every item we sold.

I now felt I could legitimately dress in Asian clothes, something I had wanted to do since childhood dreamtimes. I felt so good in them that whenever I wore a dress from the shop's stock, we sold out of that line in half the time.

Although I was hardly aware of it then, the cogs of the wheel of my life had finally found their groove and all that started to manifest itself and that was of importance to me was coming from one starting point; my resolve at the age of four to meet the god-king of Tibet.

Already this had led to "The House of Tibet", which was originally financed by a person who later assumed a major role in my life. It also led to the twenty-eighth International Congress of Orientalists, because my rugs were in a supporting exhibition in Canberra during the week of the congress. Professor A.L. Basham, renowned Australian orientalist, opened the exhibition and I felt proud on behalf of the craftspeople in the foothills of the Himalayas, who had made this possible.

Attending the congress was a dream come true, but it also opened my eyes to the immense diversity of Asia, its peoples, its cultures, its conflicts, its directions. I attended as many lectures as I could and lamented the fact that at my home university nothing was taught that remotely linked up with this fabulous smorgasbord of Asian research and studies. That is how I came to do Classics when I started my degree, a decision I have never regretted. However, when Anthropology was introduced I had only one year of study left and I pleaded to be allowed to do Anthropology I and II in one year, to enable me still to wring a major out of it. I got the permission, none too easily, and did the double course successfully, yet never completed the major. Now, there are Asian studies and Asian languages and it is time I returned to do the things I wanted then.

Mingling with other congress goers in Canberra was somewhat of a revelation as well. Most of these Asian academics had western educations and were well-travelled. I was not a scholar, in fact I had only just finished my matriculation exam. The results came out that week and I was sitting in the cafeteria rereading the results, happy as a lark, when a Chinese scholar joined me.

"Anything good in the paper today?" he queried.

"My matriculation results," I replied, and he could see from my face that they were good. He did not express surprise to find a woman in her thirties gloating over the equivalent of her high school finals, yet with the congress badge pinned on her blouse.

"And what will your next step be?" he asked with real interest. I marvelled at the absolute rightness of his question.

"University!" I answered.

"Then I wish you good luck and much enjoyment," he replied.

It was a most auspicious start to my university years and I had both luck and enjoyment in ample measure.

The most comical incident at the congress — though the other person involved didn't think so — was a freak change of identity which I would have liked to have been able to sustain. Sitting in the back row during a somewhat boring lecture, I fumbled for a cigarette.

"Not in here," whispered the man next to me, "let's go outside and have one." He too was not spellbound by the matters under discussion.

We sat in the cool corridor and had our smoke. He was an Anglo-Indian professor from some Commonwealth country, looking around for diversion. We carried our congress sachets with our name-labels.

"Lolo," he spelled. "Interesting name." Now, I have heard this before and not every enquirer gets the same story, it gets dreary.

"It's Tibetan," I answered.

"Oh, really?" he said with renewed interest and taking a giant jump to a far-flung conclusion. "When did you come down here?"

"On Monday," I said, not sure that he really believed what I thought he believed. I was very tanned, it was January. I wore Asian clothes, of course. But . . .?

"Are you going to see anything more of Australia before you go back?" he asked, with obvious plans forming in his head. It was true then. My folded eyelids, my tan, my clothes; combined, they had erased my pale eyes and mouse-coloured hair. He really thought I was a

Tibetan. Of course, if you were going to meet a Tibetan in Australia, in those days, it would most likely be at an oriental congress.

I was too honest to lead him on any further and confessed that I was going home to Adelaide. He finally twigged and his face fell. Although he'd already invited me for drinks that evening, he now dropped me like a tonne of bricks and my life as a Tibetan came to a sorry end. But he gave me ideas. After all, Alexandra David-Neel travelled Tibet in disguise for many years . . .

My growing familiarity with Asian conduct and mien saved my little import business from collapse at a time I did not want it to fold.

An entire shipment of Tibetan rugs, destined for an exhibition during the Adelaide Festival of Arts, had gone missing. The shipping agent was most offhand about it. Shipments got lost all the time and I was insured, so what was I making such a fuss about?

Here I rose up against the deadening materialism of the Australian business world. Close to tears I claimed that twenty rugs, painstakingly knotted in ancient patterns of religious significance during the last year by a group of homeless Tibetan refugees, are not something an insurance policy can replace with money. I demanded a search and threatened to be in his office every day until I saw action.

"And I warn you," I added, conscious of the fact that here on the wharfs I was in a man's world, "men get ulcers when things go wrong, but women have nervous breakdowns. And I will have one right here on your nice carpet, unless you start doing something to find my carpets!"

At that he threw up his hands. "Please don't do

that," he groaned and started to compose telegrams for Bombay, Singapore, Perth, Melbourne and Sydney, the places where the *Vishva Sandesh* had been or was going to be during its present journey.

All replies came back negative. Melbourne and Sydney reported that a search of the ship had found nothing resembling my three bales. No bales had been left behind on the wrong wharf.

I lodged a claim with Lloyd's of London for two thousand dollars, the bare cost of the shipment and a small fortune to me in those days. The claim was accepted and being processed when the *Vishva Sandesh* turned around at Sydney to load wool for the return journey.

I followed the ship's progress in the shipping news and on the day it was to dock in Port Adelaide, I once more confronted the shipping agent in his office.

What did the lady want now? The lady wanted to visit the *Vishva Sandesh?* Sigh of relief. Well, yes, it was a strange request, but there was no objection. If the lady would just follow, she would be introduced to the ship's first mate . . . have a look around on board . . . certainly. And why not?

Again, it was a soaring summer's day. The ship's first mate, a suave Punjabi, could not quite hide his surprise at the visit of the lady who had lost . . . was it three little parcels? Three bales of Tibetan rugs, I pointed out. But I was in no hurry to talk about them, now that I was on board.

Would I like an orange juice? Yes, I would. He chatted amicably about the weather and how his wife, who travelled with him, had enjoyed Sydney. I reciprocated, telling him about the delights of Adelaide. As a point of interest I told him about the Festival of Arts that was about to start, steeping the city in festivities. In passing I mentioned that it was unfortunate that the lost Tibetan carpets were to be part of a festival exhibition, and regrettable that the gallery director had rather lost his temper over their disappearance and was planning to sue the Bombay owners of the *Vishva Sandesh* for the cost of preparing the exhibition and the loss of revenue.

I was not even seething inside as I sat there chatting away over orange juice. I was merely playing chess, as was he. He barely flickered an eyelid when he asked me did I know the markings on my bales. Indeed I did. He wrote them down. He called an aide and spoke to him in rapid tones; I took it to be Punjabi. The other man's face changed from smiles to something less than joy.

I had been on board some twenty minutes now and had settled in my seat as if I was to sail to Bombay also.

The aide returned and the first mate invited me for an inspection of hold number one, where, he was told, there were some little parcels with markings similar to mine. Up we went and down we looked. Instantly I recognised the familiar Tibetan bales and my misspelt name that they'd insisted on painting on, because they didn't trust markings alone. There was nothing else in that hold, the size of a house, but my three bales of rugs.

I tried to keep my face as inscrutable as my host's when I pronounced the bales mine, produced my papers and asked for them to be unloaded.

"Now?" asked the first mate.

"Now please," I said.

Just then a whistle went for smoko, that sacred, union-decreed time of work for meditation, that cannot be interrupted by even the second coming.

I thanked the first mate for his hospitality, wished him a safe journey home and promised him good times if he ever returned for another arts festival. I said I would wait on the wharf for the bales.

He gravely saw me to the gangplank. I checked out the loading schedule and realised it would be some time before the crane would finish dropping bales of wool into other holds, so I walked to Port Adelaide township to buy a sandwich for lunch. Picking up a newspaper, and almost compulsively turning to the shipping news, I learned that the *Vishva Sandesh* was leaving that day and not on the morrow, as originally announced. In a state of shock, I ran back to the wharf, arriving red-faced and on the verge of sunstroke.

"There is the lady of the carpets again," the wharfies sang out. I had become notorious. The story of my lost and found bales had spread. I ran up the ladder to the loading master's office.

"Sit down, lady," he said kindly. "You'll do yourself in, running around like this in nearly a hundred degrees."

"A hundred?" I gasped.

"Yep. Almost. And when the thermometer hits the century, all work stops for the day."

Another union rule. A necessary one indeed, but what about my carpets?

"But the ship is leaving today!" I cried. "I'm not leaving until I've got my carpets."

"Not if it hits a hundred, she won't," said the master cheerfully.

And so we waited, the master and I and several wharfies, for the crane to finish with wool, or for the thermometer to reach one hundred degrees Fahrenheit, whatever came first.

I had recovered my decorum and decided to treat the wharfies like Punjabis. I chatted and sipped the cool water. I told them it was Chinese New Year that day and it was the year of the dog, or the hare, I can't remember, but it was auspicious for something that might please

137

anyone. Being wharfies, they were communist-inclined. Being communist-inclined in Australia meant to be China-oriented. I pulled out my drawer of Chinese stories and surprised myself. I began to enjoy myself, because I am a storyteller at heart.

Another shrill whistle outside and the heavy crane lumbered and swung across to hold number one. I thanked the master and his friends and ran down to the wharf.

One by one my precious bales came swinging through the air. My customs agent had been warned to clear the bales and was present with documents and truck. The shipping agent also had been told of the miraculous recovery, but I don't know what his reaction might have been.

The first mate was leaning over the railing with unsmiling face and didn't return my parting nod as I climbed in the truck to hitch a ride home with my Tibetan carpets.

What had driven me on to search for them, beyond the bounds of reason, was a little voice inside me that always pipes up when action is required. If I don't listen the voice becomes louder, until I have no peace left. Many of my unusual deeds and bold approaches have been due to that voice of intuition, call it what you like, and it has always turned out to be right for me.

This time I had also consulted the *I Ching*, the Chinese Book of Changes, something I seldom do and only in situations of great anguish. The book's reply to my question of what could possibly have happened to the carpets referred to a long road and a falling into big water, but the diligent seeker would succeed. It had not needed to say any more!

That evening, when my daughter Else and I unpacked the bales, peeling off one carpet after another, we found them first damp, then wet and finally sopping wet in the centre of the bales. Wool can stand being wet and the colours were fast. The sun dried them out in a few days and the exhibition went on as scheduled.

I never bothered to find out what exactly was behind the "disappearance" of my "three little parcels". But I walked into Lloyd's Adelaide office the day after sipping orange juice with the first mate.

"Ah, the lady of the carpets again," said the clerk, no doubt adding in his mind: "Dotty woman, what does she want now?" Obviously he had not yet been informed by the shipping agent. Soothingly he said: "Your claim is being processed. Do not worry. We will soon contact you."

"I found the carpets," I said.

"You what?" he asked, perplexed.

"I went on board the *Vishva Sandesh* and I found my three bales of Tibetan carpets. They are at home. I have come to cancel the claim."

There must have been quite a few red faces over the case of the lost Tibetan bales and a few lost perks along the line. From it all I gained an awareness that my mind operated alone lines which clashed with the European-Australian mentality of doing things and worked better with a way of reasoning, padding out by intuition, which was somewhat oriental. Plain mad, in Australian terms.

Life in the Indian shop brought some interesting people into my days. One was an entrepreneurial agent who was preparing a concert in Adelaide of the great Indian master of the sitar, Ravi Shankar. He was looking for incense to burn on the stage because the master played best in a cloud of fragrance.

The shop had a small selection, but I told Adrian, who was a follower of Meher Baba and wore a black

Astrakhan cap, that at home I had some sweet Indian sticks that burnt for hours and would be honoured to present these for the master's inspiration.

So it was that my incense, the incomparable tones of the sitar and the tabla filled the Apollo Hall. In appreciation, I was afterwards introduced to the master and to Alla Rakha, the great tabla player. Watching the few devotees before me do a *namasti* with hands folded before the face, I decided to be western this time, as I much longed to hold the hand that made those heavenly sounds. Ravi Shankar kindly took mine when offered and I was very careful not to squeeze his, so as not to damage it.

Rare as that concert was in 1970, Adelaideans now see several performances annually of Indian dancers and musicians. I can't think of any music in the whole world that stirs me more, that is better capable of lifting me out of the mundane and into realms where the spirits of beauty and joy reign. Virtuosi as these musicians are, it is still possible to see one surpassing himself during a concert and if the heart has sung with the strains of the music so far, it too leaps momentarily beyond the bounds of expression.

The coming of Asian and, lately, Pacific performers to Adelaide is largely due to the city's Festival of Arts, which started in 1960 and really got off the ground in the early seventies. The Festival has been the catalyst in bringing the world to this southern tip of the continent once every two years, but its impact is felt long before and after the official event, so that our sense of being in touch with the world is now constantly maintained. Arts and crafts are much less elitist since the festivals began, and immigrants take an increasingly large part in all these expressions of the human spirit.

7

Pacific sidetracks and the African connection

Over the years a conviction has grown in me that if you want something very much and your mind dwells constantly on it, forces will start to gather which bring the desired situation into being. Unfortunately this goes for the bad as well as the good, and there is a case for teaching people to control their thoughts, not to mention their words, for fear of them coming true!

In the early seventies my fixation with Tibet had further ramifications, which changed the direction of my studies, opened up a whole new culture for me, and made me sort out my love life for ever and a day! These wish-fulfilments do not necessarily progress in a straight line, neither do they happen in isolation!

Someone who frequented the Indian shop told me I really had to meet a lady who had lived in north India for ten years, where she had taught English to Tibetan children. Other people at the same time told her she simply had to meet the woman of "The House of Tibet", who could be found in the Indian shop. We would have so much in common.

When at last she came into the shop, we never talked much about Tibet, students, or carpets! She had come in to apply for a posting with Australian Volunteers Abroad, another division of Community Aid Abroad.

Leith got her wish and was posted to Papua New Guinea. For my part in handling enquiries and dealing with applicants, I was invited to be present at the farewell of the 1971 volunteers in Melbourne and saw Leith and others off at the airport. After that she wrote to me; her letters were full of exclamation marks and lamentations about the inadequacy of words for describing the wonderful country she found herself in. She talked of warm air, warm people, warm emotions, feelings, and "Oh, why don't you come to see for yourself? It is impossible to do justice to these wonderful people in a letter. There is space in my room for your sleeping-bag."

I contemplated how many times I had seen people off to foreign lands, received postcards from Bali and Burma, Mexico or Madrid. Too many, too many. And where had I been? At home, reading books about travel. True, my bank account only carried a few hundred dollars for emergencies and it was hard enough to make weekly ends meet. But I was getting older, two children already independent and Ronald away to his father next holiday. Would I garden and read travel books, or do the real thing for once? I applied for a small bank loan, quite foreign to my nature, and booked a flight. Then I carefully packed a swag, because one does not travel to Papua New Guinea with a suitcase; at least, that was my idea. Because if there was still a stone-age culture to be seen, I was going to try to meet it unhampered by western possessions.

Leaving in wintry weather, I'd packed a cotton pants-suit in my overnight bag, to change into on the plane. But I'd forgotten to pack my sandals. Arriving in Port Moresby, where the humidity is close to a hundred and falls like a smothering blanket on the unwary, I soon had puddles in my boots. I took them off and went barefoot from thereon, to the amazement of the locals and the expatriates alike. Barefoot, I arrived at Mount Hagen, where I was reunited with my swag and my sandals.

After this suitable entry into a country where ninety per cent of the people go barefoot, I landed in a crowd of thousands, made up of people from all tribes of the highlands. Leith had omitted to tell me that the Mount Hagen Show was on and my arrival coincided with the first day! The Hagen and Goroka Shows, held alternately, must be the last of the great tribal spectaculars on earth. Tribes had walked from their remote valleys and hills for as long as seven days to attend. They carried their babies, food and precious plumage, and gathered to perform their dances in front of other tribes, the existence of whom they may not have known about a decade earlier.

There was a sense of apprehension about the 1971 show in Mount Hagen, because a Scottish-Australian, Ian Downs, had just published a novel, *The Stolen Land*, which concluded with the killing of all the whites at the 1971 Mount Hagen Show by the native tribes. Fortunately nothing of the sort happened and the show was a foot-stomping success.

I sensed that Papua New Guinea was a society which thrived on a diet of rumours and reflected that given a choice of being run over by a car in Australia — an always present possibility — or being speared by a highlander, I'd choose the latter. A wise choice, as it turned out, if one compares the statistics of car accidents and spearings!

Hence I plunged into this incredibly vibrant world without hesitation. My guide was John, a British volunteer at the teachers college where Leith was posted.

"You can't go in there," John said, when I discovered several rows of long, thatched huts in a grassy area, surrounded by a fence. "It's the Instant Hilton. They built them for the show, for the tribes from outside Hagen. They'll get burnt down after the show is over."

"But those are the people I want to meet," I said. Just then a tribesman, framed in a low door-opening beckoned me.

"See?" I said. "They are asking me to come in." I didn't wait for John to argue further and would have shaken him off if I could have, with all his white man's logic of what you could and couldn't do in dealing with the natives. Trusting my intuitions, I followed the tribesman's directions and entered through a side entrance.

Inside, it was dim and spacious. Many small fires burned on the ground and each had a family group squatting around it. The tribesman motioned for me to join one of the groups. I became very self-conscious. My height, my extreme paleness, my clothes, all were out of kilter with these round, brown people who appeared to be a direct product of the earth, which indeed they were. Compared with them I was something from outer space. But I squatted down happily, next to an old man from the Wig Tribe. Their men wear wedge-shaped wigs, made of human hair, decorated with fresh flowers. He was in the process of making a new wig, plucking hairs from his beard for the purpose. I marvelled at the ingenuity and complete self-sufficiency of people who recycle the product of their own body into a decoration which is both unique and strikingly handsome. I felt a great humbleness descending on me and a new light being shed on my own inadequacy to maintain myself.

The old man and his tribe lived many days walking from Mount Hagen. They relied for everything on the forest in which they lived. Yet few whites in Papua New Guinea at that time saw themselves as I saw myself in comparison with the tribal people, but were rather full of their own competence and what they had to give to these primitive people.

The women, young and old, came shuffling nearer on their knees or haunches, babes in arms, toddlers hiding behind their backs. Their curiosity was as open and as friendly as mine. When a little hand appeared between two women's thighs to touch the skin of my leg, testing it for realness, we all laughed together. I have a strong memory of talking with them, although we shared no language. We asked questions and received answers by talking with our eyes, hands, the positions of our heads. We talked, in the end, with our hearts.

When offered roast *kaukau* (sweet potato) from two cooking fires, I managed to make a visible comparison and come to the conclusion that the two morsels were of equally high quality. This satisfied everyone and it happened to be the truth.

When a people have a major staple food, with only a few additions for a change of taste, the methods of preparing the staple becomes an art. *Kaukau*, roasted in the ashes of a woodfire, is a delicacy a restaurant chef would find hard to imitate. I found the same with sago in the western province and in cooking with coconut on the coast and the islands. And what people can do with plain rice in Asia, and with beancurd in China and Japan, deserves to have books written about it.

At last I felt brave enough to ask to hold the baby. He was a very young baby, maybe a few months old. You wouldn't think he'd have minded who rocked him in their arms. But when he looked up into my pale face with the light eyes, his own filled with terror, his little cheeks bunched up in panic and he bawled. I quickly handed him back to his mother who put him to the breast, from where he eyed me with much apprehension until he fell asleep.

These were the first people I really met in Papua New Guinea and we met each on our own terms, which were plain curiosity and a feeling of wanting to make friends.

John had come in after me and had been speaking to a young man in Pidgin, then the trade language, now one of the three official languages of the country. I was glad, however, that my first meeting had been conducted untranslated and uninterpreted. The encounter had been fresh with human fear, our equality expressed through eyes and hands, our body smells and our skins, equally warm, soft and vulnerable.

During the ten days I stayed in Mount Hagen I saw very little of my hostess Leith, who was extremely busy preparing a play with which the students were to travel to Lae, on the coast. John became my guide and dropped some of his do's and don'ts and we parted as very good friends. Later he came to Australia, married the sister of my geology teacher and had two daughters, one of whom is my namechild.

As the caterer for the college, John drove a truck and took me to Mount Hagen town or to a plantation almost every day. He also arranged for me to go to Dop's village with two Americans who had suddenly appeared at the college, on their way to the caves farther up. One was a ballet dancer on a year's travelling scholarship to study dance. The other, probably a deserting paratrooper from Vietnam, had wandered through South-East Asia for eight years. Together we went to Dop's village to spend the night and hike the next day. Dop was a carpenter at the college.

That evening I made friends with the first of a string of old women. Old women and I always get along. I am old inside. She sat beside me at the fire, naked except for a flannelette blanket drawn around one shoulder. After the sun went down and the clouds descended until they floated beneath us (elevation over eighteen hundred metres) I put on a thin jumper. Sensing I felt the cold, she took off her blanket and wrapped it around me. There she sat, in her brown, wrinkled skin, exposed to the chill of the evening. She nearly brought tears to my eyes. With much talking with fingers and eyes, I convinced her the jumper would protect me adequately. I wrapped the blanket around her and we hugged. Thereafter she sang songs for me, which is the best way of all to keep warm. Other women and girls gathered and they asked my name and the name of my husband. Then they slotted the names into one of their own songs and the effect made them roll on the ground with laughter. I imagined it sounded like:

Koima and Moni went up the hill
to fetch a bamboo container of water.
Koima fell down and cracked his skull
and Moni came rolling after!

Life at the teachers college displayed all the incongruities that arise when one culture is superimposed on another. During the twentieth century people in the highlands had played unwilling hosts to such colonisers and conquerors as the Germans, the British and the Japanese and finally had the Australians bestowed upon them as administrators. Administration was to take the place of tribal wars, the traditional way of sorting out who owed what to whom and why.

Arnold, son of a local "big man" (the equivalent of a chieftain but without the hereditary rights), was a teacher at the college. He had just returned from a conference in Japan. "Here," he said, "I stand with one foot in each world. At the college I wear clothes, eat with knife and fork. At home I go barefoot and eat *kaukau* from the ashes. I feel happy doing both." He had married a Russian-Canadian volunteer and they had a daughter. When I saw him again five years later, she had taken the baby on a holiday to see her parents and hadn't come back.

Mixed marriages were a constant subject of conversation in Papua New Guinea. The first marriage between a white woman teacher and a handsome Tolai on the rise in politics made the newspapers. People said, "But she is beautiful," as if to say "She could have married anyone with her looks. Why did she do it?" Five years later they had also parted company; to be pioneers in that lottery called marriage, while taking on the other's culture at the same time and being watched by everybody who doesn't wish you well, is no atmosphere in which to build your happiness. But there are people who do it; you don't hear much about them. I was once offered her Papua New Guinea husband by an irate Australian wife. "Complete with his extended family and the whole tribe," she said, and it dawned on me that she meant it. "Why don't you go down to the village and I'll take your place here at the university?" I felt it wasn't fair without consulting her husband, whom I happened to like very much, but I was about ten years his senior and otherwise attached at the time, although most unhappily. I remember it as one of those temptations; had I been in another mood it could have changed my life forever. Another proposal came from the man himself, this time a law student more than twenty years my junior. "Age is of no importance," he declared with a sweeping gesture as if he stood in court. But although we were terrific dance partners at the end-of-year social,

I declined his offer on the grounds that I took longer to make up my mind than the span of one evening.

It was love at first sight with Papua New Guinea, the country. After that first ten-day visit to Mount Hagen I was determined that I would return no matter how long it took. Meanwhile I told stories of my experiences in Papua New Guinea and people would ask: "How many years did you live there?" Such was the depth of my feeling and my assumption of the role of interpreter of what I had seen. I cherished the few souvenirs: a woven basket, a greenstone axe, a matchbox and a *bilum* or netbag, made by the grandmother of Sabina, a student who took me to her village. I had learned that the giving of presents was important in Papua New Guinea life and I learned that the laws of reciprocity bound me to find suitable presents for my hosts. In that respect I was better equipped when I returned in 1975.

I did not go back to Mount Hagen. Two of the Roonka workers, Tony and Jenny Crawford, had gone to the Western Province of Papua New Guinea to assist the Gogodala tribe to build a longhouse and to carve anew the artifacts that expressed their spiritual culture, which had been destroyed several decades before under mission influence. Theirs is a remarkable story.

Tony went to Papua on his own as a young man, during his holidays. A superb photographer, he would roam further and further from Port Moresby, adding to his slide collection. On the streets in the capital he met a boy of fifteen from the Lesi tribe on the Gulf. He became Tony's guide and they went north to Lesi land, boating through the swamps and on foot. Tony lived with them for as long as time allowed and he was adopted as a friend-brother, eventually earning the title *wantok*, literally "one talk" or person who speaks the same language. As a *wantok* one becomes part of a reciprocal system that brings as many obligations as rights, but assures the essentials of hospitality, food and protection.

Tony's involvement with the Lesi people resulted in a collection of Lesi artifacts being saved from rot or neglect and being deposited in the Papua New Guinea Museum in Port Moresby. Tony's obsession with preserving tribal cultures in the face of the western onslaught went further than the material artifacts alone. He understood the spiritual loss which accompanied the destruction of a material culture, resulting more often than not in dispirited people hanging around the mission, which has replaced the longhouse as a meeting place.

With many tribes the longhouse was the dwelling place of an entire tribal subgroup, housing hundreds of people. After the missions entered some areas, these longhouses were replaced by nuclear family group huts, facing each other so as to form a "street". This was said to be more hygienic. Tony's proposal to rebuild a longhouse and have it as a cultural meeting place was not welcomed by the mission and the relationship between him and "Stalag 13" was uneasy, to say the least. The mission compound had gained its notorious name because it was surrounded by barbed wire, presumably to prevent pilfering and protect the ladies from unwelcome advances. The missionaries were dedicated people and ran a smart little hospital. In their own way they had a different sort of love affair with Papua New Guinea, one that was expressed in the manner of a constantly admonishing mother who drives her beloved children on to do good twenty-four hours a day.

When Tony married Jenny — I believe it was the third Roonka marriage — they left to live in Balimo, the heart of Gogodola land on the bewitching Aramia river.

There was a small white settlement, consisting of a district commissioner and his Filipino-Papuan wife, a couple who ran the vocational school and two crocodile hunters who also kept the trade store, alias "The Lodge", for the one tourist per annum who landed in Balimo.

When I visited Mount Hagen, Papua New Guinea was still under Australian administration and very much a colony as far as race relations were concerned. It was an "us" and "them" situation virtually across the board and being chummy with the natives was certain to make you an outcast or labelled "weird" or worse. But when Tony and Jenny came on leave four years later in 1975, Papua New Guinea had become self-governing with Michael Somare as Chief-Minister. Tony had ideas of embarking, with the new government, on a program of salvaging cultures and the Gogodala longhouse was the start. Race relations were freeing up as independence approached.

The slides Tony showed at a meeting of the Anthropological Society were stunning. The longhouse soared like a ship's bow from the green grass that surrounded it like a sea. The shields, masks and other artifacts, which had been made by old men who still remembered and taught their craft to younger ones like Kali, were unique in relation to the cultures of surrounding tribes. Whereas use of colour is very much determined by the area's vegetable and mineral content, shape and pattern are a product of the mind of a people. The Gogodala produced bold, humorous and at times sweepingly beautiful patterns, while their decorations made use of feathers and seeds in a way that delighted the eye. If I had to sum it up in one word, it would be to say that it was "aesthetic", but that means aesthetically pleasing to *my* eye and *my* perception, so it may be better not to qualify it at all. But the artifacts had revived the Gogodalas' interest in their own culture and when Michael Somare gave his support to the project, they gained prestige. These days the Gogodala are admired as performers of dances and canoe races at cultural gatherings in the Pacific.

"I wish I could see it for myself," I sighed to Tony.

"Why don't you come?" he replied. So I flew to Balimo in April 1975, as it happens on the same plane that brought Tony, Jenny, their baby and Tony's mother back to the weatherboard house on the lagoon. Again I travelled on borrowed money.

In Balimo the love affair deepened. I did not want to leave after three weeks to do exams in classical architecture and platonic wisdom. Talking to Kali seemed much more important. Sitting silently on the longhouse veranda seemed even more important. Again, it is the old women I remember. Bobodawa, too old to pound sago, would sit on the veranda with her companion, another old woman, rolling twine on her wrinkled thigh. She taught me the art of making a continuous thread which can then be woven into intricate belts, netbags or strong ropes. The company of Bobodawa let me in on the gossip as well. Even though we didn't share a language, we had plenty to "talk" about as we watched the passers-by. Bobodawa was fun. I wanted to become an old woman in her image: ancient, with a pattern of straightforward wrinkles covering my body, tough, alert, highly skilled in my own crafts and with still a twinkle in the eye. I still do.

Kali came to the longhouse from his nearby village of Waligi to carve artifacts at his firepit inside the longhouse. We exchanged information about each other's family and relatives in laborious English, after which I was taken along to Waligi to meet his mother.

The main reason for the trip to Waligi, however, was to introduce Tony's mother to Kali's mother. The two men were such friends that the first meeting of their mothers, who had brought them forth, was charged with emotion and pride. I fell more deeply in love and wanted to come and live at Waligi, although I also had my eye on a button of an island in the lagoon. I felt safer with the Gogodala than with the Europeans in Port Moresby, who were a combination of geniuses (or genii, as the correct plural appears to be), rogues, desperados, bureaucrats and alcoholics. It is perhaps significant that the Australians in Papua New Guinea referred to each other as Europeans. As Australians, they were neighbours of the Papua New Guineans, as Europeans, they were of a race that spread as colonisers over the globe. As most of them were of Anglo-Saxon origin I did not regard them as Europeans, because Britain has always been an island to itself, not sharing any borders with the continent. Although the Australians were not colonisers and bowed out as administrators in September 1975, they are still learning to be neighbours. Not sharing any physical land borders with the surrounding countries, Australia suffers from the same isolation as Britain, although Britain at least has the Scottish problem and the Irish dilemma to make her aware that other peoples have other sensibilities. The Australian attitude has long been that what is good enough for Australians should be regarded as God's gift by the neighbours, and even our past minister for Foreign Affairs couldn't properly pronounce the name of Papua New Guinea.

My 1975 visit to Balimo ended in a delightful trip down the Aramia and the Bamu rivers to the island of Daru on a leaking boat owned by the crocodile hunters. We had every trouble a nine-metre riverboat could present. The pumps broke down one by one, an old leak grew bigger, we baled the water out by hand with containers and stopped the leak with underwear. The engine often would not start after we'd been laid up for the night and neither engine nor steering seemed able to cope with the strong tides that washed in and out from the sea. Crossing the fifty-kilometre-wide mouth of the Fly River to reach Daru was nothing short of insanity in that vessel and we nearly drifted off into the ocean to be lost forever. The lights of Daru in the night were a sight more welcome than Father Christmas!

The wet monsoon had much delayed my exit from Balimo, and the boat trip had come about because planes could not land on the grassy stretch where Brahman cattle grazed, called Balimo airfield. I'd sent a telegram to my examiners at the university to warn them I would not be in time for term exams. "Stranded Fly River. Request supplementary", it read. I felt there was little use in wiring that I was stranded in a palm-covered paradise called Balimo, eating lotus seeds and fresh coconuts and gossiping in the longhouse. The Fly River was the nearest landmark they might know the existence of. Not that they were impressed. It hadn't been done before, getting a supplementary exam because of trouble on the Fly. As if a supplementary was fun, having to study again during term and getting questions that have been painfully thought up to make it hard for you. But they compromised and set me an essay question that made my hair curl and led me to abolish sleep and gardening in order to get it researched and written on time. But then the essay earned a distinction and it had all been worth it to float in a leaky boat on the Bamu while my study mates were doing their duty.

I was doing the last year of my degree and trying to map out postgraduate studies. I had already turned away from two honours courses for fear of specialising too soon and Australian Literature did not offer one. I still had to complete the major in Anthropology, but could not afford to spend a whole year on that alone. Moreover, I wanted to get back to Papua New Guinea.

Where there's a will there's a way. The saying took on a whole new meaning as I set about combining my two desires for 1976 into one. None of what I planned had been done just exactly that way before; it was a first for every authority I had to deal with. However, just as I had obtained permission to do a double anthropology that year, so too I persisted until I had 1976 mapped out, organised and financed. Years later a friend recalled that I seemed possessed at the time.

I would do a Master of Arts Qualifying in the Literature Department of the University of Papua New Guinea, for which my studies in anthropology and my unit in Religious Studies at the teachers college were good background. A charming man with a Chinese name was chairman of the Literature Department in Waigani, the suburb where Papua New Guinea's then nine-year-old university stood. He was much in favour of my coming, although the Academic Registrar had not as yet approved. This did not worry me. I was too busy arguing my case with the South Australian Education Department which paid my scholarship.

"We have never let anybody out of the country to study, not even out of the state," they moaned. "Not that we suspect you of wanting to have a good time . . ." But of course I *did* want to have a good time. I wanted a good time studying subjects which were by now more fascinating to me than Elizabethan history and Chomsky's theory of language. I'd also come up with a different interpretation of Plato from the one approved by the classics lecturers, which had cost me a distinction, and I felt a bit like the author of *Zen and the Art of Motorcycle Maintenance*, having a need to divorce myself from the scene of my intellectual awakening and branch into uncharted territory where they could not, and doubtlessly would not, follow me. Under the auspices of the Australian literature section I was doing a piece of private research into ethnic writing in Australia, which resulted in a small bibliography. I worked furiously away on this to complete it for the printer, as well as slogging away on my finals for the Bachelor of Arts degree. It all came together when a person in Education, who remembered me from the agricultural school where I had been a secretary, came across my file and said "Let her go!" His trust in me was backed up with authority and other supervisors had to groan and give in. It had taken five months to achieve.

Meanwhile I was trying to brainwash Ronald for his imminent stay of at least a year in Port Moresby, but this young man, born in Australia, had no plans to leave the soil of his birth. I cooked him sweet potato in coconut milk, sago pudding and fried banana, but he would not budge. I bribed him with promises of holidays at Mount Hagen, but he wasn't interested. I told him of the prestige he would gain with his peer group when he returned, but he was not impressed. In the end I blew up and accused him of being a male chauvinist piglet. "All children," I shouted, "follow their fathers when they move house to further their career, WITHOUT asking questions! Why can't you do the same for a mother? Would you say 'no' if your father was transferred to Hawaii and you were told to pack up and go with him?"

"That's different," said Ronald. "Why can't I live here by myself? I can cook and clean and make my bed and it is only for a year.'' He was fourteen, going on for fifteen. But the law would have cast a crooked eye on me had I agreed to this request. I could understand it though. He hated change. Finally it was agreed he would live with his father for a year and decide at the end whether to move back or remain. As he still hated change, he remained and still lives only a suburb away from where he started his Melbourne life.

I left for Port Moresby soon after I got my final results, carrying my *bilum*, a sago-bag from Balimo, a swag and a portable typewriter. The bundle and bags contained all I needed to live for a year without spending. My scholarship would have to be stretched to include the airfares to and fro. Tony and Jenny now had a house in Boroko, a suburb of Port Moresby where Tony worked with the National Culture Council. They offered me a room, which I accepted with deep gratitude. Without their help I would have been lost, because the university still had not accepted my application. This did not worry me, because I trusted that the nice Chinese man, who had been writing me very encouraging letters, would support me even more when I actually turned up in the flesh and the powers that be had to say either yes or no. If they said no, I planned to put one argument after another for my admission, until they said yes to get rid of me.

My intentions were of the purest order. I wanted to study the country I loved through its languages and literature and make it known in Australia as a culture of as yet unappreciated merit. I wanted to build bridges between reluctant neighbours.

As soon as I was settled and unpacked, I took a PMV, or Public Motor Vehicle, the common public transport, to Waigani. I still had to pinch myself to believe I was really here for a whole year, academic registrars willing of course. The blanket of humidity felt like a second skin, the way I liked it. My long Indian skirt swung around my bare ankles. One layer of cotton and nothing underneath is my idea of comfort. Crossing the busy Boroko shopping centre, I walked elastically to the bus stop at the junction. The future was before me. A year had never seemed such a wonderful hunk of time as it did that day, for I felt I would pack it to the rafters with experiences. It was even then quite clear to me that I came as a student in more ways than one. What I had to offer would come afterwards, or so I thought.

At the university I searched for a point from which to begin. A friendly girl in an office dialled an extension for me and on the other end spoke the deep husky voice of the friendly Chinese man. Yes, he said, I could walk over to the Literature Department to discuss my application, seeing that I had arrived and was in the university grounds. Given directions I found the building, kissed the hibiscus flower by the entrance for luck and strode up the stairs. I knocked on the door which carried the number I'd been told, heard a voice say "Come in" and opened the door on two years of relentless agony. My friendly Chinese supporter sat in a swivel chair. He was a big, black Ugandan with a sly smile which I took for a kind welcome. It was the welcome of a spider who had just seen an insect land in his net.

There is no doubt that Taban enjoyed being the spider in the web, just as it is certain that there was another Taban who despised himself for doing so. For he also had his dreams. His Chinese sounding surname was but one lead into his speculations on race, identity and descent. He had been across the Atlantic to live the other dream of many non-Americans. He had studied in the United States. He carried a fading newspaper cutting of an interview with Taban in the *Washington Post*. I looked at the boy in the photo and recognised the dream, but the man had by then lost it. Not only were Americans not uniformly kind and cooperative in their dealings with him, but they had often mistaken him for a descendant of slaves. Neither he nor the slave descendants wanted to be mistaken for one another. Their goals did not even run parallel.

Taban was the last son of a mother who had sensed he was hanging around, waiting to be born. To facilitate his entry into the world she had not only consulted a witch doctor, but had returned to an already rejected husband for the act of conception. Thereafter she had loved her son and spoiled him rotten, as probably only an African mother can. His head was swollen with his own importance, but underneath his ever-confident exterior he cried out for the loving hand of his mother. No woman had ever loved him as much. One woman's love had turned to hate and he had ideas of training some new woman for the empty space beside him, one who would pander to all his whims, take the brunt of his switching moods, play hostess for his many friends and never, never, never speak when he wanted silence, or query where he had been, or refuse his simple demands. He'd had a brief training session with a tall German beauty, who had finished up by throwing her thesis the length of the department corridor, shouting at his closed door: "You are afraid of me!" whereupon she had left for Germany. This piece of gossip I translated in my own way as being the sort of culture clash that could not happen to someone like me who had seen Paul Robeson in *Bosambo of the River* and read Joseph Conrad's *Heart of Darkness*. Culturally speaking I was prepared to meet Africa on its own terms. Taban's obvious overtures of friendship would find a response in me that would lead to a magnificent cooperation, resulting in an academic victory for cross-cultural studies. Or something like that . . . anyway.

By New Year's day, 1976, I had had two yelling fights with my future supervisor, during one of which I had told him he was a liar and a cheat. He had smiled that wily smile, worthy of a Mills and Boon hero, intimating that I was probably not far from the truth. Although we had visited the Academic Registrar together, the board which decided foreigners' applications had gone en bloc to Africa for a study tour and were "lost". That meant they should have been back a week ago but hadn't turned up. By New Year's day Taban was not speaking to me or anybody and I took that very personally. Later I learned that his house had been broken into on New Year's Eve and the thieves had made off with all his favourite African shirts. This had put an enormous dent in his dream of black brotherhood, coming as he had the previous April with a dream of teaching his black brothers on the other side of the world the gems of world literature, and bestowing upon them his many lines of poetry which sang of the injustices and ambitions of his own life in that wide, hostile world so far. To have his homeland shirts stolen at the start of a new year, the year in which he was going to achieve this, was more than he could bear and he disappeared for days, after leaving the office with glazed eyes, silent for once.

I felt I had run out of credit for the time being and, with the beginning of term many weeks away, I took my uncertain plans, my written proposals and a book or two, and flew to Balimo with an American sago expert called Jim, who was to study sago culture in Isago, a longhouse village further up the Aramia river.

Seeing the lagoon appearing beneath the wings was

enough to make me forget Taban, academic boards and cultural bridges. I was in love with the land once more and the city was a bad dream, where people lost their good dreams; or worse, tried to adapt them to asphalt unsuccessfully. I knew I would get my sanity back in Balimo.

Far from getting my sanity back in Balimo, Taban's spell had lain a hold over me that troubled me even in paradise. Strange things happened and uneasy dreams disturbed my sleep. Eventually I went on a trip up the rivers on a double canoe with one of the crocodile hunters, whom I had earlier considered as just about the ideal living partner, considering my inclinations for tropical adventures. I tried to revive this old interest, but it was of little use, although we were friends of course. He had his children and his eighteen-year-old nephew up for a holiday. With three of the Papua New Guinean boys, who worked off and on for The Lodge, and Joe, his Sepik cook, we steamed down the Aramia into the Bamu and up the Gwari River, which came tumbling from the Southern Highlands. This is the heart of the country. Rainforest stands like a green tapestry screen on both sides. Birds of a beauty unsurpassed fly through the tree tops. Cries of wildlife unseen cut through the stillness. Crocodiles splash in the water. There are leeches at every landing place and mosquitoes everywhere. You accept that you will be bitten and stung and sucked to a pulp for the privilege of just being there.

Dusk was the hour of the flying foxes; they wheeled low over the water in a dance of dalliance until it was time to hang upside down from the branches of trees, the likes of which did not exist anywhere in the world. I drank it in. The beauty, the strength, the vigour and energy of that world.

Each village housed a different tribe, each with its own language. Papua New Guinea has over seven hundred languages and the cultures they represent differ widely. One language on the Gwari sounded superficially like Swedish and I would have investigated but for falling ill with malaria. It was a beauty of a bout. I ran a fever which sent me into delirium. At the same time a cut on my right hand festered into a tropical sore and my right arm, which had its lymph glands interfered with during a cancer operation in 1974, swelled up to twice its normal size. When I was lucid, I crawled from my bed to the edge of the deck to dip a towel in the river. Wound around my throbbing arm, it would dry to a tinder within an hour. I was horribly, horribly sick and the skipper later told me he feared I would "kick the bucket". Having a sick woman on board tarnished his idea of a trip up the river and our friendship cooled off rapidly. Joe the cook cast me a glance of pity now and then and this was the only compassion I was aware of.

The double canoe was lumbering on its way back to the Bamu, loaded with empty oil drums, when I recovered from the fevers. I wanted to wash the sweat off my body but privacy was hard to find, so I settled for a good hairwash. I was sitting in the sun on deck for the first time, feeble, but still alive, my arm a monstrous purple-blue-yellow-green, drying my hair, when the skipper yelled: "Women and children on the aft deck! The bore is coming!"

I had heard plenty of stories about bores and placed them in the same category as fishing stories. I looked ahead, and what I saw coming rolling towards us over the wide, wide waters stopped my breath! The bore was a rolling wall of water, a metre and a half high, advanc-

162

ing at the speed of a running cassowary. This was the tide from the sea forcing its way up the rivers. We had just entered the head of the Bamu, where it is at its narrowest, but still easily five hundred metres across. The bore, squeezed by the banks, roared towards the landspit where the Bamu divides into the Gwari and the Wawoi and we were floating mid-river in between, with the jetty of Emeti just coming into sight on the right-hand bank.

It took less time than it takes to tell this, before the bore hit us with the force of a tornado. Nephew Peter was eating a bowl of cornflakes in the galley when the roof fell in. The right-hand dugout canoe split fully down its length, before most of the deck splintered off the left-hand dugout. Eight people were hanging on to the wreckage and sinking, while I was being swung in the air by a deck pole. I tried to grab the little boy's hand, as he was nearest, but his leg was caught. His father freed him and both children clambered up. Soon we were all in the left-hand dugout, shaken, but uninjured. Drums and wreckage floated over the width of the river, which was again as calm as on a lovely summer's day.

We floated back up the Gwari with the tide for four hours, before we could turn and float back to the Bamu. All the men had performed heroic deeds to rescue belongings from the wreckage and, because I always packed my things in plastic bags, most of mine were retrieved. The skipper's moneybox was delivered back to him a year later, completely intact, by local villagers.

Arrival at Emeti, six hours after our ordeal, was heaven on a mudflat. Squeezing the soft, brown, waterlogged earth between my naked toes, I knew I was an earth person, a landlubber, a true Capricorn. The people of Emeti were wonderfully hospitable and concerned. The only white person who lived there was Eva, a missionary who had lived on the Bamu for forty years. Her husband lay buried there and she soldiered on for the Lord and the sick. A trained nurse, she trained others to patrol up the river with medical supplies to help those in need. She talked more about crocodiles and outboard motors than about the ten commandments and I felt there were many people there who loved and respected her. Yet she too carried the white man's burden, thinking of herself as a bringer of civilisation and Christianity, the only true creed. She felt that Papua New Guineans could never rule themselves and Independence drove her back to Australia. She still keeps in contact with Emeti people and all who visited there. Now in her eighties, she is daily homesick for the Bamu. A medical condition keeps her in Australia, but she hopes to be buried with her husband at Emeti. Her friends there would prefer her to spend her remaining years with them and when I read her letters, full of pining for the beloved place, I wonder at the choices people make on the basis of religion, politics and convictions about race.

Eva gave me medical care before we went on to Balimo by flat-bottom motorboat three days later. There the doctor at the mission, who hailed from Adelaide, advised me to get to Port Moresby as quickly as possible, or even better, to Australia, to have my arm seen to. It still looked quite horrible, as if it was quietly rotting away, independently from the rest of my body, which seemed to have recovered from the malaria. I was put on a little plane to Daru, where I delivered a message from the skipper to David Chan, the local storekeeper, who served all the settlements up the river. Hearing the story of the shipwreck, David burst out laughing. He slapped his thighs with glee. The croc hunters had been bad debtors on and off and, as long as nobody had really been hurt, he was having a good laugh over their misfortune on the river. When I asked to see a brown roll of batik-print cloth to buy myself a new laplap, having lost some in the shipwreck, he said to the girl who served me: "That one's on the house!" I thanked him almost in tears, a sign of how weak I still was, but also because I did not quite know how to take his callousness towards the losers. After all, they were my friends.

But Daru is full of callous friendships. So interdependent are people on that small island for their social traffic, their livelihood, their emotional needs, that they love and hate each other simultaneously. Every evening they gathered in the club, drank beer, told stories. All the races that had ever passed Daru on the way inland had mixed and mingled and were represented.

I stayed in the house of David, a tall blond Englishman, whose partner in love and life was Stella, a Highland girl from Goroka. They were incredibly hospitable and I came to love Stella like a sister. A fellow from Port Moresby was travelling through with his guitar and also staying at Stella's. As he played and I sang, we worked out a repertoire and soon the room filled with people who listened and listened and asked for more until my vocal cords collapsed. One member of the audience was Frank Narua, a marvellous old man, who spoke in a whisper due to an operation for cancer of the throat. There was a Polish mechanic, filled with mixed-up homesickness for a Europe that had ceased to exist, and Ella, a tall mixed-blood girl who had grown up on her father's plantation and wanted to be a model in Queensland. The air was always heavy with scandals in Daru and gossip was the heart of the town. But there was an endless supply of generosity amidst the jealousy, suspicion and petty deceit. Except for the true Daruans, whose tribal land this was, one got the impression that everyone was hiding from something, had fled from self-created situations which had got out of hand, threatening life and liberty. Maybe they were all prisoners by their own hands, but if they were, they made the most of it.

Back in Moresby my arm settled down, the lost board had returned and approved my application to study in the University of Papua New Guinea and Taban had called around at Tony and Jenny's place to find out where I was. He could in no way understand what could move a person to go into the jungle and when he heard of my having malaria and getting shipwrecked on a crocodile-infested river in the same week, he cried out: "If you want to die, you can do it in comfort in the city! What moved you to go so far away?" He had these endearing traits which reconciled me to him again and again and as term got underway and I was deep in my studies, it almost seemed as if the whole of life had come to its final destination under Taban's guiding hand. Despite periodic clashes or days of coolness, our relationship managed to coast along until Easter with some occasions of deep mutual understanding, the like of which I had only known in my fantasies. Fantasy was of course Taban's specialty and the life he led in his mind constantly clashed with the realities that surrounded him. I would have understood this had I been informed of all the whirlwinds in his mind. On the occasions that he did confide in me, we had unlimited peace between us. But paranoia would always return and the vicious cycle of suspicion, rancour and revenge would start up again.

At Easter, which we were to spend at his house with a pile of books and a fridge full of food, a few things started to dawn on me. Taban suffered from an ugly complex that had probably beset him in the United States. It was the white-woman-conquest by the slighted black man. I became aware that there was a whole historical movement of slighted black men who had made it their business to do to a white woman what so many white men had done to their black women: use them, then drop them. I became aware that Taban had gone through some warming-up exercises in this ugly quest. Neither the rumours about him nor his explanations were the truth, which was squashed in between. To be used in putting down the white woman who had preceded was hurtful in the extreme, as I loved the man despite all his idiosyncracies. In his best moments he knew this and became like a lamb, or like a saint, or a sinner redeemed.

Every discovery about him that evoked my anger or disgust seemed to be balanced out by one that convinced me the real Taban was hidden under layers of acquired attitudes and mannerisms, which only had to be peeled off to reveal the aspiring rescuer of humankind underneath.

In his book case I found the Buddhist Dhammapada, the underlinings accentuating the same verses as in my copy of that book. His favourite books were the *Wisdom of the East* series and there was little doubt in my mind that he aspired to be a future buddha or bodhisattva, or wandering sadhu, and at least a guru in this life. Children and animals loved him and people were constantly asking him for little loans. He wanted to be everyone's friend and regarded it a sin to cause pain or suffering. Yet he made enemies and hurt others when his exalted principles got too heavy to carry through the weary days.

I have a memory of a very uncomfortable week, when we were both struck with tonsillitis and visited a doctor.

We walked from the car to the surgery arm in arm and he said: "It is good to feel the sun on one's face." His gratitude to be alive at that moment was simple and touching. In that crowded street I also became aware, for the first time, of people staring at us. He was darker than most Papua New Guineans and distinctly different in features. I wondered whether it would have bothered me that people stared, had I been the black person and he white. There was no sign that he had become aware of me as white during that little walk, but in the surgery we both knew that the doctor's disapproval for two such disparate people sharing one and the same infection hung like a stink in the air. We nursed each other for the rest of that week and having tonsillitis with Taban remains one of my better memories of him, I'm sorry to say. I would go so far as to believe that had he incurred a chronic tonsillitis, we might have made a go of our partnership outside the academic concerns that had thrown us together.

He already had several books of poetry to his name and jealously guarded his reputation as Uganda's wonderboy poet. But he could not quite tolerate another talent beside him, however modest, and I learned to keep my writing to myself.

One of my teachers in the Honours course was an African woman of great beauty, Adeola James. She was a Yoruba from Nigeria and always wore Yoruba costume. In the long, slim skirt she loped on sandalled feet as if crossing deserts, her matching head scarf crowning her ebony face. Every time she walked into a room to tutor us in literature, it took me several minutes to concentrate, as I was always overcome by the beauty of her appearance. A few times we had short conversations which made me feel strongly that we could have been friends, if too many things had not stood between us. She was no friend of Taban. An east-coaster and a westerner in Africa trust each other as little as in America, it seems. Yet she always remained fair in speaking about him, although she often disagreed with the way he ran the department. Once she told me how she had seen her mother's face in that of a Papuan woman who sat in the street in Port Moresby selling bracelets. I confessed I had seen my own mother's face in that of a Chinese woman in Daru. Our perception of people was guided by the same concerns, but Adeola felt much more burdened by the fact that she was a woman than I did. Of course, she was married and I was no longer so. If we could ever meet when we are old women, I think Adeola and I could be friends at last, because the politics of men and academic pettinesses would no longer matter.

The Festival of Arts in Adelaide was on that year, incorporating Writers' Week. My friends wrote me descriptions of the Tibetan Dance Theatre which I had missed and I wished they'd come to Papua New Guinea on their way back to India. Instead there came a writer whom nobody had referred to, but who had made quite an impact in Adelaide. He was the Nigerian writer Wole Soyinka, who eventually won the Nobel Prize in 1986. His lecture at Waigani was impressive for its socio-political insights, as well as for his minutes-long sentences which arrowed their way with unnerving accuracy and self-assuredness to an eloquent end, carved in English more beautiful than the Queen's speech-writer can muster.

He also gave an off-the-cuff seminar during which he was asked to recite his famous poem "Telephone Conversation". It tells of a phone call to a landlady in London about renting a room and the landlady wanting to know how black he is before asking him to come and see her. He was obviously quite sick of the poem by now, but had to recite it. I was probably the only white woman there and it was easier to fasten on a white face to recite it, so I got a personal delivery, so to speak. That evening Adeola was hostess at a party for Wole and when we were introduced again, he bowed slightly and said: "It is you, isn't it?" I confirmed that I was me, but unfortunately I had not then read his masterly novel *The Interpreters* and so I missed the point of his remark; disappointed that I didn't seem to want to play the game by the rules, he turned away to charm others with his wit and intellect.

Taban was doing one of his turnabouts that evening and I left with a Papua New Guinean friend, also a poet, to listen to his reminiscences of his lost white lady love for half the night. I knew from the gossip how he'd lost her and ventured to ask him a question.

"How can you love someone and beat them at the same time?" I asked.

He fumbled at first, trying to evade this crucial issue. But as I insisted he formulated a startling thought. "When you beat the woman you love," he said, "and you leave the house angry to go and have a drink with your friends . . . and when you come back and she is still there, you love her more than ever."

In view of the fact that the woman, in order to leave the house, would have had to lift her sleeping children from their beds and venture into the dark in a town where the street life after dark is not exactly safe, this seemed a completely unreal argument to me. But he stuck to it. He too suffered from the white-woman syndrome, but after a drunken accusation that I was a white exploiter, early in our acquaintance, he turned around and became one of the best friends I had that year. With him I was at ease and could talk freely of all that bothered me about race relations and even about Taban and his unpredictable moods. He tried to convince me to give Taban up, but my stupid heart would not listen and he gave up trying to convince me and began to cultivate another white woman friend of mine. For he was lonely also and could not waste his time on a woman who consorted with the enemy. He and Taban had no love lost between them.

After three months with Tony and Jenny I had been allowed to rent a room on campus in the women's house, Luavi, which meant friendship in one or another Pacific language. All the student houses were called "Friendship" in different regional languages.

The student houses were for Papua New Guineans and other Pacific students and I was lucky that Luavi was not quite full so that I could move in. It meant a great deal to be on campus and part of the life there, as well as being able to go to the library at all times and not be housebound in the evening. On weekends I always visited Tony and Jen, looking forward to sharing the week's happenings and feeding the baby his porridge.

Life in Luavi, the only women's house on campus, was full of gentle faces, shy greetings and yodelling laughter in the evenings. I was of course a bit of an oddity, even though there were officially three other white women who had rooms in Luavi. But two used their rooms more as a base, one living with friends in town, the other coming back after a relationship with a boyfriend broke down. The third one had grown up in Papua New Guinea (I think her father was a lawyer) and she shared a room with a Papua New Guinean girl, being thoroughly part of the local scene.

I did not feel alone in Luavi even though no one dared

to approach me in the first weeks. They were right of course in sniffing me out, waiting to see what sort of a person I was. After all, there was no past record on me, whereas they all had their tribal affiliations and usually had one or more *wantoks* on campus to vouch for their identity. But bit by bit relations loosened up, as they must when you share washrooms and toilets and staircases together.

I had a lovely little room facing the enormous lawn that stretched to the main road. The lawn was dotted with trees and the hills rose up behind it. Right beneath my balcony was a little courtyard with a brick wall, clothed with ever-flowering bougainvilleas in deep purple and orange, and some hibiscus bushes. The wall was a recent addition to prevent ardent young men from scaling the balconies to visit the ladies of their choice. Sometimes the lady did not know she had been chosen and objected to the late caller. For the same reason, a guard took up position in the hall at six pm, and every male visitor had to sign the book and record the room number of his lady and promise to be out by eight. If he was not, a second guard who had come on duty by then would rouse him up and walk him out the front door, often with the lady's approval. It stands to reason that if, in a community of two thousand, only two hundred are women, there is going to be some lively campaigning after dark!

My first friend in Luavi was Mary Luke, a remarkable Bougainvillean woman who was doing her second degree and also acted as house-mother for Luavi. She was somewhat older than most of the inhabitants, but her suitability for the job came from an inner strength that shone out of her, and a compassion that never failed. She had been a nun, having grown up on an island where the Catholics beat the Lutherans to it. She must have been regarded as a promising religious sister because she was sent to Rome during one of those winters when Italy too receives its blanket of snow. The thought of this beautiful black woman in the snow in Rome created such a strong mental image in my mind that I am not sure whether she showed me a photograph of herself in the ancient city, or whether it was produced by her storytelling. Mary Luke had given up her religious vocation when she realised that she too wanted to have children like her friends and age mates. She finished her studies that year and became a student counsellor at the Bougainville copper mine, which had paid her scholarship. She was highly qualified, but I heard she eventually gave it up because all the apprentices she had to instruct for their own good were males and traditionally they did not take advice from a woman kindly. The modern world had arrived and with it a modern infrastructure, but the old one was only adjusting where it suited the men, who regarded themselves as sole keepers of the culture.

My second friend was Nakanat, who came from Manus Island, made famous by the American anthropologist Margaret Mead. I learned that the Manus Islanders were hardly on friendly terms with Ms Mead since the contents of her book *Growing up in New Guinea* had become known. It is one thing to be a treasured visitor who takes an interest in your culture, but quite another to turn out to be an author who interprets without checking and then tells the world all about you as you are not, or do not think yourself to be. Anthropologists have learned since Margaret Mead and the better ones explain at more length what their purpose is and try to verify the interpretations they put on things with tribal elders. I remember how carefully Tony juggled his words to get it just right, after scores of consultations with his Gogodala informants. They always knew that one day Tony would put them in a book and that they would get to see it. Fortunately, *AIDA; Life and Ceremony of the Gogodala* (National Cultural Council of Papua New Guinea in association with Robert Brown & Assoc., Bathurst, New South Wales 1981) turned out to be a book of great physical beauty due to Tony's talent with the camera.

Nakanat used to come to my room in the evening, alone or with other girls, and we'd talk about our relatives and childhoods. Grandmothers, I found out, are much the same in most cultures. They speak in proverbs and are endlessly resourceful. Nakanat's grandmother and my Opoe had even expressed the same proverbial advice to us on similar occasions! Nakanat was often homesick for Manus and that went for many of the young women of Luavi. They came from many tribes, from the highlands and the islands, the coastal swamps or the small trading towns. But they were all homesick for their mother's cooking and full of disdain for the mess food we lined up for three times a day. Some lived solely on bread and butter and what fruit turned up in the mess, unable to stomach the cooked offerings, not even the rice. Rice, after all, was an introduction to Papua New Guinea, and although many came to like it, others clung to the idea of sweet potato roasted in the ashes, or sago fried or steamed in bamboo. Sometimes several of us went to the market at Koki or Waigani to buy *kaukau*, coconut, fresh greens and pawpaw and we cooked ourselves a feast in the kitchen on the ground floor. Meat or fish was beyond our means, but *kaukau* cooked in coconut is satisfying enough if eaten in sufficient quantity. The local greens had local names, but most were spinach-like and sometimes you could get the leafy tops of the sweet potato plant, which are delicious when stir-fried. Pawpaw, or papaya, is a food fit for the gods. I tried to have two papayas a week, giving me a slice for breakfast every day, and it was probably the reason my health didn't collapse entirely during that year.

My scholarship being just marginally more generous, I was able to buy coffee, sugar and milkpowder. Thus the evening congregations often took place in my room and I was glad to serve my guests that small luxury in exchange for their highly valued company. Few of them smoked, but Marianna did and when life got on top of her, which it often did because of her flamboyant romantic involvements, she knocked and came in to talk and puff smoke out the open balcony doors.

I had noticed Marianna often in the university grounds before I came to know her. She was petite, extremely pretty and so confident and almost haughty that one had to notice her. Also, she wore shoes. Not just rubber thongs, but shoes. I heard she had been to Fiji on an exchange scholarship and had just returned. One afternoon, in Mary Luke's room, I was introduced to her. She came from Kwotto, an island off the Papuan coast. I told her I came from Adelaide.

"So did the father of my little boy," she said, with a voice that betrayed nothing of the drama that sentence contained. With a shock I realised who she was. One of my tribal brothers and close friends from Roonka had gone to Papua New Guinea, spurred on by Tony and me, to take up a job at the university. There he had met Marianna, then a first year student. They had fallen in love and a relationship developed, becoming stormier as time passed. Eventually my Roonka brother almost fled the country, returning to his old job in Adelaide, thoroughly dislocated in mind and spirit. But Marianna was pregnant and when he heard he arranged to be there for the birth and get his name in the records as the boy's father. That might have been a promising new beginning for the repopulation of the world with a more tolerant race of multicultural people, but Marianna had other ideas. She accused my tribal brother of lack of support and desertion and she fought him like a tigress on his return, which should have been a lovely reconciliation in his expectations. It was a clear case of man not understanding woman and woman feeling victim but not taking it lying down. The little boy was growing up with Marianna's aunt at Kwotto and although the father maintained him and went to visit him several times at great expense, no reconciliation ever took place.

Yet, despite my Adelaide connection, or perhaps because of it, Marianna and I became close friends and shared the sorts of thought one only lets a sister in on. Once, after seeing a film in the campus lecture theatre, in which a Japanese man explained how he would cut off a hand or a finger for his brother, we were walking home, deeply enmeshed in the story, when Marianna suddenly gasped.

"Blood! There's blood on us!" We looked at each other with a mixture of horror and desire to believe. There was blood on our hands, in tiny specks, but when we touched it, it came off as dried flecks and there were no wounds. How and where we'd picked that up was a mystery in itself and we preferred to interpret it as a sign that we were bound in blood as sisters.

Marianna's stormy life on campus and problems with her studies caused her to leave and take a job in a government department. The last time I met her it was to present her with a parcel that had just arrived from her little boy's father. It was his Christmas present to her and I was to be the mediator once more. She accepted it with little interest, but when out of the wrappers came Kath Walker's most famous book of poetry on the struggle of the Aboriginal people her whole face lit up and she said: "I always wanted to have this book." I said softly: "He must have known."

Marianna joined the diplomatic service and lived in Indonesia for several years and I am sorry that she lost touch with me, but perhaps it was better for her to lose the Adelaide connection altogether.

There were two lovely New Britain girls, who never failed to stop when they met me in the grounds and have a chat. It is customary in villages to hold hands with the person you meet on the path while you talk to her. This is done amongst women as well as men, but I never observed it between a man and a woman, unless they were more deeply attached. The New Britain girls would hold hands with me as we talked in the sun and the custom impressed me as one that could bring about world peace if practised widely. One of them, Ruby, invited me to the New Britain end-of-year social where I discovered I could dance! Having missed out on learning to foxtrot and waltz because of the aftermath of the war, here I was, at age forty-two, stomping away barefoot on the concrete dance floor to the music of a Papua New Guinean live rock band and finding I had patterns inside me that only my feet could express. No foxtrot or waltz would have done for what I danced out of my system on that night and on the evening of the East Highland social, to which I was invited by Naomi. I owe these two women a depth of gratitude for an opportunity that never came back again, but is remembered with unadulterated pleasure.

Naomi became acquainted with me later in my stay. She had inhabited the room I then lived in, but had moved in with another girl. I was never quite certain whether my application had been the cause of her shift and so I was shy of speaking to her. When we finally got to talking she assured me it had been her own choice to move, as she felt lonely at the time.

Naomi was a Bena-Bena girl from around Goroka and she had lived six years in Sydney attending high school. I deeply admired her strong ties with her relatives and the soil of her birth. All she wanted to do was finish her degree, go home and plant her garden, which she expected to do no matter what sort of official job she would get. A highland woman's garden is like an Englishman's castle; you don't give it up if you can help it. Her mother was looking after Naomi's garden then, producing *kaukau* and greens for the family.

Naomi's life has worked out a little differently and she now has a responsible job in Goroka. I don't think she sees half as much of her native ground as when she was a student in Port Moresby and had the long holiday to go home and get reacquainted. She is, in a sense, westernised beyond repair. I think this has caused a tremendous loneliness in her life, which eventually has to be filled. As she corresponded with me for eleven years, I am aware of the schism a western education caused in her life and suspect something similar may have happened in the lives of the other women I knew in Luavi. Nakanat and Mary Luke kept in touch for a few years. By the time I went back for a brief holiday in 1980, I had already lost contact with Mary Luke and Nakanat was herself on holiday in Manos, with her little daughter. Naomi had probably passed us in the air, flying to Goroka when we flew to Port Moresby. Such is life, but the disappointment was great.

Maria from Madang was also a later acquaintance and the only one I caught up with in 1980. I made a terrible mistake which shouldn't have happened. We were staying in the Islander, a costly hotel on the coast and not quite our style, when I rang Maria at work to arrange a lunch date. Hearing where I was she was eager to come to the Islander, but as it was well out of town and I didn't want to get her in trouble with her boss, I suggested we meet and eat in town. As it turned out, there was nothing better than a department store cafeteria, where we shared a listless beef-and-mustard sandwich and talked about her life and mine.

Maria had a finely tuned mind and vulnerable spirit, which had been hurt in the multi-tribal goings-on at campus to the point where she had needed to give up her studies, go home and rest. She had been surrounded by caring hands in Luavi until her departure and I had been deeply moved by her own summing-up of her state of mind. There was no rancour, no hatred, no desire for revenge. Drawing a little flower, she said: ''That's what's in my mind.'' She corresponded with me for a few years, but after our meeting in 1980 she never wrote again. I realised too late that had I invited her to lunch in the Islander, she would have treasured the meeting for the local prestige that could be gained from being in that place. Maria had changed and so had I, but I owed her more for her friendship than a lousy white bread sandwich on a cafeteria stool. Mistakes like that bother me for years and the regret can never quite be wiped out.

Ronald's visit during the September school holiday posed a problem of accommodation. No men, not even a fourteen-year-old man, were allowed to stay in Luavi after eight pm. I approached Melvin, a Solomon Islander studying geology, about whether the men's house might have a spare bed. He found one, bless his soul, in the room of Poram, a law student. It must be said that young Ronald felt apprehensive when I told him where he was going to sleep, but that apprehension fell away within hours. Poram and his friends adopted

Ronald as a younger brother, slotted him into the *wantok* system for the week of his stay and allowed him to sit in on their late night palavers about politics and everything else that concerns students. Soon he left Luavi straight after dinner to join his new friends for the rest of the evening.

Friends took us out and Ronald, pale, blond and blue-eyed, had dinner with a Bougainvillean as black as ebony and found they had many things in common. He'd had for some years an Aboriginal friend at school, but that was about all the exposure to non-white people Ronald had chalked up. At Koki market the women looked, pointed and laughed at him and he liked the attention, though he didn't understand it. A New Zealand friend drove us into the hills to see Errol Flynn's goldmine and we met a boy she knew from up the Gulf, who came along. Within minutes Ronald and the boy spoke like old school-mates. It was a lovely process of unfolding that week and I still lamented that he had not come to spend the year.

The National Art Gallery had an exhibition on and the National Dance Theatre danced on the lawn under the stars and it was hard to tear Ronald away. At Luavi all the girls knew his name and greeted him, ''Hello Ronald,'' with wide smiles, more than once a day. When it was time to leave, we scraped money together to buy Poram a cheap watch, for he did not have one, and Ronald went to present it, coming back with red eyes. That was one kid who might grow up without prejudice.

Had I stayed longer in Luavi, by continuing studies in the following year, I would no doubt have become second mother to some of the girls. Late in my stay there were sometimes quiet knocks and a young woman would come in for a private talk about a private problem. Not that I had solutions, but I had problems too and I was older and perhaps a little more experienced. In the end it was just having a talk and a coffee that was appreciated. By the time I left I was just about what the male student counsellor had hoped I could be, an older woman to present a more moderate model of behaviour to the younger ones than had been done in the year before by white feminists, who had spread their liberation gospel to no one's benefit but their own; they relieved their spleen. It had resulted in campus strife and my Roonka brother always claimed it was behind Marianna's constant reviling of him. But of course as a male he had to be biased.

I could certainly see the strictures which some tribal systems and the male bureaucracy imposed on Papua New Guinean women, but I had already learned too much about tribal society to believe that you could simply import a new slogan and wipe out injustice in a country not your own. The Papua New Guinean women will struggle in their own way for the positions they want to maintain and gain in modern Melanesian society and they have different methods from those that western women have evolved.

In Tony and Jenny's cookhouse lived a young couple from Dobu Island. John had recommended himself as a house servant and although Jenny wanted no servants, the fact that the cookhouse stood empty had brought a string of enquiries for the job. In the end she took on John and soon his wife Sini arrived from Dobu to set up house with him. Later Jenny found out that Sini was only fifteen. But she was mature in many ways and well up to her task as wife. Happiness still reigned in the cookhouse during her pregnancy and Sini and John and I became good friends. I used to come to their house and share a smoke with John and talk in halting English with Sini. After the birth of their son, John came to me and asked me to name the child. This was a great responsibility. The baby looked weak and after a day's thought I decided on Daniel, explaining to Sini the biblical Daniel and the strength he had displayed. She said she knew the story and they were happy with the name. I asked whether they would also give Daniel a Dobu name and they said they would. The name giving was accompanied by suitable presents.

We learned to our dismay that Dobu women don't leave the house for a month after giving birth and live on water and taro. Sini was a frail girl to start with and we feared she would fade away, especially now that she was feeding a baby as well. I came weekly with tins of milkpowder and other strength-giving food, but she did not break her tabu. There is no querying such customs, which no doubt sprang up for a reason that we, from afar, would not appreciate. Jenny and I were immensely relieved when the month was up and Sini came out into the light and started to eat and put on a smile again.

But John began to make trouble. The baby cost money and he felt there was not enough left for him. His *wantoks* required him to take his turn, as a married man and father, in the fortnightly beer-drinking events, which could slurp up a month's wages. John started to beat up Sini and Sini would flee to Jenny, who would take her in. At last, when I happened to be there with an Australian guest spending the night, it all came to a head in an ugly scene, with John's relatives coming in with an axe and threatening us for having Sini and Daniel in the house. John had stood under my window part of the night, claiming I had to give back his baby, while I appealed to his good sense and our friendship and promised we'd sort it out in the morning. Tony was away and Paul, the guest, took the brunt of the bare-handed defence against the axe-wielders. Somehow we all got into the car, Sini, the baby, Paul and I and Jenny drove to the Boroko police station.

At first the reception was cool. Papua New Guinean police at that time were not impressed by whites coming to complain about axe-wielding natives. But when it became clear that we feared not so much for ourselves, but for Sini and the baby, they did, to their credit, become interested. The way they handled the affair deserved nothing but praise. Themselves of other tribes, they came, a carload full, to palaver with John's *wantoks*, to explain the law of the land. They took Sini and baby to an uncle on the other side of town, where John was not allowed to see her for the time being until peace had been restored.

It was close to my date for departure and when I walked for the last time up Angau Drive to visit Tony and Jen, I suddenly heard a voice from the bushes and out came John's face. He had found another job and he put out his hand to shake mine. He was sorry, he said, and he obviously felt no rancour and did not expect me to feel any. I tried not to, but my responsibility was to his little son, whom I'd named, and his mother. I delivered my departure presents to the uncle and included one for John, because by then they were together again.

Women labour under such circumstances in Papua New Guinea, in the same way as women in Australia labour under their husbands' affiliations with "the boys" and the pub and the domestic violence that often results from that. Female liberation is only half the answer. The other half is that men everywhere need to be liberated from their obligations to each other, at least to the extent that they can see and recognise their obligations to the women in their lives.

I packed up with feelings of deep regret, taking down

all the little things that make a room a home. In Luavi friendship had become more than a word. The Luavi women have been the only group of women in my life amongst whom I have lived with mental comfort. Nakanat had nursed me when I developed a mysterious illness, probably on account of being cursed. *Puri-puri*, or witchcraft, exists of course. There are plenty of people who have died from it, no matter what scientific tag you put on it. The girls recognised the symptoms as belonging to *puri-puri* and asked where I had spent the previous day, a Sunday. I'd been on an island with Monica, a Gulf student and her Australian scientist friend David and some others. Among the group was a Motuan of the local tribe, who asked me how I liked Port Moresby. It so happened that I had a lot of objections to Port Moresby society, meeting ground as it is for disconnected people who have thrown the home rules away and indulge in living it up in the capital, far from tribal mores and discipline. Voicing some of my pent-up criticism was the wrong thing to do. The Motuan fell silent, turned to another Motuan and spoke in his own language. At goodbyes he had fixed me with a piercing stare without the customary greeting. The next morning I was paralysed in the legs and had to crawl for help.

Nakanat and several other women kept up an all-day routine of dropping in and chatting to me. Nakanat also got western medicine from the campus sister to settle my stomach, which was weirdly careering in my body. I dozed and talked to the women who dropped in and by mid-afternoon they said I was looking better and I would be all right. The next day I was back at classes, a few pounds lighter, but not altogether wasted away.

My education at Luavi was at least as important as my education in the lecture halls and tutorial rooms at the

University of Papua New Guinea. And looking back, it has been of more value to me. The acceptance of myself, as a foreigner and a woman of a vastly different culture, by so many women, themselves of so many different cultures, speaking different languages, enriched me far beyond what a formal study program can do for one's mental and spiritual development.

Having been part of a Pacific nation in its first year of independence was also a formative experience I would not like to have missed. The generosity extended to me by many Papua New Guineans in all walks of life was as unexpected as it was real. Having shaken off the burden of Australian administration, they could have acted otherwise, had they been a less magnanimous people. I had been catapulted forever out of that dangerous duality of mind that afflicts the migrant, the "us" and "them" syndrome. In Papua New Guinea that syndrome did not, on the whole, exist for me, as in so many situations I had been made one of "them".

In preparing for departure I bought unbleached cotton in which to send my books home. I had the end of the roll which carried the manufacturer's stamp: "Taban — Eagle on Rock", complete with graphics. It came from China. Recognising I could not win, I cut it into a shirt, embroidered the legend and wore it to the last public occasion where I had to meet him once more.

It is hard, exceedingly hard, to separate the "leit-motiv" for this part of my autobiography from the totality of experiences during 1976 in Port Moresby.

For me, Taban's race had become more specific, from African to East-African. He was not really Ugandan, because the borders were colonial leftovers. His tribe, the Luo, spread across these borders into Kenya and the Sudan and he in fact carried dual nationality in the modern world of passports. I read what I could about the Luo, which wasn't much, but it helped me to understand some of the things he referred to, though not his moods. The strident, fun-loving and energetic Luo only surfaced occasionally in Taban and increasingly I realised that his acculturation in America had destroyed much. When his great blood-brother and the nation's other wonderboy came to Papua New Guinea to read his poetry, I expected at last to see the real Luo vitality. Instead we saw and heard an old man who had, not wisdom, but a scathing disregard for the people he was addressing and a preoccupation with women and alcohol. Even Taban was relieved when he left.

As far as identity was concerned, Taban was to me the number one, the beloved. My identity in his eyes was at rare moments "she who cares", but mostly the white woman who could produce the milk-coffee-coloured child he so longed to see. For he believed in the mixing of the races, one of the points we agreed on. I see the future world, if we can stave off nuclear disaster, as peopled by humans of a middle brown hue, able to stand the higher temperatures that the forthcoming greenhouse effect will cause. I think the earth is working on a survival plan herself (see James Lovelock, *Gaia — a new look at life on earth,* New York: Oxford University Press, 1982), and she works at various levels simultaneously. I was not surprised that I should play a role in that survival plan, difficult as it is to be a white parent to a brown child. But Taban's musings revealed to me that he merely wanted to see the child, to satisfy his curiosity, to have a glimpse of the future world race to be, what its hue was and whom it resembled in features. After that the child was to be fatherless. I'd been there and done that and it didn't fit into my view of the earth's survival plan, so I backed off, not without pain at the parting. I'd already been putting up with accusations that I was secretly taking the pill, to which I could have replied that he was often impotent through alcohol. I often thought of his mother in those days and came to understand her, because I too could feel a child floating around, waiting to be born. There may have been more than one. Not in the sense of twins, heaven forbid, but one after the other. After all, it must be exceedingly frustrating to hang around waiting for a man like Taban to sober up in more ways than one. There was a girl perhaps at first and definitely a boy later on, and then a femaleness again that could be sensed. I even believe she was born eventually, not to me but to someone close to me at the time. Unfortunately that girl, too, has to live apart from her daddy, but she is the product of two races and a human being of the future.

I came to some understanding of the man who was so cluttering up my life and my studies that year, when the Trinidad Steel Band came to town for Independence celebrations. Their music was strangely reminiscent of my father's organ playing and, in a flash, I equated my father and Taban, both artists, both possessed by their talents and totally egotistical on that score. In neither's life was there room for me.

8

The second wish-fulfilment

Landing in Cairns, Queensland, where the people were pink and fat beyond belief, and the supermarkets full of inessentials, brought culture shock.

People smelled of chemist shops instead of carrying their own scent and sweat. People moved away from each other in the crowd and apologised if they touched you. No holding hands on the streets here, while some-one talked to you.

The thesis I had delivered at the university I had just left was called "The Theme of Love in Papua New Guinean Literature" *(Bikmaus,* vol. III, no. 3, September 1982, Port Moresby). The writers I had inter-viewed had spoken of their love for their village, their parents, their siblings, their land and their culture. It went to a depth I felt was missing here. I took the train south, to acclimatise slowly.

Acclimatising to the weather was equally difficult. From north Queensland to Brisbane was not too bad and I still managed with my cotton clothes in Sydney in November. I had a long conversation on Central Station with a Jordanian platform officer. He was young and bright and had won the top prize for English when he finished high school in Jordan. He had received his prize from King Hussein himself. I asked how he found his life in Sydney after such glory. "Oh, all right," he answered with a smile that was just a little wry. He had plans for better things and the mind to do it. "I'm half Jewish, you know," I said, "in Jordan you wouldn't be talking to me." He stuck out his hand. "Let's make peace here then," he said. He was the first sign since Cairns that there was still an interesting human experiment going on in Australia, which was worth watching and perhaps even worth being part of, after all . . .

Melbourne, where I was to stay with my eldest son, turned on its usual blustering, rainy, marrow-chilling weather. I had to borrow Adam's jeans-suit and jumper and he still mentions the electricity bill I ran up to keep warm in front of the radiator. Return to Adelaide and my hills cottage brought me finally to the beginning of my new life. A new life without dependent children. A new life in which I could make plans to use the things I'd learned for the benefit of humankind.

One takes from others, one gives to others, with knowledge as with everything else. Papua New Guinea had taught me quite clearly that one cannot live as an individual without paying one's dues to the group.

But I was far from well. There was still a teaching diploma to be studied for under my scholarship arrangement, but I asked for a year's deferral to get my strength back. A part-time job as researcher for a Blake scholar at the University of Adelaide would keep me alive, though barely. Within two months the malaria reared up again and my eyesight degenerated. I had hallucinations in bright daylight, seeing Adelaide features as Port Moresby features and waving to unknown people I mistook for Moresby friends. I was living in the past.

The past returned with a sweet smile of reconciliation

at a conference in May attended by several Papua New Guinean writers. Amongst them was Taban and from the way he talked you would think that he'd finally seen the light and sorted out his life. He would leave Papua New Guinea by the end of the year; the brotherhood myth had died. His mother had died in his absence and he wanted to go home to tend her grave. Then he wanted to settle in the Sudan, get a job he knew was coming up, and build a house. And when that was ready, I could come and we could settle down and he would write and I would cook.

I told him this was a ridiculous idea. I could cook in a tent or a rented flat. I did not want to wait for years until I was grey and wrinkled. But he spoke about the house that Jack built, because everything he did or planned was first put through the sieve of literature or proverbs. And Jack took his time and so would Taban. We would talk about it at Christmas. He would attend a conference in Australia after packing up, then stay with me in the hills for some months to write the first of several books he had stored in his mind. He had not been able to write well in Papua New Guinea. I had written better and more there than ever before and was still living on the momentum of it. We parted with peace between us at last.

In August I took a bankcard holiday to visit the country of my birth for the first time. I had not seen my mother since she had visited Australia in 1970. I landed in London, took the bus to Victoria Station, saw a familiar African face in a booth and booked a room in a small hotel in Notting Hill. Then I walked into the street to the subway.

London was a revelation! Instead of bobbies and nannies and gents in bowler hats swinging black umbrellas, I seemed to be in little Africa and little Arabia and little

West Indies. I wore a long brown dress with pockets made form a Pakistani cotton bedspread and heaven only knows where people thought I came from, but what did it matter in this marvellously cosmopolitan city, where the world was coming together.

I got into the subway train to Notting Hill with my swag and my *bilum* and it took off so quickly that I lost my balance slightly. My swag touched the hat of a seated lady. I apologised and quickly sat down with my bundles.

The lady had a female companion. She felt moved by my clumsiness to tell her friend what she thought about foreigners, particularly those foreigners who thought they could come to London and take over the city of the English and most particularly those foreigners who came from the Middle East, as this one evidently did, the one who had just bumped into her. "And well-heeled too, I'd say!" she continued, examining the fresh airfreight labels on my luggage. "If you ask me, they all ought to be sent home to where they came from."

This tirade took several minutes and her companion only reacted with "Hmmmmm" and "Uhh uhh". I sat through it as if I had just fallen from the moon. Not a year ago I had been called a white exploiter by an irate Papua New Guinean and an African had made me pay the colonial bill, and here I was told to go back to the Middle East where I came from, instead of cluttering up a once nice, white country, like dear old England!

Two young men sitting opposite, eyed me with incredulous eyes, obviously waiting for me to turn and say my bit in reply. They looked like Australians and in any case weren't quite as fooled by my yellowed skin and bedspread gown as the English lady. But I fully accepted that at this moment I was a bit actor in the drama of history. And besides I had no objection at all to being a

Middle Easterner without a veil. So I enjoyed my new status of unwanted foreigner for the duration of the trip.

It was a beautiful late summer's day in London and the Notting Hill hotel room looked out on leafy trees, under which stood three enormous ambulance buses with about a dozen first aid personnel. Hanging out of the window, soaking up my first London atmosphere, I detected the sound of many people shouting, singing and making music about a street length away. Remembering news reports, I decided it had to be an English football match and the ambulances were waiting for the casualties.

I went down and out towards the people-noise. Rounding a corner, there it was. Far from a football match, I had landed in the middle of the famous bank holiday West Indian carnival of Notting Hill. I worked my way into the crowd, my feet tapping, the sun beating down on brown sweaty faces. Was this London? Or was I back in Papua New Guinea? But in the centre a tall English bobby was dancing arm in arm with four West Indian beauties, other dancers clapping the beat, the drums climbing to a pitch.

The bandleader on the truck grabbed the microphone and addressed the public. A sea of people of every hue, all of whom were enjoying themselves.

"There has been trouble in other years," he shouted, "but you will have to agree that we are having a wonderful carnival today and that's how we're going to keep it. So tell your mothers and your brothers, tell your sisters and your lovers, that today you danced at the West Indian Carnival and that we had PEACE! Tell your mothers and your brothers, tell your sisters and your lovers, that today you sang at the West Indian Carnival and that we had JOY! Now take each other by the hand

and dance . . ." His words were drowned when the band struck up again and the people yoo-hooed their agreement.

As the procession rounded a corner, I noticed a telephone booth and remembered I should ring Christine, my ex-colleague from the Adelaide English department, who had returned to her homeground. I darted in and found the number in my little book. She picked up the phone herself.

"I've arrived," I said breathlessly. "I'm having a wonderful time."

"Where are you?" she asked.

"In Notting Hill, at the West Indian Carnival," I replied.

"Oh, my God!" was her retort. "That's dangerous! Get out, collect your bags and come here. We can put you up."

"No way," I said, "though I don't want to sound impolite. There is no danger here, just a lot of people dancing and singing and having peace and joy. And there's a bobby dancing in the middle of it all."

She clearly didn't believe this, but as the bobby hit the morning papers next day, I was vindicated.

So this was the famous bank holiday carnival that ended in riots and murder every year. I wondered how it had built up that reputation. A radio reporter was interviewing carnival goers as to their opinion whether violence would erupt or not. His ancestry was African, his suit from Bond Street, his accent made him a Londoner. The girl he interviewed had peroxided her black frizzy hair that surrounded her West Indian features and her accent also made her a Londoner. This was their conversation.

Reporter: "Do you think there will be trouble this year?"

Girl:	"Yes, I think so."
Reporter:	"If there is trouble again, whose fault do you think it will be."
Girl:	"Oh, the young guys . . ."
Reporter:	"Do you mean the black youths?"
Girl:	"Yes. They will cause the trouble."

On radio, two London voices discussing the West Indian Carnival and Christine and other British listeners saying to their spouses: "See, it's not safe there. It's going to happen again." Nobody would ever need to know that the girl and the reporter were framing members of their own race. What sort of game was this? It is of course the game of the western media, in which the reporter was caught as much as his white colleagues. If there is no news, you make it, and you make it every day if you want to keep your job. The girl, his willing victim, had the honour of knowing her voice would be on the air.

The carnival folded that evening without any hint of turmoil, but afterwards, when most people had gone home, some violence broke out between gangs of youths and some twenty-two were arrested. So much for the carnival as the origin and cause of violence. It's a pity it doesn't come off so well every year, because the organisers certainly promoted a message of peace, brotherhood and good will between people of all the races who, through a whim of history, share a London summer's holiday.

I love museums and London has some wonderful ones. Rounding off an afternoon in the British Museum, I visited its cafeteria, joined the queue — oh, if there is one thing the British are incomparably skilled at is forming queues — and eventually paid for my coffee and bun, foot-slogging it to the sitting area. There were no free tables. I chose a seat opposite a man who was staring into the crowd. Most of all I needed a cigarette, but my matches were all burnt ones. The staring man's arm shot out with a cigarette lighter. He was staring at me now and he did have nice eyes. And a smile as well.

Soon we exchanged our museum favourites and arrived at some common interests. This Moslem had a genuine interest in Buddhism, but wouldn't believe that I, a non-Asian, could be a Buddhist. He set me a few exam questions to answer, and it appeared he had read books about it. He was also versed in classical mythology and could sing Arabic poetry.

Naturally, if one is going to meet such a talented man, it has to be in a museum cafeteria. He'd come from his Middle Eastern country to have a London holiday, but had become increasingly bored and lonely, with no one to talk to about the things that interested him. Yes, he'd taken an English girl out and told her Greek myths and she'd laughed at him and called him silly. The relief on his face to find a person who was prepared to discuss Plato, and at least listen to his ideas about Carl Jung, was as genuine as his knowledge, all gained through ferocious reading while he did his degree in engineering.

Khalil and I spent three days seeing the sights of London through our particular lenses, coloured as they were by mythology, literature, philosophy and Jungian psychology. He didn't like my long brown bedspread dress with the handy pockets because it made me look like his grandmother, so he said. I felt rather honoured. On a cold day, he gave me the cardigan he had bought in a London department store for his mother and said that I looked wonderfully modern in that. It made me feel like *my* grandmother. I doubted whether I would tell him of my thin stream of Jewish blood, but as our friendship grew, I took courage. When I told him he was almost elated. It proved, he claimed, that people of enemy races could get along together, something which he had always believed. Unusual as Khalil was, I felt there had to be more Arabs like him and I still hope that in time they will come forward and grow numerous. But it will take a lot of them to silence the voices of the fanatics on both sides of the firing line.

Khalil kept up a correspondence with me which sang the same high note of idealism, until, after a long silence, a letter came which gave me cold shivers up my spine. I had a feeling as if someone was standing behind me as I began to read. I even turned, but I was in my own house and there was no one. As I read the letter, the chill grew. The sentences were stilted, as if dictated. They made excuses which did not quite make sense and spoke of the difficulty of writing and a hope I would understand. His father had died and life had changed for him. I turned the envelope to look at the address. It was still the same, but under it was a charity postage stamp, printed in English. The proceeds were to go to the PLO. I could only wonder whether my foreign letters had brought Khalil into trouble and we were once more caught in the cogs of the crushing wheel of history. I burnt his letters and kept only the memory of the Moslem who had extended friendship to a Buddhist Jew and wanted peace with the world.

Coming home to Holland brought confrontations of a different kind. As a foreigner I was requested to report to my hometown's police station every eight days, a rule which made my mother cry: "But you were born here!"

She went with me to vouch for my identity, carrying her umbrella to lay siege if there should be an assault on my status as a Dutch-born daughter. It must have been the last year for that rule, because when I returned in 1978 they waved me through with the left hand. I don't suppose they recognised me!

Trying to speak Dutch all day was no sinecure. My grammar was back to front and sometimes I didn't know whether a word I used was English or Dutch. I'd been away nineteen years of my adult life and I was scared to cross the street filled with lethal traffic. Yet my mother rode a bike! I realised I was less Dutch than something else, though what I wasn't sure! And I knew I would never live in Holland again.

Holland was also full of the children of its colonial history. West Indians congregated in the big cities or drove buses in my hometown. Moluccans, racially indistinguishable from other Indonesians to the Dutch eye, were staging the odd protest to get repatriated to their home island. The Moluccan train hijack in north Holland, staged by a handful of desperate, acculturated youngsters, had caused racial disharmony which took years to settle down. During these two visits, in 1977 and 1978, I did not often feel proud of my Dutch birth, for the prejudices were openly discussed and they were petty and small-minded, as all prejudices are. The causes lay in the gaps between people's cultures and the fact that from the West Indies, for instance, mainly young people had come, and with them a drug cult which scared the pants off Dutch parents; for good reasons of course. The subcultures here were in many ways similar to those in Port Moresby. Once the familiar environment has fallen away, the home rules are abandoned and the individual, no matter from which race, does his or her own thing or follows a peer group if he or she needs security in numbers. Those who came out with families, as many of the Turkish guest-workers did, had other problems of non-acceptance, based on their different dress and ways of housekeeping. I can only say that it gave me a thrill to find, on the corner of my mother's street, a small group of Turkish women, wrapped in their big headscarves, having an afternoon gossip, while one of them was spinning wool on a drop spindle. Little Turkey in my old street. Had they only been there when I was a child, how different my childhood might have been. My hunger for faraway places and people who did things otherwise could have been satisfied right here at home. I might never have migrated!

I'd had faint plans of returning via India and perhaps visiting Lobsang Rabgay and the Tibetan carpet weavers in Dharamsala, in the foothills of the Himalayas. Spurred on by an Indian from Bombay, who I met on a Dutch train, and a young American divorcee, whom I met at New Delhi airport, I booked a train to Pathankot at Old Delhi railway station.

It was my first visit to India and, contrary to my expectations, I immediately felt at home. The humidity, the dusty lanes and the brown people everywhere made me forget myself and my tenuous future, about which I should be so serious, and the fate of the world, which was always hanging in the balance, and the whole meaning of life, which was on the skids.

I was booked in a ladies' compartment with five Indian ladies of all ages. One was a slightly built widow, dressed in white. Another, a large woman, larger than I am, with steel-grey hair, fixed me with a stare of dislike. There were two women my own age, one of whom spoke enough English to ask me a string of questions about my past and where I was heading. There was also a young girl whose English was school-perfect and the three of us were in conversation for some time. Then it was the hour to bed down and on each wall two planks clapped down, hanging from chains. Those, with the seats, made three bedplanks on each side. According to the booking I had a bottom plank, but the large, grey-haired lady decided she wanted to swap her top plank with mine. I was rather grateful even though it took some athleticism to swing up there with my swag. The idea of having her sleep above me caused me no comfort. The chains looked strong enough but also ancient, dating from early colonial times, and one of them would snap one night, according to the laws of probability. We all had our heads away from the window and on top of our valuables, in order to keep them out of reach of thieves' hands during night stops. There was no glass in the windows and it was pleasant to have the cooler night air flow in.

The next morning was spent in and around Pathankot railway station, as I couldn't deposit my luggage and the bus for Dharamsala wouldn't leave until midday. Again, there was a ladies' waiting room and it still had all the comforts British ladies would have expected on their way up to the hills at the start of the hot season. Couches, a lovely round wooden table and a washroom.

I attracted interested looks from everyone who came in. Pathankot evidently did not see too many foreigners. A flock of Indian schoolgirls on an excursion queried my origins. I let them guess and it was of course unfair. With my Dutch-Melanesian accent and its newly acquired Indian inflexion and my clothes, which were made in India but which no Indian woman would wear, it was a hard task to pin me down. So I told them. And left them to think that I spoke pure Australian!

"You have a funny accent," said one girl. I agreed.

"Do we have an accent?" asked a bright-eyed one. I

hesitated. To me they did. But they were in their own country and they spoke English as it is spoken in India. Anglo-Indian English had evolved in their homeland because of the input of Indian languages into the imported trade language.

"No, you have no accent," I said. She nodded, because she hadn't thought so either.

A young Indian woman in a lustrous sari, with her hair beautifully coiled and her arms heavy with bangles, had eyed me since she had come in. Now she began to talk to me. After the initial polite exchanges that people everywhere use to test the water, the temperature and the wind velocity of the stranger's disposition, she began to tell me a story of woe. She had, she claimed, run away from her husband and mother-in-law in Delhi, because of maltreatment by both. She had left her baby son behind. She could not go back because they would break her bones and beat her. She had decided to commit suicide. What did I think of it?

Maybe I was naive believing everything she said. Maybe I was compassionate in just the right amount for saying what I said. Who shall know? Young women are maltreated at an alarming rate in India by their in-laws and husbands. Some are murdered once the dowry has been paid up, so that another marriage can be arranged and another dowry added to the family fortunes.

I tried to convince Nimi that suicide was not the right thing to do, that it couldn't be undone if you later regretted it. I spoke of the long life in front of her, but if her story was true then that thought would drive her closer to suicide rather than keep her from it — for what might be her expectations for a better marriage deal, having run away from one already?

I asked whether she had relatives. Yes, she said, she had a brother in Bombay. I leaped at this. She had claimed to have only a few rupees on her, so I had been buying her tea from the little platform tea cart with its wrought-silver decorations and samovar. I would, I said, pay her fare to Bombay. This would cut my stay in India, but that was of no concern if it saved a life. I was elated at the solution.

To my startled surprise, Nimi turned down my generous offer. No, she couldn't front up at her brother's house. I asked whether her brother would be sympathetic to her case. She claimed he would be, but she still couldn't go there. She still thought she'd better commit suicide. This baffled me and I told her I'd go to the ticket office to find out the price of a ticket to Bombay, while she made up her mind.

She was still sitting there in her finery, cross-legged on the brown leather couch. Her sari was peacock blue and green, her bangles gold, her skin light brown and unblemished, her hair glossy. There was a composure about her that I found uncanny.

I told her I would buy her the Bombay ticket the moment she made up her mind to go to her brother. I would also give her rupees to buy tea and food during the journey.

She glanced at me with a look of severe disappointment. Then she presented her alternative. Why, she tendered, could she not come to Australia with me? That would solve her problem. Her mother-in-law and her husband could not find her there.

I realised I had again run into a case of cargo-cult, which in Asia takes the form of thinking that any foreigner is made of money and can, at a touch of a bank's doorknob, produce passports and currencies and airline tickets for whomever they choose to thus endow. It was my turn to look severely disappointed.

I did of course explain to Nimi that my funds would

just stretch for the nine days I had left in India, that my return ticket was paid for by a loan and that she could not go to Australia without applying to the immigration authorities. She nodded vaguely, losing interest.

It was nearly time to pick up my bundles and walk to the bus terminal, so I told Nimi to throw herself on the mercies of the stout cleaning lady who kept the ladies' waiting room spotless. No doubt, being a Pathankotian, she might find Nimi accommodation for at least the first night and who knows, maybe a little job that would pay for her food?

This suggestion made Nimi look down her nose and toss her long plait in defiance. I shrugged. No doubt the cleaning lady was of the wrong caste to do a favour for Nimi, who was obviously of high caste. Well, if suicide was better than the mercies of an untouchable, so be it. I was still perturbed, but tired out by arguing according to my logic, which was not Indian woman's logic.

Nimi and I parted with a friendly farewell and I wrote a poem about her later, in Australia. She kept preying on my mind. Was her story true, or was the look the cleaning lady once threw her an indication that Nimi was a prostitute, whiling the time away, waiting for the next train with potential customers to come in? Remembering the women on the train the night before, who had fallen into three groups, keeping apart from each other, I decided that Indian women, despite the problems they faced, did not stand united. Again, it is not for a foreigner to ferret out the causes of that disunity, male-imposed as it may be. India's women have to do it themselves and, judging from the increasing public profile of Indian women, some are doing just that.

For the good reason that I would like to return to

Dharamsala one day, and because it has no airfield, I prefer not to go into detail about the three hour bus trip along hairpin bends, where one bus would have to back up if another wanted to pass. I was sitting on the wrong side of the bus most of the time. The valleys I looked straight into were of a bewitching beauty, but the precipices too close for comfort. But from the race and identity point of view the bus trip brought another experience worthy of recording.

There were some young western men sitting in front of me, in pink *kurta* shirts and carrying prayer-beads. One had a nasty cough. Seeing that they spoke Tibetan with a Tibetan passenger and were obviously "local foreigners", I wanted to ask them about the best place to stay in MacLeod Gunj, the settlement above Dharamsala where the Tibetan refugees live.

I popped my simple question, got a blank look from one and a turned shoulder from the other. I pondered the possibility that they didn't understand English, but any sojourn in India long enough to learn Tibetan would have brought them at least enough words to tell me so. No, this was a case of spiritual *hubris* and I had come across it before.

The waves of hippies and other bliss-seekers descending on India and Nepal during the seventies had a number amongst them who were quite serious in their desire to learn about other religions, usually one in particular. Depending on which religion they settled for, they could either open themselves up to the world or close themselves off. In Buddhism there is a strong tendency to turn inward and seek isolation in order to achieve a spiritual clarity which is then used to the benefit of all living beings. Unfortunately, some western followers go through a period when inexperience of the totality of all life forms, combined with a hang-up about

people outside their particular group, makes them unap-
proachable, almost arrogant. It passes, I suffered from
it myself.

The bus terminal of MacLeod Gunj must be the smallest
in the world. The tiny village square at the top of a steep
ascent, surrounded by stalls and teahouses, was made
for walking only. At a pinch one could imagine a small
donkey train coming to a stop here, but not two full-size
buses! Each had to back into street openings to turn for
the descent.

To find Lobsang I entered the Tibetan teahouse. It
contained two clusters of western hippies and a Tibetan
boy who offered lemon tea. No, he didn't know Lobsang Rabgay, but the carpet-weavers lived at the end of
the street. There being only one street, divided by a
Tibetan temple and prayer drum gallery in the middle,
the weavers' workshop wasn't hard to find. I recognised
it from a photograph Lobsang had sent me.

Soon I regretted not having sent Lobsang a photo of
myself, because he was most suspicious of this stranger
walking in and claiming she was Lolo from Adelaide.
That my name floated around the Himalayan foothills
as a possible benefactor I knew myself, for I received
letters from places as far apart as Darjeeling and
Srinagar, asking for money or "scholarships". I even
suspected there might be someone making an extra
rupee by selling my name and address to hopeful candidates for my charity. I am only sorry I was such a
crummy bet!

Lobsang scrutinised my passport, my face and my
words, translated by another Tibetan. Then a young
woman he had summoned came in and I recognised her
from a photo in which she appeared with a friend of

mine, who had come as my "ambassador" and stayed for two months. I knew the girl spoke English. I told her I had her photo and that she sat next to my friend, whom I named, and held a little *apso* dog in her lap. She smiled and translated, whereupon Lobsang's big face broke into a wide grin and he stood up, indicating the interrogation was over. I had to be Lolo!

Relieved, I let him take charge, as this was what he obviously wanted to do. Lobsang, appointed by His Holiness the Dalai Lama as director of the MacLeod Gunj refugee weavers, had started with fifty people in tents and ten years later had them living in newly built apartment blocks, working in a sunny workshop with plenty of windows to let the dust out, and would soon have them eating their meals in a canteen under construction. The toddlers and babies were looked after in a tiny creche opposite the workshop, so that mothers could hear their child's cries or laughter, pop over to breastfeed and generally remain in touch. One of the apartment blocks had a new Tibetan hotel on the first floor, also belonging to the weavers' cooperative. I was to be an honoured guest.

"Follow me," indicated Lobsang in Tibetan and as we went out he swept up a gorgeous Tibetan rug from a ready pile, dark blue with colourful dragons chasing flaming pearls. In the hotel I was given a fine room on the street and the rug was placed on my bed. I was overwhelmed by the grace of his hospitality.

My memory of that week in MacLeod Gunj is dominated by Lobsang's powerful personality. Although he neither spoke nor understood English and there was always an interpreter with us, my memory of our conversations is of a direct contact. He told me how my first order for rugs had been their first export order and how he'd sent a bright, educated young Tibetan to

Delhi to learn all he could about customs, documents and shipping. Once their rugs and my borrowed money had been safely exchanged, Lobsang cast an eye on the wider export market and by the time of my visit they were exporting to America, Europe and Australia. I couldn't have been more pleased. It had bothered me that I had not been able to continue to purchase goods from them, and to learn that my bold little venture had brought them the experience needed to branch out was a lovely consolation. Once more I explained my financial situation and my inability to run a business on a scale larger than I had done, and thus make it viable. He understood and I finally accepted that his gratitude and hospitality were in return for past favours and not for any hopes of reviving "The House of Tibet" in Adelaide.

On Monday Lobsang asked if I would like to meet His Holiness. Thinking there might be other high lamas in town, I asked which one. His Holiness the Dalai Lama of course! I was stunned.

When I recovered my breath I said: "Lobsang, I have wanted to meet him all my life! But I can't believe he will want to see me. It is too much trouble for you. I am pleased to have come so close, I have known about him since I was four years old."

"Leave it with me," was Lobsang's reply in Tibetan.

On Tuesday he came running up to my room early in the morning. He had received a phone call from "the top" and I was to present myself at noon to His Holiness's secretary in the bungalow. The Dalai Lama's residence sits on a rocky spur above MacLeod Gunj and is reached by a lovely winding road that leads first to the most important Tibetan temple, containing a statue of the future Buddha.

Kelsang, the girl who spoke English, had taken me for

a guided tour of MacLeod Gunj and Dharamsala, during which we had bought a charcoal-coloured heavy cotton, from which the local Tibetan tailor made me a Tibetan woman's dress in one day. I also had a pink and white blouse made with long sleeves covering the hands and a shawl-like collar. It all fitted like a glove and thus attired I went with Kelsang up the winding path to the temple. There we made three circumambulations and worshipped, before Kelsang returned and I entered the portals of the bungalow's grounds.

Lama Tenzing Geshe received me smiling and courteously, speaking beautiful and fluent English. The Tibetans had come out into the English-speaking world one year after I arrived in Australia. For many there was no immediate need to learn so foreign a language in countries like India or Nepal. But despite Tibet's long isolation, the Tibetan government in exile had taken their new status as a sign that they had to meet the wider world and the learning of English was taken up amongst its leaders and school-going population.

Lama Tenzing Geshe's mind was like quicksilver, darting swiftly from topic to logical subsequent topic. I had to shake myself out of my traveller's torpor to pay him the respect of coming up with some intelligent replies. He described in lively detail how surprised His Holiness and his retinue were when, in Europe, they were greeted by westerners in Tibetan dress, prostrating themselves onto the ground before His Holiness. His Holiness felt that people ought to keep their own customs in these matters and, where Buddhism was concerned, he felt that instead of flocking to Buddhist countries or places of worship, they ought to practise it in their own countries to the benefit of their own people.

I felt conscious of my Tibetan dress, the most comfortable garment I had ever worn to an official occasion. I wanted to defend my predilection for it.

"Asian people," I began, "have adopted many items of western clothing and worn them for over a century. Men's hats, coats and trousers have become popular wear in many Asian countries. Recently Asian clothing has found its way to the west and has become popular there. I think it would be nice if people wore what they felt comfortable in."

Lama Tenzing Geshe took this point in good grace and asked me what sort of questions I was planning to put to His Holiness. "None," was my reply. This took him by surprise. "No questions?" he asked, raising his eyebrows to elicit explanation.

"I have dreamed for years of meeting His Holiness the Dalai Lama," I said truthfully, "and when I was young I had many questions. But one by one they have either been answered or become obsolete. I have nothing to ask, but as His Holiness is the head of my religion, I would be honoured to meet him and pay him my respect."

This satisfied him. He was still worried about the possibility of arranging an audience that week. Could I stay longer? I felt terrible, having to say that I couldn't, but he understood my problem. I was grateful for his sophistication and alert tuning-in to my problems.

"His Holiness does not see many people these days," he said, "but we will try. I will be in touch with Lobsang Rabgay." He stood up, indicating the interview was over. Our most interesting conversation had lasted half an hour. It had been a very useful exchange of cultural ideas.

The fulfilment of my second wish came about two days later, on a Thursday afternoon in October 1977. I was fitted out with a silk presentation *kata* by Lobsang. *Kata* are white scarfs which the Tibetans present to each other as a greeting, on arrival and departure and on special occasions. Usually they are a cheap gauze weave, but only silk would do now.

I wanted to give His Holiness a present, but could scarcely have bought him anything in the local bazaar! In my luggage, however, was a spherical orange candle, which my mother had bought for me the Christmas before. When she found that the postage was as much as the candle, she kept it in case I should come. I felt she would agree with the candle becoming part of the Dalai Lama's household and so I wrapped it in tissue paper, with the *kata* around it. Despite Lama Tenzing Geshe's remarks about westerners in Tibetan garb, I decided to stick to my own opinions on this score and donned my Tibetan dress, with a clean, Australian blouse.

My thoughts as I walked up the now familiar winding path centred on the spiritual aspects of the forthcoming audience. In the intervening days I still had not conceived of any question worth asking. Not that I knew all the answers, far from it. But I had arrived at an understanding of how questions cancel themselves out if one pursues the Buddhist path, which is so simple a child can understand it. I knew that solutions to the problems of my own life lay in my own attitudes and efforts, no matter how small. And the solutions to world problems lay in the hands of all the world's individuals, each pursuing a path toward peace according to their own religion or philosophy. I had felt for some time that one had to aspire to a position in between, from where others might be inspired to believe in their own power for good. To do this, one had to rise above one's own problems, without forgetting what it is like to have them! At that time, my only remaining problem was Taban, a person to whom I had made some commitment but who, after two hasty letters, had dropped out of the news again. I knew I had to start to build up a life for myself when I returned and not count on his vagaries any longer. That decided, I really did not have any problems left. Building up new lives was my stock in trade!

In a suitably empty state of mind, ready to receive impressions, spiritual guidance or simply be alert to the moment, I entered the watch house, where I was searched by a Tibetan woman after being checked through by the Sikh guards. The candle took some explanation, but after examination it too was allowed in. The walk through the lovely garden to the bungalow was a bit of a dream. Was it really happening? Was I really about to meet the god-king boy with the peaked cap, who sat on a pile of silken cushions when he was four and I saw him in the newspaper?

I had some more time to think about this as I was let into a waiting room, where an Indian family of husband, wife and daughter was also waiting for an audience. After they left I had time to look around. In a corner was a television set with doors in front of the screen. On top of the set stood a glass case with a scale model of the Potala Palace. This made me very sad. The Potala must be one of the most imposing and unique buildings in the world. It had been the Dalai Lama's home for more than twenty years. I could only wonder how it affected him to see this model as a reminder. His religious training has no doubt taught him not to covet material things, but a home is a home, and he was known, for instance, to love the Norbulingka, the summer palace outside Lhasa.

I sat on a well-worn yellow brocade couch. The French doors were open, looking out on the garden. I sat there, much as I had sat in Koonalda Cave some years earlier, in a state of suspense.

The secretary, Lama Tenzing Geshe, came for me. Appearing in the open doors, he beckoned me onto the veranda. Together we walked along it to another set of French doors. In the door opening stood a familiar figure in the familiar maroon robes, slightly hunched with the head bent in our direction.

As I walked towards the still figure the thought went through my mind: I know this man so well, have known him for so long, have read his books. But he does not know me at all. This cold realisation, after forty years of veneration from afar, was wiped away by the deep smile on the Dalai Lama's face as he greeted me.

I already had the silk *kata* and the candle in my outstretched hands. Thrusting the candle into Lama Tenzing Geshe's hands, I bowed my head and offered the *kata* to His Holiness. After that, I took the candle back and, presenting it in the same way, I told him it was a small present from my homeland for his temple. Both lamas appeared amused by the gift.

I was shown a chair and the Dalai Lama sat down not far from me to the right. Lama Tenzing Geshe sat opposite us to handle the translation. In those days the Dalai Lama's English was good enough, but he still preferred to speak in Tibetan and be translated.

He began by asking me from where I had travelled and, on hearing of my visit to my mother in Holland, asked me how old she was, who looked after her and whether I had brothers and sisters there. His concern was neither personal, nor just a formality. I knew his own mother was also very old and living nearby, surrounded by some of her living children.

He would ask the question through Lama Tenzing Geshe and listen to my English reply without needing a translation. His questions came quick. Soon he was asking me about my life in Australia and I was more at ease, sensing the informality of the man and his gentleness.

At some stage he asked whether migrants experienced any prejudice in Australian society. Maybe I hesitated for an instant, it is possible. But my answer was that we didn't. I could not let my new homeland down in a conversation as important as this one. I listened to the next question in Tibetan, but when Lama Tenzing Geshe translated, it came out exactly like the previous one: Did migrants experience any prejudice in Australian society?

It was the only question I had not answered truthfully. I realised I was sitting opposite a human lie detector. The Dalai Lama's ploy of repeating the question without variation, without rephrasing, pulled me up sharply and the second time I did answer it truthfully, speaking of the problems migrant children sometimes had in schools, the teasing about names, food and appearance, the problems of people from very different cultures in gaining acceptance. This time the Dalai Lama was satisfied and went on to another topic.

I could sense the interview was coming to an end. There was a momentary hesitation in the Dalai Lama's attitude, then a nod to his secretary and we all rose from our seats.

As my chair had been positioned conveniently close to the French doors, it wasn't difficult to take a few steps backwards and not turn my back on the room and the two lamas. His Holiness came quickly to the doors and, as I bowed again, placed the same silk *kata* around my neck. Then, to my great surprise, he put his hands between the two hanging tails of the scarf, grabbed my hands and held them firmly between his, with a quick pressing gesture. As I looked up, there was the same deep smile and the gentle eyes behind the glasses. The message was: "You can relax now, it is all over!"

Lama Tenzing Geshe led me down the veranda and some way down the path. "He isn't very well, you know," he said. "He is not very well today."

I took it as an excuse for the length of the interview, which had lasted for about twenty minutes. I thought it was long enough, seeing that I had no questions and that no matters of any great socio-economic, political or religious nature were discussed. For a person who simply wanted to pay her respect to a revered figure, I had been royally received. From the point of view of a secular leader it could have been a waste of time, but the Dalai Lama is more than a secular leader. In recent years he has even branched out from being his people's spiritual leader to being a world figure for peace and cross-cultural consultation with other world religious leaders.

Stopping briefly at the temple for a moment of stillness, I then descended the winding path in quite an unforgettable state of mind. My second wish had been fulfilled. For a person with three wishes, I had done better than expected. When I was young, only the last wish seemed to offer the possibility of fulfilment. Living under palm trees and meeting the Dalai Lama of Tibet would have been put down as plain impossible by anyone knowing my circumstances then. Now, as I slowly walked back to the Tibetan settlement, I spontaneously threw away the third wish of being found by a compatible man with whom I could share the rest of my life. I felt it was greedy to want more than I had achieved in wish-fulfilment. From now on I would concentrate on living alone and making my life useful to those around me. I would lead a life of peace in the hope that it too would spread. I would not be depressed by the errors I would undoubtedly continue to make, but would remember this day and start each day anew in this spirit.

The evening was spent at Lobsang and Ani-la's apartment over a delicious dinner of Tibetan noodles, while Lobsang extracted from me every word that His Holiness had uttered and had it translated by a most companionable young man who wasn't too shy to offer his own opinions to the conversation.

"Westerners come here," he said, "and ask His Holiness such religious questions as the nature of the Great Void. How could one speak about it?"

Indeed. This young man understood my lack of questions to the Dalai Lama. It would not have been difficult to cook up an interesting religious topic; I was well-read enough to do so. But it would have been dishonest and a waste of everyone's time. Yet I had a feeling Lobsang was somewhat disappointed at the small harvest of words from the audience and the lack of important pronouncements made by his revered leader due to my lack of queries.

That night I dreamt. I was sitting with a lot of people in a dim room on chairs arranged around the walls. To my right sat an English girl who wore glasses and was telling others that she was going to get married soon. Between her and me sat the ghost of Mao-Tze-Dong. He must have been a ghost, because he was very pale and even in my dream I knew that he had died the year before. Someone asked who the girl's future husband would be and she indicated someone across the room. I looked and there sat Taban, looking at me and smiling sheepishly. The dream faded out.

Taban had said that he wanted to travel to China while he was on this side of the world, so I assumed he had done so and met the girl on tour. She was a nice girl and for her sake I wished she was only a dream-girl! But the dream had been clear and concise and it enabled me to put the past behind me. The future, however, looked as empty as the Great Void and I remembered that the day before, as I walked down the winding path, the thought had crossed my mind that I could now safely die!

That thought was neither welcome nor unwelcome. It had simply occurred because the conditions for it seemed right. I had, for the time being at least, come to the end of desire, that urge that keeps the flame of life burning until decay gets the better of it.

I was, however, still breathing and putting one foot in front of the other, so on I would walk, taking life as it presented itself.

Apart from the second wish-fulfilment, the week at MacLeod Gunj was filled with activities, including a Tibetan picnic on a Tibetan public holiday. The picnic was held for all the Dalai Lama's workers, those in government, leadership or any other function directly connected with his establishment. Lobsang and Kelsang took me along. The picnic was held in the garden of an old English bungalow, where the wonderful white Tibetan tents with black scroll decorations had been set up. The *chang*, or Tibetan barley beer, was going around and I was offered more than I wanted of that potent brew and had to empty it out near the bush behind me. I was the only foreigner there and it was so pleasant to sit on the lawn in the sun in an oval ring of gaily dressed Tibetan women, whose conversation undulated like water lapping gently on the shore. I had been sitting there for hours, perhaps, concentrating on the sound of the language, their gestures, the expressions on their faces. I did not have to talk and my observation of the women became like a penetration of their mood. Suddenly I found myself laughing at something one of them had said, with a nudge of the head to indicate a playful boy who was making a slightly rude sign about a man outside our circle. I had understood the content of her remark. Several women turned towards me and Kelsang asked: "Do you understand Tibetan?" I had to answer that I didn't, and yet, at that moment I had. It became a treasured memory as my exploration of other cultures has always been aided by learning something of the language, yet in this instance I had but one word of Tibetan to my credit: *Tudeche*, or "thank you".

Kelsang also took me to visit a goldsmith who made sacred objects for the temple and the Dalai Lama's household. He had come from Tibet at the same time and was regarded as one of the best goldsmiths in the country. He was a middle-aged man with a young wife and young children. Their frugal hospitality was touching and this time I was caught out without anything I could give or do in reciprocation. He showed me his stone-walled workshop and it was no hard task to voice my admiration for this man's craftsmanship. But to him the sweetest thing he had to show was his little son, taking up an embellishing hammer and skilfully belabouring a piece of brass with it. Of all his young apprentices, his little son was one of the most promising, he admitted, glowing with pride. His apprentices weren't there that day, but looking at their little seats, I hoped they would carry on this aspect of a unique culture, now defunct in its land of origin. The world's store of spiritual art is rapidly diminishing.

During the week I was introduced to a four-year-old boy whose nickname was Lolo. I asked what it meant, but there was no satisfactory answer, just a nickname it seemed. I presented Lolo with a silver teaspoon, also carried from Holland, and he folded his hands solemnly in front of his face and bowed his thanks. I wondered whether his name meant the same as the name Lolo given by the Chinese to the Nosus, a tribe of eastern Tibetan regions. There Lolo means robber, highway robber, in particular. But I didn't dare to mention it to little Lolo's aunt, because jokes can fall awfully flat between cultures, something Americans find hard to learn.

From my window in the evenings I watched Lobsang and half a dozen of his workers meet on the roof of the workshop across the street. They would stand in a circle and bend their heads inwards. So they stood for a long time in the dusk, with the red, green, white, blue and yellow prayer-flags fluttering around them in the breeze, connecting the corners of the flat roof. The snow-capped mountain peaks stood like sentinels behind them.

When they departed, the sound of little home looms would start up and, amidst the playful squealing of children, singing, talking and the snapping of little *apso* dogs, there would be the constant boom-boom of the beaters, until, as if by agreement, all sound stopped at eleven o'clock. Six hours sleep for everyone, because at five in the morning the same noises would start up, accompanied by the clattering of food pots and again the beaters of the home looms. By eight the children went off to school and the parents to the workshop or other activities.

The hotel was on the higher side of the school and, by climbing on its flat roof, I could look down into the schoolyard and hear the songs and see the games the Tibetan children played. When the teacher came they formed rows and all together sang the Tibetan national anthem. Nothing seemed to be forced upon them, few directions given. Their behaviour was self-disciplined, positive and an eye-opener for a westerner, especially someone who had been on the teachers' end in Australian schools. There is no need to ask what their secret was. It always lies in the entire culture. If one wants to know the future of a nation one has only to look at the population of its schools. The Tibetan children I saw at MacLeod Gunj promised a wonderful future for a Tibetan nation. Unfortunately they had no country of their own and there is no saying how they will be influenced by their refugee status as they grow up and come to realise their losses.

I had given Khalil's mother's cardigan to the woman who managed the Tibetan hotel, because she had admired it and obviously would not be pleased with my Pakistani bedspread dress. She brought me to the bus early on Saturday morning, after I had taken leave of Lobsang, Ani-la, Kelsang and many other Tibetans I had become acquainted with that week. I knew several had put themselves out to make me feel welcome and had honoured me with food and ever-full cups of Tibetan butter tea — a delicacy if you don't try to equate it with English tea — and hospitality in their colourful, ever-tidy homes. I felt I could not have stood another week of being an honoured guest, without being able to do something substantial in return for the community over and above what I had done in the past. I was more than happy I had made the visit. Now it was time to start my new life. Wole Soyinka had said in one of his plays: "Those who have much to give fulfil themselves only in total loneliness" *(The Strong Breed)*. I'd had these words pinned up in my room at Luavi and remembered them now. I had received enough. The time for giving had come.

Much of my changed attitude to the value of my life had grown since the middle of 1976, when a crisis in my relationship with Taban had made me search for enlightenment in the few Buddhist books I had with me. The events surrounding that crisis were, in retrospect, miraculous. I plan to tell the story in full in my autobiography of religion, but suffice it to say that from that time personal wishes took a back seat and I began to see my life as an instrument, to be played melodiously or to be silenced by the burden of craving. Strangely enough, since that time, almost everything I have ever wished for in the past has fallen in my lap without any efforts to gain these things on my part. Not that my life is without tediousness or difficulties. It has its share. But none take over, their importance is not what it used to be.

Neither have I become the sun of friends' and relatives' lives! I have a long way to go in that respect. But the turning point was reached in 1976 in Port Moresby and confirmed at MacLeod Gunj in the foothills of the Himalayas. All I need to do is wake up in the mornings, find that I am still breathing and commence my day in the spirit of the decisions I made there.

9
New directions

To tell the rest of the story up to the present time would be somewhat like sweeping up after a banquet, if it weren't for that fourth, belatedly conceived wish and the ripples of past actions coming back to their point of origin.

I set about organising my life and enrolled to do the Graduate Diploma in Teaching in 1978, while continuing my part-time research job. I had been publishing articles and short stories for some time, but now the stories I produced centred around the meetings of people from different cultures. It was there that the seed of world peace was to be found, if it didn't get trampled in a rush of misunderstandings.

In early December Taban's letter arrived. He was off to his Australian conference and would land in Adelaide shortly before Christmas. I reversed gear and prepared for his majesty's coming. Another letter rang with a note of the old familiar hysteria and megalomania and I was beginning to feel I was being used as a convenient stopover place on his way to the stars, so that he could shake out his baggage and get his laundry done on the cheap. I cabled that if he was just going to pass through he might as well pass overhead and not bother to land. The cable reply was that he would come as planned.

I must have known in my bones that this was going to be the last act of the masquerade. But I primed myself to be positive and to admit once more a concept of the future that lay somewhere in Africa, cooking for Taban, washing his shirts and writing my stories on the sly. *Que sera, sera!*

He stayed for two weeks and the most interesting thing we did was pile tent and camping gear into the Moke and head north, to the dry parts of the state and the Flinders Ranges. At last he gave in to the country-side, instead of hiding in cities and cloistering himself in public institutions where glory of one kind or another was to be had. He started to talk about the wide land of Uganda, similar to the undulating land of Orroroo. He'd herded the goats when he was a boy and for a while that boy returned and was quiet, just looking at the passing landscape. But there were the towns and each town had a pub and he would not pass one of them without a drink or two. Sipping my lemon squash I would record the reactions of the locals as they tried not to look at the black man in their midst. They knew he wasn't an Aborigine, but weren't game to ask. In one pub in Burra the comments were vile, coming from drunken mouths of blinkered louts; being colloquial I hoped they passed Taban by. But I felt hurt on behalf of both of us and prodded him to leave the place. There was a caravan park caretaker the next day, who was curious and friendly and whose little son was absolutely enraptured by Taban's smile and appearance. The man who loved children and animals was at his best, discussing the concerns of a six-year-old who suddenly saw Africa drop into his own backyard and didn't want it to go away.

Back home in the hills, with the city half dead after Christmas and New Year and many places closed, the day-to-day routine became tedious in the extreme. We'd talked about all that had befallen him during the last seven months, for what had befallen me was of little interest to him. He had been to China; I'd found his postcard on my return from India. I did not ask about the girl. The Chinese, Taban confessed, had not been as kind to him as they ought to have been to a person with a Chinese-sounding surname, who was prepared to consider a possible Chinese input in his ancestry. He'd been reprimanded for laying a friendly hand on the female interpreter's shoulder. Physical contact was not on and a dip in the Yellow River, which Chairman Mao-Tze-Dong had once swum across, was equally chilly.

We'd spoken a little about his future plans, but as all depended on his personal appearance in the right place at the right time and with the right disposition, this topic also fizzled out as a bonding glue to keep us in communication. He said he could never live in Australia and, knowing the society well by now, I agreed that he would find it more than merely uncomfortable. Not because he was black. The society was growing up. Rather because he craved so much attention and went so much out of his way to get it, the town would be too small for him within a year or so. This had been the case in Port Moresby. Sydney would have accommodated him and his eccentricities, but he wouldn't have been able to shock Sydney-siders and to shock and then to beguile people with his wit was his purpose in life.

When finally I got hold of an academic who was a specialist in African literature and wanted to meet Taban, we heard there was another African in town, who had married an Australian and became a resident. When I told Taban the name of this person, he

222

discovered to his delight that they were related and entitled to call each other cousin! Off he went for a family reunion and two days later I received a message to come and pick him up. He had not yet dried out from his binge on the booze and I imagined the cousin was glad to offload this heap of a morose roisterer, whose witty little sayings started to sound like repetitions of an advertisement for a mental disinfectant.

We drove home in partial silence — my silence. The next morning, when he had sobered up, I told him we had come to the fullness of our time together and I would drop him off at his cousin's office, from where he could no doubt find his way back to Africa. Inside I was torn between disgust and pity. I blamed myself for not having understood earlier that he was an alcoholic. During the last fortnight, with morning drinks at coffee time, the pub crawl in the country and the final binge in the city, the penny had dropped. I had a fair idea what life with an alcoholic would be like and I passed it up. With it went a love that had lasted for two years and weathered neglect and many an insult.

After the initial shock of the discovery and my decision were over, my deepest regret was that I had not been able to hold up the bridge between our cultures. But I knew the effort had been so entirely on my side that a collapse, sooner or later, was a foregone conclusion. A pathetic bit of proof came one-and-a-half years later with the arrival of a postcard in Taban's handwriting. It came from Copenhagen and he indicated that he'd thought of me on my homeground. He'd never been able to remember where I was born and often called me ''You Scandinavians''.

There was also a reference to Hans Christian Anderson and his fairytales and I knew he hadn't changed. And why should he? There was obviously no incentive to do so. The world loves a fool. Except that Taban was not the fool he presented to the world. But why he played the clown and cried under his make up, and drove himself to drink, only his mother would have understood. Perhaps.

A friend from Port Moresby had meanwhile come to settle in Adelaide and from him I heard the snippets that filled in the rest of Taban's story. The English girl did exist. She had gone on the China trip, together with other students. But she had not wanted to marry Taban. In fact, she had refused his advances. When he told her that he would fail her in the exam if she did not give in, she had gone to the academic registrar to complain. I had done the same thing in 1976 when Taban had refused to read my thesis which he had supervised. I'd left him a copy of my letter of complaint and I've always suspected that he'd rushed over to the academic registrar's office to talk my letter out of the secretary's "in" tray for quick and desperate destruction, because I never received a reply. But it brought some action and I found a new supervisor who examined my work before the year was over.

So many women ask themselves how the hell they landed in the sorry situation where love led them. It took me a while to appreciate that every situation makes some contribution to one's growing up, or, in other words, everything in life is deductible, sooner or later!

Much of that year has a veil over it, as if my mind had gone into retreat. My brain was working, however, and my very final exams (which would make me a qualified teacher) were in sight when disease struck once more. Somehow I battled through, handed in papers and tried to sit tests. But before the end I was in hospital with severe hepatitis. I came out the day before Christmas, barely able to sit upright. A woman friend took me to her home for a few days and I remember sitting in the sun on her terrace, shelling peas or peeling potatoes, panting with the effort.

In January I handed in the last essay and got my results. I had qualified, though not as well as I had hoped. I applied for jobs as nothing had come of the overseas applications I had sent out that year. I was vitally interested in furthering my language research in areas of cultural confrontation, where pidgins arose as trade languages and creoles as the native tongues of children of mixed marriages. My three referees had all received a request for information from a university in a small country on the west coast of Africa, where I had applied for a teaching post and declared my interest in that particular branch of linguistics. All three said I ought to have a good chance, but I never heard again, not even a rejection. I could only reflect that the letters of my referees had unmasked me as a woman, whereas previously my name ending in an "o" had protected me! None of my other irons in the fire brought results either. It was time to sever the African connection, make space and see what would come. Meanwhile I began to organise myself for creative unemployment and planned to make and market crafts, lay out a vegetable garden and write books.

Looking back I shake my head over my persistence to get a job. My liver count had been five hundred when I was in hospital. It was still three hundred in March. The allowable count was forty-five. Energy came at such a premium, that in order to do my household chores and plant my little garden, I had to sit in the sun every half hour, to rest and soak up energy. Food didn't benefit me, appetite didn't exist, I was very, very thin.

Despite all that the creative unemployment suited me. I was happy at home with just mundane chores to do, crafting in the afternoons. In the evenings I read books I had not had time for during my ten years of study. I'd forgotten how to read a novel for pleasure. My hand automatically went for a pencil and pad to make a note or underline a sentence.

But what spurred me on to apply for positions was the knowledge that jobs were running out fast, the fact that my age was against me and the attractive idea of earning enough money to buy shoes when I needed them after living "below the breadline" for twelve years. Not that I had not managed exceedingly well. Growing up in poverty has the advantage that you learn how not to spend your money. I knew what was important to me: books (second-hand of course), petrol for the car to go places, the occasional bargain antique, and bank loans to travel on. Unfortunately I didn't pay much attention to my diet. Having grown up in times of hunger and shortages I tended to think that as long as I had something to fill my stomach when I felt hungry, it didn't matter what it was, as long as it was cheap. If I got a job, I promised myself, I would do something about meals . . . read a cookbook or two.

In March a telegram arrived offering me a job as a teacher in Darwin High School. I was overjoyed. I had refused a job in Mount Gambier, in the south-east of South Australia, because I knew I couldn't stand the cold climate there. I had no resistance against temperatures which went below the temperature of the body and felt best in heat of 37° Celsius. Darwin would cater for that, I would live under palm trees again and I could dress in one layer of cotton and go barefoot in my private time.

I accepted by telephone and received instructions about where to store my belongings, how much luggage to bring, and how much money to live on until my first salary. Eight hundred dollars, the voice said. "Sure", I replied and dismissed it. People who lived like other people lived needed eight hundred dollars a month to live on. I'd never seen such an amount together, unless I had borrowed it. This time I would sell some of my furniture and I would live on the proceeds of that. I would live in a hostel and be on probation. They'd pay for my airfare and transporting my car on the Ghan, the old cross-continental train. I was to start on the first of April. No joke!

Much as I regretted saying goodbye to my beloved rented cottage in the Adelaide Hills, I knew it was time for a new start. The doctor at the hospital said I could not work full-time. I cried and said I had to. To gather the physical strength to do the packing up was like climbing a mountain barefoot with a load the size of your own body. The day came and I put the Moke in the transport yard and handed over the keys. I can't remember the last days in the cottage. Grief and grit would have mingled, I'm sure.

There were some Roonka friends in Darwin and one met me at Darwin airport. There was a saying amongst Roonka people that wherever you travelled, there would be a New Ngaiawang waiting for you. One of them, a writer and teller of stories, had presented us all with a copy of a little book of New Ngaiawang legends one Christmas (Helen Tolcher, *Myths and Legends of the New Ngaiawang,* Adelaide: Tolerable Publishers, 1971). In it we found sensitively drawn pen portraits of ourselves and tales told in the style of Aboriginal myths.

In it I was a black swan, Loloa, who had once been a woman who had tried to suppress violence in the tribe. When she was unsuccessful she left in sadness and changed into a black swan, swimming away from her tribal land. The Roonka brother who met me at the airport was Bata, the keeper of the stones of wisdom, who danced and sang and fell asleep while the stones were stolen from his cave. He was a librarian of course and it so happens that the library he worked for had recently been burnt out, but I doubt it had anything to do with his song and dance!

At first I lapped it all up: the tropical sunrise, the tropical dusk, the tropical sunset, the frangipani-strewn footpaths, the humidity like a second skin. I was saving energy by not having to keep warm any longer. The hostel was on the shore, the food was good, the room small enough for me.

The school was not what I had expected. Housed in the old meatworks, it was a concrete collossus, a twentieth-century Stonehenge on the rocks. Half a dozen young trees struggled to make a living on the lawn. Shade was provided mainly by the buildings.

But there were the kids. I threw myself into the work of preparing lessons, with little to go by as there was no teaching program as far as I could make out.

Darwin High School had to be the most multi-cultural school in Australia. There were strong Chinese and Greek communities, but every other European country must have been represented, as well as several from Asia. The Aboriginal school population was much more varied than I was used to. There were tribal Aboriginal students from the inland, but also islanders from the north. There was a large mixed-blood population in Darwin and the racial strands that had been interwoven ranged from the whole Pacific basin to the Anglo-Saxons and Europeans.

I had several tribal Aboriginal girls in my home-class. I didn't teach my home-class, only gathered them in the morning to read and discuss the school's daily notices. I would very much have liked to teach them as well, to get to know them better, apart from the usually rowdy fifteen minutes from eight o'clock onwards. Those Aboriginal girls I had in my teaching classes were shy, not at ease with me like the ones in the home class, who saw me every day. It takes a long time to build up confidence, and some left school halfway through the year. I had an Aboriginal boy in one class who could neither read nor write and I thought, by the time I realised this fact, that the school had done him a disservice by promoting him year after year, without anyone lifting a finger to remedy his lack of skill by special tuition. He was a fabulous illustrator and a footballer of local fame and I only hope he won appreciation for those talents.

His talents and his lack of reading and writing skills in year 11, as well as those of many other students, glaringly showed up the deficiencies of the education system as it then was. Whereas my days were packed to the hilt with preparation, marking and teaching for five classes from year eight to eleven, my evenings, if there was no marking to do, were spent in fretting over how one could change the system from within so as to bring out the best in each young person. This of course was no new idea. Indeed, it is the slogan under which most education departments wield their power, without ever reaching their goal.

The management of the school was most probably determined by its size. There were eleven hundred students and some eighty teachers on a campus the size of two street blocks. The principals were probably as conservative as they come, although the deputy head mistress, who had an afro hairdo for a while, was popular and won two hundred dollars in the new casino in opening week. I always felt that if I could talk to her, we might be able to cook up a plan for people like Joe. But she was forever busy and one stuck to what was regarded as essentials when given an interview. It might have been different had I been strong and energetic and had I stayed on after the first year . . .

The Chinese students were a teacher's ideal. They were diligent, always did their homework, spent time on their projects and gave intelligent answers when questioned. Otherwise they were quiet and fairly silent. When, at teachers' discussions about assessments, it became clear to me that participation in class was seen as voicing opinions and debating, the faces of several of my Chinese students came to my mind and I knew they could never be assessed that way. I explained that they were the best listeners in class debates and that listening was also participation. Indeed, many of the others did not listen, full as they were of their own opinions which they wanted to voice. As a result their essays merely reiterated an entrenched position, whereas those of Chinese students more often reflected all opinions given, with a preference for one or two. I suggested that listening was to be made part of the assessment. I was turned down with all votes against. Participation was talking in their culture.

The only two Chinese teachers in the school were not present at that meeting. Most teachers were of Anglo-Saxon background with only a thin sprinkling of foreigners. Naturally they saw school as they had experienced school, with modern improvements and more freedom as to choice of subjects. I saw something very different. I had already formulated a ten-page plan for a total education for life, rather than for a job, for people who left the school system. I could see that half my students in the upper classes were ready for that plan, if only someone would listen long enough to take it seriously. Certainly, the Aboriginal and Chinese students would have come into their own in an education geared for total living, because they did not come from cultures in which the goals of life stand separate from what one does every day, all day.

In 1979 the Australian-Chinese population of Darwin showed all signs of being a very successful subculture. Their ancestors had been imported to work as coolies on the railway line and road which were to link Darwin with Adelaide. The route cuts across desert practically all of the way. The railway still only reaches from Adelaide to Alice Springs in the centre of the continent, although every so often a politician promises to complete it if he or she gets voted in again. The project has become almost legendary in the same way as did the tunnel under the English Channel which had become proverbial even before construction had started. So much so that sometimes one isn't sure whether the line is there now, or yet to be built.

The Chinese coolies soon found there was little to eat in the desert and, coming from a race of agriculturalists reaching back forty centuries, they made small patches of the desert bloom with edible vegetables. They also went into laundry services. In fact, they soon did the housekeeping of the Northern Territory. When I became aware of these facts, I remembered the brochures I had read from the Australian Immigration Department, while I was still living in Holland. Darwin, they had claimed, was proof that the white man could build, maintain, and live in a city in the tropics. (Darwin lies halfway between the Tropic of Capricorn and the

Equator.) That turned out to be but a partial truth. The Chinese were there from the beginning and the city is still served by a business community which is largely Chinese. The white Australians who live there now are mainly public servants in one capacity or another, or two-year exiles doing a stint in their company's Top-End branch. The two-year exiles mostly go back to where they came from in Sydney, Melbourne or Canberra and are usually attracted by the extra money in their paypacket, given for the discomfort of living in the tropics! My paypacket also contained this tropical loading. As practically all food and other consumer goods are imported across the continent, the extra money went into paying higher prices, sometimes as much as four times the southern price for everyday food items.

The fact that the Australian-Chinese in Darwin have managed to preserve their culture as well as they have is probably an effect of the racial prejudice they experienced in this "white man's city" of the brochures.

They kept to themselves and built their temple. After cyclone Tracey in 1975, the Chinese temple was the first building to be rebuilt, purely because of the efforts of the Chinese community. On Fridays, after the school week was over, I would go to the temple, standing at the end of a street at the end of town. Entering between the stone lions, I would buy a two-dollar pack of incense and walk into the cool main hall, where the shrines stood against the back wall. There I would burn incense for Kuan Yin, the goddess of mercy, telling her some of my troubles and worries of the week just completed, and also honour the other deities, with whom I was less familiar. Sometimes the temple keeper would come in and bang the giant gong to wake up the gods so they would listen to me. The Chinese temple was my point of rest in Darwin. Once we had a Chinese relief teacher for a few days and she was also a Buddhist. As we talked I wished she could become a permanent teacher, so that I would have at least one soul to talk to without having to polish up special topics for polite conversation.

I don't think any justice has yet been done to the history of the Australian-Chinese in Darwin, without whom there might never have been a Darwin. The catalogue of the travelling scroll painting *Harvest of Endurance: History of the Chinese in Australia, 1788–1988*, published by the Australia-China Friendship Society, reveals that there is an unpublished MA thesis on "The Darwin Chinese: A Study of Assimilation" by C.B. Inglish at the Australian National University (1967) and a work by T.G. Jones, *The Chinese in the Northern Territory*, in press with the Darwin Institute of Technology. There is also a reference to *The Northern Territory Dictionary of Biography*, Vol. 1, as containing biographical details of the Chinese in Darwin. At the time of writing, Darwin has a mayor of Chinese extraction.

Judging from the 1979 profile of Darwin society, whites alone could never have built or maintained that city for a century or more. After cyclone Tracy, building crews of mainly young men came from all over the continent to rebuild the devastated town. Many stayed and after Tracy the population almost doubled in a decade. But this time the town had not been built from scratch. An infrastructure, although cruelly interrupted, had been in place. In 1979 most whites led lives of air-conditioned comfort in their offices and homes. Their relaxation was drinking alcohol in all its forms. It is the boozing capital of Australia, if not the world. The yearly flotilla races on the sea are their great annual effort, when all empty beer cans are made into floating crafts to sail into the sunset. The prizes are no doubt booze as well, I didn't check. For a non-drinker it isn't much of a place to build a new life. Orange juice oozed out of my pores after every party.

Even at the fortnightly dinners of my Roonka brother's circle of agreeable friends, I was the only one to abstain from the juice of the grape. But I did enjoy those meals, which sometimes took place at my flat, which I rented from an on-leave academic. The other memorable party was at the house of a teacher who hailed from Singapore. It was a "steamboat" dinner and I was deeply impressed with the grace and devotion with which she had sliced and cubed mountains of raw vegetables and meat. We sat around a round table with the steamboat on a charcoal burner in the middle and picked and chose tiny titbits of food, cooking them in miniscule wire baskets in the hot water. This was the opposite of the guzzling, gorging type of eating that is Australia's cultural pride. Food became almost a sacred substance here and people had to wait for it and became hushed and gentle in their conversation. The beautiful tropical garden setting, the tropical night sky and the atmosphere of good company, somehow all seemed an achievement of our accomplished hostess.

There were too many parties in Darwin, the city of exiles. Exiled from their hometown for financial reasons, or escaping from disagreeable spouses, dictatorial parents, or unmentionable situations they had gotten themselves into "down south". The influx of new people in all seasons is also one of the secrets that keeps Darwin going. Without new blood the population would soon become inbred and run to pure alcohol, apart from the Chinese and a handful of other puritans. Much construction work that goes on there is done by crews which come up from "down south" and work like slaves for four months (or as long as it takes), taking home huge bank balances from overtime and tropics loadings to pay off their debts or put a deposit on a home. My eldest son did the Darwin stint for several months, working sixteen hours a day, every day, sleeping, and eating and not much else. To his credit he visited the temple just before he left and took me the photograph I so much wanted. Then he left and paid off his debts. That's Darwin to many people. The entrenched Darwinites said the place had never been the same since cyclone Tracy, and I fully believed that. The dislocation and destruction left its mark and, despite new buildings and flash shopping arcades, will not be wiped until people start to love the place again in great numbers, instead of milking its economy for their own short-lived ends.

I made some friends in Darwin whom I will never forget, who made settling in and battling on a perfect joy! But the transience of people and life meant that I, too, had to decide whether to stay or to leave. I had a try at buying a block of land in the bush, eighty kilometres out of Darwin, thinking I could be happy there in out-of-school hours. The French teacher had done the same and when I saw her bush paradise with tent and water containers, my mind was made up. I had nearly reached the point where the bank would decide I might be worthy of a loan, when a letter arrived from a person I had not seen in ten years and whose face I could not recall in detail.

The letter came from the man who had financed the first shipment of Tibetan carpets and taught me how to go about the venture in a business-like way. At that time he was a lecturer at the university department where I worked as secretary, one of quite a few people who had admired the first rug I imported and collected from customs during my lunch hour. I'd been a little afraid of his high-powered manner and the amount he lent me gave me sleepless nights. However, he had stuck to his word and saw me through the first exhibition which convinced him I would soon be able to pay back the loan. After this had been accomplished I lost touch with him. I left the university, as, soon after, did he, to set up a school for a different type of education. I was interested in that but, after helping to paint the hallway of the old house he had bought to set up his school, I realised I couldn't afford to send my son there and that was the end of our contact.

The letter attempted to fill in the intervening ten years. He had gone to the Buddhist Society in Adelaide, which I had helped to set up, and a letter from me, describing the Darwin temple and life at the Top-End, was read out loud. He wondered whether it might be the same Lolo — I had resumed my own surname in the year I obtained my degree — and was given my address. With the letter came a parcel containing a book he had borrowed from me and which I'd given up for lost.

He told me his marriage had split up, he had rented a house and a woman of his acquaintance had spurred him on to get his life together, hence his visit to the Buddhist Society. He also had plans to go perhaps to Japan to live in a Zen monastery for a while. As he was an American by birth this didn't surprise me. Conquering countries often take on part of the culture of those they defeat and it certainly was the case in the America of his generation, which had adopted the little Buddhist Zen sect as a role model for the new American spirituality after World War II's upheaval of the New World's social atmosphere.

Going on the reciprocal system I had learned so well in Papua New Guinea, I owed him a favour. It sounded as though he was in need of a break from his present environment, which had brought forth the disturbances in his present existence. He sounded a very tense person. So I wrote back, telling him what I had done in the preceding ten years and added that, if he needed a holiday, I had an extra room and Darwin was a nice place for taking a break.

I had forgotten this once-in-a-decade correspondence, when a telegram came to say he was coming to Darwin. I quickly ticked off in my mind how many places of interest I could show him, and nearly didn't make it to the plane, because I gave a lift to a hitchhiker who lived further out of town than I had anticipated. But as I ran into the arrival hall, the first passengers were just coming through the door and so we met, ten years older, in a crowd of escapees in which he, I guess, was one.

Burr stayed for several days and I did drive him around to the tourist spots and some nice little eating places. We nearly made it to the Sunday evening folk concert in the bunker on the rocks, but a tropical rainstorm made the Moke almost take wing and we had to turn back. That suited him well as he mainly wanted to talk. If it was a midlife crisis, a looking back and asking "Where did it all go wrong?", it came out in a well-thought-out manner. He had taken his time to make his decisions and questioned his own motivations and actions. But there were a few surprises. The Zen monastery was after all not very high on his agenda. The lady who had spurred him on to take his life in hand was not his lover, as I had assumed. And thirdly, his latest idea was that he would like to live with me. But not in Darwin.

I realised I hardly knew him and I wasn't going to sacrifice my lifestyle, so painfully achieved, nor my philosophy of life and value system, for another

237

experiment in a department where I had hardly been successful. At the same time I recognised that he was not the only one who stood at an intersection trying to look in four different directions all at once. I'd just had an offer from Aunt Truus to come and live in Amsterdam and share her antique stall in the big, covered antique market. This was attractive, although I only wanted to do it for a year, or two summers at the most. I'd also contemplated taking the money I couldn't spend in Darwin — I still didn't have the OK to apply for a loan to buy land — and going to West Africa to find a job in a school or teaching institution. But in some ways I wanted to teach one more year at Darwin High to see if things improved; if they didn't I could aways get out then.

And now this. Then I remembered something. My life in Darwin revolved around teaching and making efforts to do my bit to improve this world. Some of those efforts went into gathering people of like mind to establish a branch of Amnesty International in Darwin. It was just beginning to take some shape. I was also working on a paper to be delivered at a conference in Fiji, in which I was trying to clarify the connections between language and culture to an international audience. I was on the brink of discoveries I needed to spend time on. Then there was my writing, which had become increasingly important to me because I felt this was the way to reach a world which would not listen to people like me, who have trouble finding their words when it matters most. In trying to do these things on top of the teaching load, I felt I was just scratching the surface and the world would not be a grain the better for my efforts, unless I could put more energy and time into it. I had neither. I was still very thin, very tired and not interested in food, unless I didn't have to prepare it.

One evening, feeling despair creeping up when my life seemed so ineffective, I spoke to my deity and said that if I was supposed to continue this path of putting myself out for good causes, I would need some help, because I couldn't handle it all alone.

Admitting that I was not coming up to my own expectations made me feel better and I had already forgotten that little summons to other realms. Yet weeks later, here sat a person who said he could help, that there was no reason to give up the things that concerned me, that I could write and get involved in things and that he might join me in some of those efforts. It seemed incredible that someone else wanted to live as I lived, but I knew he meant it. I wasn't sure though whether he realised what it entailed. But I contacted my deity and said: "If this is your answer, I will give it a go."

I told him I was prepared to give living together a try. "But you are the last one," I added. No more experiments if this one failed. He agreed.

The last month at school suddenly became easier with the knowledge that I was going away. I almost regretted it, but I had made the deal and had to go through with it. But not before one more temptation came my way. I was asked to consider a new position as ethnic arts officer, which would have entailed dealing with all the ethnic communities in and out of Darwin, covering all the arts and crafts. I nearly flipped at the idea. But Burr had said he couldn't stand the humid weather in Darwin, so I had to decline. I probably would not have been up to it physically, just as I wasn't up to a full-time teaching career.

So the Moke went back on the Ghan to Adelaide and I flew back to unpack my stored goods. There were a few weeks before Christmas to get used to each other and then we took a plane to Fiji. It was December 1979.

There's no better way to get to know each other than to travel through foreign parts. The cyclone season was not at all to Burr's liking and it was clear we would never settle down in the tropics. But he immensely enjoyed the life of the streets and the singing and music making, the people and the bits of indigenous culture they showed us. Fiji has two beautiful races, the native Fijians and the Indians, whose ancestors were brought there by the British to work as coolies. It is easy to understand as an outsider that both groups regard Fiji as their country of birth, but it is harder to understand why they can't come to a cultural understanding, seeing that the country is doing so well. It is the cultural centre of the Pacific, as well as the intellectual centre with the University of the South Pacific in Suva. It also receives most of the tourists who come this way and both races profit from all these aspects of their society. But as is so often the case when there are only two main groups, one accuses the other of encroaching unlawfully on areas of life each sees as necessary to their own survival. It begs the question of course as to why two groups can't become one group, without losing the valuable cultural assets each has to offer to the whole.

One night I wanted to see an Indian movie. Being used to seeing movies in foreign languages, without subtitles, I assured Burr it would not be a waste of money. We went to the big double cinema and Burr queued up for tickets. Some Indian ladies, waiting for husbands doing the same, conferred and one came up to me and said we were in the wrong queue. I told them we wanted to see *Meera Raksha*, cracked up to be the epic movie of the year. They asked did we understand Hindi? I said we didn't, but still wanted to see *Meera Raksha*. At this they organised that they should sit around us to translate, and so they did during the three-hour epic. It was the most enjoyable evening we had in Indian Fiji.

The loveliest evening in Fijian Fiji was New Year's Eve, which we spent in our small motel near the beach. A marvellous old man with a guitar had come to entertain, we don't know whom: the guests, the owners of the place, themselves, their friends? Anyway, there he was in the courtyard, a replica of Louis Armstrong with a raucous sense of humour to match. A young fellow accompanied him on a bass, made out of a tea-chest and a broomstick. We hummed and tapped feet and clapped until the year had changed.

My paper was well received at the conference and I had the satisfaction of having people from at least four regions of the world, including a poet from the Pacific itself, fully understand what I was trying to grapple with.

We returned, doing an island hop to the Solomons and thence to Papua New Guinea, touching down in New Britain, then the mainland coast, Mount Hagen, and finally Port Moresby.

I felt it was good for Burr to see the country where many of my ideas originated. Mount Hagen, after nine years, was a bit of a shock. There was a squash court, a hamburger stand and coca-cola shops everywhere. All the people wore clothes. Whereas a decade ago one would have pointed out a person wearing western dress, however much adapted to the region, now I discreetly pointed out a man in "arsegrass". "That's how everyone used to get about," I told Burr. Knowing the expense of buying clothes and the extra work for women washing them, I regretted the change. The only good point I could find was that the Mount Hagen women had learnt to handle sewing machines, and they sat in the market place running up skirts and blouses. At least they'd kept part of the trade in their own hands. The cloth of course had to be imported.

Papua New Guinea appeared to be doing well. The people in the cities certainly were looking more prosperous, although it was hard to tell whether that applied to the villages as well. The few we saw looked no different from ten years before. I thought of all the expatriate remarks about the country being incapable of running itself and of the increasingly severe problems Australia was facing at home, with economic decline, unemployment, soil degradation, deforestation and crises in education, family life and juvenile delinquency to boot. Papua New Guinea had its share of these, but they were more the result of western interference in the first place, than of the departure of western administrators. It was hard for expatriates to accept that Papua New Guinea would eventually not function according to the Australian model, but find its own, Melanesian way of doing things. If Papua New Guineans have a different sense of time to Australians, then Australians ought to realise that they themselves have a different sense of time to Europeans. I vividly remember waiting in offices for officials who would say "Just a minute . . ." or "Wongbesek . . ." ("I won't be a second"), and turn up half an hour later, often without the required reply or item. All peoples in the world have their own sense of rhythm and therefore their own sense of time and no one is better than another, they just suit the places where they developed.

After our Pacific island hop, we decided to settle in the Adelaide Hills, which we both loved. In April we saw a block of land which still had native vegetation and in September we moved there to live in a tin shed, while building our own house. Meanwhile I had found a part-time job teaching English to refugees and new migrants and here at last I was in my element.

My students were of all ages, but they were adults and they were motivated. Although the first ten weeks of English language learning were more or less compulsory, after that it was very much up to the migrants themselves to attend classes, which were free. Our salaries were paid by the government. At some stage during my two-and-a-half years with the Adult Migrant Education Service, I also taught a day course at a factory where many migrants worked, but mostly classes took place in the city and, as far as mine were concerned, in the evening.

To teach people who really want to learn and to know, from one's own experience, what their difficulties with the language are, made it a tremendous challenge to come up night after night with a lesson component that they could carry into the next day, finding it did work! The lessons were couched in a bed of social information, to enable them to recognise situations they would find themselves in.

Although I was teaching intermediate classes, the students' ability still varied greatly. On top of that the students each brought their cultural baggage to the learning. At one stage I was teaching people of seventeen different ethnic groups in one room. They came from the following countries: Vietnam, Poland, Kampuchea, Germany, Laos, France, Bangladesh, Denmark, Uzbekhistan, Sweden, Bulgaria, Switzerland, Greece, Italy, Hungary and Yugoslavia. One girl was a Tartar and I also had a Korean, a Japanese and a Chinese-Russian student.

I spent a good deal of time telling stories. Not stories from books, though at times that also came into it, but stories from my own life as a migrant. This certainly elicited responses, but in order for them to express their own needs, ideas, and lives in the new language, something else was needed.

I came to the conclusion that food was the first culture item that they looked for in the new country, sometimes finding specific ones, sometimes carrying it as a nostalgic memory. Secondly, many began to discover the structures and points of logic in their own languages as compared with English. Therefore it was possible to make them put pen to paper to write about these topics close to their hearts. For many that was the first piece of writing they had done in English.

After that I gained courage and would write on the board some five different dates at which people in various parts of the world celebrated their new year, together with their calendar systems. There was always someone in the class who had grown up with the Chinese moon calendar and from such a departure point we would get an exchange of New Year celebrations from Sweden to Laos, from Russia to Italy. This was followed by spring celebrations, Maypole dance festivals, Macedonian wedding feasts, Chinese name-givings and Vietnamese courting customs. In order to jog their memories, the students often prepared for the writing of these essays by sitting in pairs and telling each other about their country's festivities. To see a Swede explain Midsummer feast to a Vietnamese and to watch a Chinese demonstrate to a Swiss how a dragon dance is performed, makes one realise that the exchange of cultures must be the basis of all further contact between peoples of different ethnic backgrounds. Economic exchanges only go so far and often run into trouble. Tourism without cultural understanding does more harm than good. And political exchanges without cultural understanding . . . well, the less said the better!

The teachers agreed amongst themselves that the best thing the students were learning in our classes was to be tolerant of each other's different ways and views and to come to understand and like some of the customs that have come to Australia with the influx of refugees and migrants. If we taught them some English as well, all the better.

I treasure a little cyclostyle-printed booklet that I was able to put together from the work of several classes. It contained delectable recipes for Korean pickled cabbage and Vietnamese spring rolls and stories of schooldays in other lands, memories of festivities or what grand-mothers had taught, linguistic arguments and treasured memories of homes which were now lost.

These years were the most fruitful of my multi-coloured career. I gave up when the night teaching became too much for me physically. Despite another operation for a cancerous condition, I had become somewhat healthier than I had been for a long time, but as I wasn't getting any younger, I just could not shake off my fatigue. A rest was in order.

I meant to return to teaching after the New Year's break, but it never happened. I am a great lover of space in life, space for things to happen. I had thrown myself wholeheartedly into the growing of vegetables and fruit for our own consumption and this work, though hard, was proving beneficial to my health. On top of that, we had started a branch of "Men of the Trees", an organisation which plants trees to combat soil erosion and climate degradation. For a year-and-a-half the office was in our tin shed and often the phone went all day, every day.

We started to travel around in a small van to country areas to talk to farmers about the need for trees on their land, and the building of the house was put off until the organisation was a growing concern. Thanks to some very talented people which the movement attracted, we could retire from office duties after a few years, but by that time I had tasted the delights of "being retired" and discovered there were a thousand things waiting to be investigated that I had never had time for. By that time we also had behind us the disastrous bushfires of 1983, in which we had seen much destruction and thus changed our ideas about living tucked away in the bush. Hence, we had a lot more work to do on the block to change our dwelling place into something safer than we'd had in mind when we started.

Living in a dominantly white society has taken away, for the time being, the acuteness of opposing racial prejudice on a daily basis, as one did in Darwin, for instance. My main culture conflicts over the last few years have come from living with an American-born Australian. For a long time I had been far from complimentary about Americans and American ideas of what was good for the world. It so happened that this American had fled from the same things I criticised, but that didn't mean we understood each other perfectly! However, having a philosophy (borrowed from Asia), in common, and enjoying the same sort of things in life, made the experiment work.

Visiting America explained a few things about Americans. In preparation for our trip, I asked Burr a lot of impromptu questions about life in the US. He would try to describe and I would conclude by saying: "Just like on TV."

He got close to stamping his foot at times and shouting: "No! No! No! Americans are not like what you've seen on TV." But mild-mannered as he is, he would start again and explain that television stories are

246

vastly exaggerated blow-ups of basically friendly, easy-going people, who lead quiet lives of routine patterns. In the end I accepted his version.

Until we arrived at Kennedy airport! From the word go-go-go we found ourselves on a vast television stage, required to act as extras to the star performances of taxi drivers (ours looked like Bill Cosby and acted like all the Three Stooges at once while I had kittens in the backseat!), striking airline pilots, robot waitresses in period costume, shopkeepers looking like Al Capone and funny little smart arse whiz-kids who could talk for fifteen minutes non-stop about whatever money-making racket they were in without saying anything memorable! Gulp! So this was America.

"It is just like on TV," I said to Burr after a few days. He nodded silently. He had been away too long.

Either American film and television producers make exceedingly exact reproductions of real-life people and situations, or the American people have come to believe in the blow-ups on their screens and learned to behave accordingly! I would rather believe the latter . . .

The only purpose for our travels together has been to visit our elders, but since they happen to live in Holland and the USA, it means a world trip every time. To break the long flights, we usually stop for a week in a tropical place on the way home to Australia. Thus we became acquainted with the troubles in the island paradise of Sri Lanka, where another two beautiful races of people, the Sinhalese and the Tamils, deny each other the light of day and existence in peace in the land they were all born in. When we came in 1983, they even fought over the tourists and their luggage, so that we spent days in hiding to avoid the clashes we caused in the streets.

Three days after we left, the streets of Colombo ran with blood and the state of emergency was declared.

In 1980 we had hastily left Holland when the Iran-Iraq war broke out. We wondered whether we would ever make the long journey again, at the risk of being intercepted by one violent conflict or another somewhere along the route. But in 1985 we tried again and for the first time travelled without wars breaking out on our heels, or cyclones demolishing habitats as when we were in Fiji.

Our stopover this time was Singapore and for the first time we country bumpkins fell in love with a city! Not, mind you, with the gaudy tourist strip where most tourists stay, but with the underlying infrastructure that keeps this city of two-and-a-half-million people, from three dominant and many minority races, running smoothly and efficiently and seems to have most of them satisfied with their lot.

Staying in Chinatown was like staying in a village. Soon the Indian hawker on the street corner knew us and we could find our way "home" in the dark. We have a Sikh and a Chinese friend in Singapore who are married to each other. She was disowned by her father for marrying a Sikh, but as a modern Singaporean she took her independence in her own hands and defied traditions which did not fit life in a multicultural nation.

Singapore recognises four Singaporean languages: Malay, Mandarin, English and Tamil. A lot of the Chinese in Singapore are not Mandarin speakers. They may speak Hokkien or Cantonese or any of the languages of Southern China where most of them come from. With the children learning Mandarin at school, as well as English and the other Singaporean languages, there are many grandparents living in Singapore now who do not understand their grandchildren, even though they all live in the same house. I asked several people of the middle generation, the parents of today, whether they will try to teach their children the old language, but invariably the answer was "No time!" By the end of the twentieth century the old Chinese languages will have disappeared from Singaporean life and, with the advent of Mandarin in China itself, where it is taught to one fifth of the world's population, a sound picture of the world of the mid-twenty-first century may well be one of just Mandarin and that brand of cultureless international English that is being learned so fervently in classrooms on all the continents and islands of the world.

I remember a touching incident when we visited the beautiful Singapore museum. One room is filled with scale models of Singaporean life since its beginnings. One model depicted coolie quarters of the nineteenth century. These men from South China were brought to Singapore to build the southernmost outpost of the British empire in Asia and lived in tiny huts, the walls completely taken up with bunks, a table in the middle. The model showed, I think, about a dozen or so men going about their after-work activities in that cramped space.

In front of the model stood a Chinese woman, not yet middle-aged, and a boy of perhaps seventeen. She talked with excited gestures to the boy, whom I assumed to be her son, and pointed out details in the coolie quarters.

I caught her excitement to such an extent that I walked up to the pair and asked the woman to please explain to us what she knew about the scene. She did not understand me, but the boy did. After a quick consultation he said: "My mother says my grandfather was like this," and he pointed at one of the tiny coolies in the model. Feeling we had interrupted a family reunion, we thanked them both and went our way.

I reflected how marvellous it was that within three generations changes had taken place that had made the boy a part-owner of a city to which his grandfather had been brought almost as a slave and through whose toil it had come into being. There are losses and there are gains in the short history of Singapore.

Chinatown, at last, will be preserved. To many who knew the city from olden days, this is the living heart of Singapore. Yet every time one visits, one finds that new, tall, concrete apartment buildings have encroached further on the tiny enclave of crooked streets and ancestral temples, where one can eat, sleep, get tailored and buy everything that is needed for a richly varied life. If one never left Chinatown, one wouldn't lack a thing, least of all company, conversation, music and festivities.

During our stay there we were approached by two students from the University of Singapore doing a survey on Chinatown; ought it to be preserved or what? The girls seemed to know Chinatown less well than we did after our week of streetwalking. They lived elsewhere in the metropolis. So we told them of the little temples, the flea market, the street of the image makers and so forth and asked them to put in our plea to stop all development work right there and then. They wrote it all down with characteristic thoroughness and we expressed the hope that they would spend some time seeing for themselves what was in danger of disappearing forever. Yet saving Chinatown has become an issue more through the outcries from non-Chinese, who come to soak up the atmosphere, than from the people of Chinese extraction themselves.

"Little India", not too far away, is experiencing a similar fate. Rows of open shopfronts, redolent with spices or the colour riots of saris make way for mammoth hotels and offices to serve the perceived needs of twenty-first century humankind.

Still, Singapore is a happy place to visit, a restoring place for a rest. I'd never thought I would rest and unwind in a city, but is the open friendliness of Singapore people, no matter what their racial background, that makes one forget fatigue and go out in the streets day after day to be part of the positive energy they collectively generate.

Meanwhile, visits to Holland revealed that another phase of multiculturalism had been reached there. By the 1980s, the children of the Turks, Moroccans and West Indians were mainly Dutch-born. They spoke Dutch without an accent and received a Dutch education. Their foreign fathers too had learnt enough of the language to get by and had been there long enough to make friends with Dutch people at work.

I heard about one such friendship. A man my own age, with whom I had played when we both were ten, told me of his Turkish workmate in the factory.

"He brings his wife to the annual factory dinner with her cowl on," he said disapprovingly. "You can hardly see her face. I said to him 'If you can look at my wife, then I want to be able to look at your wife. She should not wear the cowl to the factory dinner.' "

Maybe he was somewhat surprised that I didn't agree with him and we argued about the point for a while, until I said: "We minorities have the same sort of trouble in Australia."

"What minorities?" he said. "You are not a minority." Perhaps in his opinion minority peoples wore exotically different clothes to distinguish themselves on purpose from the mainstream.

"Yes," I replied, "I and a few million other people from about one hundred different countries are ethnic minorities in Australia and our customs and ways of living aren't always appreciated by those born in Australia and even used to be publicly criticised until recent years."

He looked at me in perplexity. Then he said: "Yes, but you are an ordinary, decent person!"

It was my turn to be perplexed. Yet, as the evening wore on, he made it clear to me that the Turkish guest-worker was one of his best workmates and by the end of the evening he said: "You've given me a few things to think about."

I hope to take him up on that during my next visit to my hometown. He made me think too . . . of how ordinary, decent people like him can ever shed their natural prejudices if their knowledge of other cultures cannot be deepened by the media, today's main educator of adult people.

Having my third wish bounce back as a perfectly possible fact of life, after I'd so blithely tossed it away in the foothills of the Himalayas, recently made me dare to make a fourth wish.

With the opening up of Tibet to travellers by its Chinese rulers, the wish began to form of one day setting foot in the country of my many contemplations and seeing Lhasa. In 1987 I travelled to Nepal to join some other aspiring travellers. But somehow the timing was wrong. Kathmandu was full of tourists recovering or coming down with viral infections and the tour organiser had just contracted hepatitis. I caught something myself that gave me such a raging fever that I wished to roll in the snow on those rarely visible mountain peaks that line the Kathmandu Valley to the north. For a person as tropically oriented as I am, that meant I was really sick. But making the most of my new walking boots, I pushed on, holding maps upside down, getting lost and living on canned drinks. When I heard that three travellers had just died in avalanches on the road to Lhasa, I felt I'd had enough signals and booked a plane back. It took two months to recover, but there is the Nepal diary I wrote and the unforgettable memory of seeing Mount Everest suddenly appear from the clouds in a splendour which is indescribable and climbing Swayam Budnath on Buddha's birthday — celebrated four days later than in Adelaide — with hundreds of pilgrims and the happy Tibetan children having a holiday at their local monastery. And the dog who didn't recognise half a bun when he saw it . . . never having been offered one before. The half-starved pup was gnawing on three chicken feathers with a devotion worthy of a nobler goal, when I, unable to eat because of the fever, put the half-eaten bun under its nose, expecting it to leap up with joy and gratitude. But he went on gnawing his feathers for another minute, until suddenly he must have had a whiff of bakery shop smell and connected it with the rock-like shape before him. The last I saw of him was his tail, low-down, disappearing behind a bush. The bun was gone also. I pictured him sleeping in the shade that afternoon with a new, never-known feeling in that high drawn-up stomach of his. I don't know what sort of conclusions one is supposed to draw from encounters like that. The pup and the bun somehow became symbolic for Nepal's situation. Kept afloat by tourism and aid, it is one of the poorest countries in the world. All the time I felt I

253

shouldn't be there, using resources that were too scarce to share. The tourism is not entirely welcome. My presence was offensive when I rested by a holy river and I was stoned, probably by little boys hiding in the bushes above me. But the tourist dollar gives its moment of satisfaction, although it doesn't do much for infant mortality and life expectancy.

Since I was there, an uprising took place in Lhasa, and Tibet was closed to tourists. I would gladly forfeit my fourth wish if the situation would improve for the Tibetan people. The gradual destruction of such a unique civilisation in the name of progress, without the rest of the world objecting, is a sad sign that it can happen to all of us. I'm sorry to say that so far Australia has also largely ignored that situation in favour of the sale of wheat, wool and steel. The only role Australia seems to play in Asia is that of a seller of commodities. Hopefully this will change when young Australians, speaking Asian languages, grow up and take over the reigns.

10
The future Australian face

To come to the end of an autobiography, even a partial once such as this, is a letdown. For the writer it is like coming too close to death too early.

The mood has changed entirely. What was begun in heady exhilaration, knowing the store of experiences I could choose from to support a view of life and the human condition as it had grown away from the soil of my birth, comes to an end in mostly sombre tones of grey, with just a few flecks of colour here or there. Rather a dull piece of tweed, so to speak. Suitable for everyday wear, but hardly the garb for celebrations.

If I were writing only of my own life, I would end in a minor key as I close off one life and start another. But a minor key representing reflection after many a major chord and with an intimation of a fuller sound yet to come. But, strangely enough, the more I live the quiet life away from the crowds, the less my own life seems to matter, whereas the lives of the individuals in the crowds worry me daily.

There has been little cause for complaint from this migrant. I've had quite a bit of luck and my sense of the "possible impossible" brought the world to me, even in the years I had to stay put, at the bottom of the world, in lovely, sedate old Adelaide.

But I am not an island. I live the lives of other people. On behalf of the old and the new tribes I have axes to grind. Having woven my tweed, I found I had nothing to wear to the celebrations of the Australian bicentenary in 1988. (And when I was called up on stage in March 1988 I wore an "ethnic" blouse over an op-shop skirt!) This event had been anticipated by some of the descendants of the original white settlers as a display of wealth, achievements and fireworks. The government built itself a new parliament house, the cost of which could have wiped off a goodly slice of our national debt. It has not refined the behaviour of parliamentarians.

To celebrate after two hundred years' exploitation of a continent, with a debt the size of Australia's, is a travesty many an early settler of any nationality would not understand. Despite its ample natural resources, starting off in this country has never been easy, an existence is only won by frugality and hard work. For so many the time of their reward has come. Instead they see their Australian-born children estranged and unemployed.

As I was preparing this last chapter to summarise my experiences from the aspects of race and identity as an Australian citizen in this part of the world, the news broke that a top ex-public servant, now a senator, had voiced an objection to the immigration of non-English-speaking peoples, because of the cost to the nation of their free English lessons!

This sort of attitude painfully ignores the fact that a nation's topmost resource is people. That the people of Australia are not united as a nation is very clear from the opinions they express through the media. We are a multifarious mob. But what better way to forge a national conscience than to have those who know the language teach it to those who don't? Language is the culture carrier. Language classes are the places where people recognise each other as people and find their common ground.

The senator's attitude also ignores the contributions made by peoples from non-Anglo-Saxon backgrounds, during more than forty years of post-war immigration, to the industry, agriculture, society and cultural breadth of Australia. The senator's shirt and pyjamas are, in all probability, the work of the hands of migrants who can't speak English, as indeed may be his car, the walls and roof of his house, most of the vegetables he eats, the washing machine that washes his socks and his undies, and the fridge that cools his drinks, bottled by non-Anglo-Saxon hands. One could go on.

Non-English-speaking migrants have been the "guest-workers" of Australia since the end of World War II, enabling most of those who did speak English as a native tongue to fill up the ranks of the white-collar workers, the public service, the retail and business world and also the world of art and theatre. As migrants slowly but gradually enter all these areas, new waves of refugees and migrants arrive to take their places in the factories of industry, the sweatshops of the clothing trade, on the construction sites and the fruit-picking circuit.

Many of these wage slaves are also the buyers of the goods they make or the consumers of their own industry. And any excess of their labours is exported to other countries, including the countries of their birth, adding to Australia's foreign exchange which supports our high standard of living.

The complexities of immigration as they affect the economy of a country are many. Some believe migrants cost money, others believe they generate it. I am not qualified to unravel the knot. But I remain offended by the senator's remark on behalf of such non-English-speaking immigrants as Dr Henry Polak and Dr Alexander Gallus and others I have known, who have made their considerable intellectual contributions to the Australian reality of the late 1980s. I feel hurt on behalf of the ethnic writers, who live largely unrecognised in this country, and whose accumulated experience, skills and talents I recorded for ten years. And finally — and why not? — I feel peeved on behalf of myself. I also had free English lessons and the senator has implied that I wasn't worth the outlay. Wouldn't that make you feel at home after thirty years?

Since then the Fitzgerald report on migration has pulled me up even sharper because on its recommendations I would not be able to enter Australia today. My only skill as a spouse was typing and that was rendered useless in the absence of knowledge of the English language. My only scoring point would have been my youthful age in 1958.

I don't suppose two prize-winning books were worth my importation, but I still think that the senator, with Dr Fitzgerald and his team and others who argue like them, dreadfully underestimate what space and opportunity can do with human potential. The world of Australian migrants is full of miracle stories, an oral history hardly yet recorded.

The instantly economically viable migrant that the senator and the Fitzgerald team want to import has other choices open to him or her. The great attractions of Australia are its uncrowdedness and relative lack of pollution. The latter can be undone speedily by the actions of the population we already have — it is only a matter of time. Our asset of space is as deceptive as that of the Sahara desert. Space for what? There's a lot of land out there but the topsoil is blowing away, crops are diminishing and, where some states are already perceiving environmental degradation and a drain on natural resources caused by increasing tourism, a responsible government should seriously engage in estimations of how we are going to feed even twenty million at the start of the twenty-first century, let alone keep up food exports.

Economically viable migrants in my book would be people who understand soil, reafforestation and sustainable agriculture. People who understand these complex issues speak in deeds and are well worth free English lessons!

Are there more diehards like the senator? Alas, too many. But less as time passes. It is a matter of holding your tongue until they die out, or laughing the last laugh before it is due, which is the same as being found wrong because of being right too early! The fact must go on record though that, more often than not, when such inbred opinions as the senator's are being expressed, some politicians and sections of the public and media rise in protest to redress the balance.

On the even more positive side there are many Australians who have found their life's work in promoting the multicultural society, who cannot conceive any more of a life without friends who were born overseas. The very concept of the multicultural society has proven to be an excellent job-creation scheme!

Multiculturalism enables people to shed harmful traditions which confine women, force children, and keep men in the bondage of a perceived image. At the same time it is an opportunity to find out which traditions and customs are worth perpetuating and to demonstrate them for our common enlightenment. No less important, Australia is becoming a depository of interesting cultural expressions which have lost ground to the point of extinction in their countries of origin, just as our free libraries hold books which have been burnt on the soil where they were written. Demographically speaking we are a living laboratory and we are building up the archives to support it.

In May 1987, there took place in Adelaide a Wesak celebration for Buddha's birth, enlightenment and death, in which five Asian and three western Buddhist groups took part. The host temple was that of the Vietnamese-Australians, who showed us all what hospitality for the sake of good relations really is. I was often moved to tears during the ceremonies and the festivities thereafter, when children and artists of all participating groups presented their acts and sang their songs. Australians who have admitted such events into their lives must suffer in silence over the periodic utterances of the diehards. It is to be hoped they won't build up another national guilt feeling, such as already exists over the treatment of Aborigines, because this will only retard our final coming together.

Guilt is like a wasting disease. I feel that guilt may have retarded the coming together with the Aborigines. I recall sitting in on a lecture given by a missionary priest, who described how he inflicted himself again and again on a Northern Territory tribe, to suffer any insult and accept every accusation they levelled at him, in order to pay his debt and the debts of his ancestors. He then belaboured his audience by laying his version of the debt at their feet, denying them sleep, daily food, their health or peace of mind (if they still had any by that stage), until they'd gone to be purified through vilification, as he was being purified. I'm sure he had a need to do what he was doing but it was negative in the extreme and defeated the purpose. I suspected that "his" tribe simply didn't like him very much if they insulted and accused him as much as he claimed, for Aborigines also have rules for treating long-term guests.

No one appears to have asked the Aboriginal leaders of today whether they see it as a possibility that they could have remained the only inhabitants of the Australian continent till the present day. As this seems rather an improbability, I wonder if they would have preferred another conqueror to invade the Great South Land, such as the French, the Portuguese, the Dutch or the Japanese, all of whom came to have a look. Or one of the other great nations who patronise minorities: the Russians, the Americans, the Chinese, or the people who became the white South Africans?

The Aborigines may have scored better in some aspects with any of those. More cultural integration from the French, more intermarriage from the Portuguese, more education from the Dutch, more cheap technology from the Japanese, approval of their communal lifestyle from the Russians and the Chinese, but, from the Americans, just more of what they got. But more than likely they'd be fighting to claim back their land now, just the same.

Lack of education has left many Aboriginal people with a lopsided worldview — which they share with older white Australians — in which comparisons with other indigenous peoples appears limited to American Indians, although, in essence, the Estonians and the Tibetans are struggling just as desperately and without legislation coming to their aid, to retain their culture and regain their land, with less success to date.

Long-term guests are what the white settlers are to the Aboriginal tribes who have lost their land in the process of white settlement. Undoubtedly the biggest question the 1988 bicentenary has thrown up is the question of what indeed the Aborigines had to celebrate. Despite efforts in recent years to redress the injustices of the past two hundred years, their status in society, their health, education, life expectancy and opportunities to fulfil their own ambitions on their own terms, are lower or less than that of any other minority group in Australia.

The virtual epidemic of Aboriginal suicides in gaols all over the country must have been going on for a long time, but since it has come out in the open and a Royal Commission has been appointed to investigate these deaths, the rate of Aboriginal suicide attempts seems to have increased dramatically.

Most of the victims appear to be young men, put in the lock-up for minor offences, such as drunkenness or resisting arrest in public disturbances. Many of them had not even been brought to trial and were not expected to get long sentences. Yet they hanged or tried to hang themselves, with their socks or strips of bedding, in most cases dying without leaving a trace of an explanation why.

Is this a national Aboriginal protest of the most gruesome kind? A string of self-destruction, organised in unseen Aboriginal ways, to draw attention to their deplorable status after two hundred years of white rule? or is it racial suicide, the seed of which was sown generations ago, when the grandfathers and great-grandfathers of these young men were shot as intruders on their own land, their women abused, their children disowned and trained in institutions to be housemaids and carriers for the white conquerors?

I was an island when I came to this country as a migrant. I was truly an atoll floating in a sea of attitudes and activities I could not understand. I was shielded by my linguistic shortcomings and cultural inability to fathom what was taking place. And yes, I was shy of the shy Aborigines and wanted no part of the historical struggle that was going on between them and the other "them". Just as I had wanted no part in the Dutch national guilt over colonising the Indies, which had brought to us poorer people of Holland no more than cheap pepper to put on our staple diet of potatoes.

But nearly thirty-one years of residence in Australia has given me a few insights, and free communication with other peoples in the Australasia-Pacific and Asian regions has formed my opinions. They are, by the nature of their arising, neither based on misplaced patriotism, nor on a magnified sense of historical guilt. For that, I never became enough of an Australian, remained too much an outsider, longed too much to be a citizen of the one world.

Yet I have to acknowledge the freedom I am given in Australia to voice my opinions and comment on events. This freedom is even more appreciated by migrants from oppressed countries, though often less used by them, because old fears are slow to die. And true enough, one pays a certain price for speaking one's mind. I had more friends when I was still unable to express the thoughts growing in my mind, or chose, for fear of offending, to hold my peace and remain dumb.

It seems to be natural for some people to love their nation and justify its needs, no matter how objectionable. They will have the same attitude to their children and will never understand how it is that little Johnny ended up in court for robbery with assault.

There are still politicians who feel like that about Australian society, some in very high places where they are sadly out of touch with what goes on at grassroots level. They travel around the world, telling other nations how noble our intentions are, how badly we are sometimes treated and how richly we deserve to be held in higher regard. Such approaches to international politics and diplomacy will only condemn us to the backbenches of the world parliament to come; for as a small nation, population-wise, we are of little importance in global affairs, unless we use what we have intelligently and with wisdom.

What do we have in Australia that other countries do not have?

We are a country-continent and enjoy an absence of land borders with neighbouring countries. This better enables us to live in peace with the people that surround us.

Australia is the only continent that has not known a major war on its soil. Australian soldiers have traditionally fought their wars overseas. The tragic near-extermination of the Aborigines was not a war as the victims were no match for the guns of the invaders, neither did they know in many cases that they were being overtaken. Although Australian soil is not free from spilled blood, it is the least abused continent in the sorry history of humankind. Therefore there still exists here an atmosphere in which people can visualise that a life of peace may be preferable to a constant standing up for perceived rights. I speak as a child of war whose perceived rights diminished as I grew.

Australia can become more than the last frontier, or the last refuge, where people flock from war-torn countries to grab some land, to make good before it all ends. Australia, the last outpost before the moon, can become the new frontier where peace is put into practice, where peace pays! A frontier pushing outwards into the world where its people came from, offering patterns of peace out of our experience.

It would take another book to outline the details of how this could be done, but there are people in Australia who have the wherewithal to put it all together.

Too often it has been argued that Australia has imported conflicts by admitting immigrants from warring nations or ethnic groups, who can't get used to being fellow-citizens with the old cause of their conflict reduced to historical animosity. But their destructive influence has been overrated. They are minorities within minorities and their children usually outgrow the xenophobic patterns of hostility the parents could not leave behind.

Anthropologists have traditionally studied ethnic groups for their peculiar differences from surrounding groups, so that a worldview of countless ethnic neighbourhoods arises, where intermarriage is bound by strictly controlled tribal rules. As most ethnic groups, no matter how small, have, over the centuries, had a tendency to reject offspring of liaisons not approved by the tribe or culture group, the very numbers of these so-called miscegenations will be forever lost in the vagaries of sanitised oral geneaologies. This forces the offspring of cross-cultural marriages and relationships to choose allegiance with the group that is most accommodating and to repress all tendencies and attributes affiliating him or her with the other culture, in order to belong. In order to make up for their genetic shortfall they may become holier-than-thou members of the accommodating tribe.

It is high time for people of all cultures to stand up and be counted for all the various strands of ancestry that went into their making, acknowledging each one they can trace, even though one may be the preferred culture for living in. After all, one only has one body and has to choose one place for it to live in.

At the same time anthropologists should do a global survey of interaction, not just intermarriage, along all the trade routes and borders of the world. They may come up with surprising results.

For instance, it has occurred to me that people who profess anti-semitism are suppressing, knowingly or unknowingly, a trickle of Jewish blood in their own veins that they don't wish to acknowledge for fear of persecution, or because they never liked Uncle Abe or hate bagels. It is natural to turn against one's progenitors while one is young and doesn't understand the consequences for the psyche. Once repressed, the need for strong allegiance is created and the holier-than-thou protection shield soon put in place.

You cannot persecute a tribe for two thousand years, chasing it all over the globe from continent to continent, without it leaving traces. It is my gut feeling that most of the world's population by now can claim Jewish ancestry, no matter how minimal. This probably is so for other persecuted races on the continents they inhabit, for I have seen African features in many white Americans and Aboriginal ones in white Australians.

Nationalism fosters racism and is not the same as national unity. What all people have in common is their capacity for suffering and if we wish it more on others than on ourselves we are guilty of racism.

If Australian leaders talk in terms of a loss of Australian lives then that is racism. It implies that Australian lives are more precious than non-Australian lives. If we are reminded that Australian lives were lost for a past cause and a present way of life, then that is racism too. It implies that the lives lost on the other side of the conflict do not have the same value and that others do not have the same rights to defend their way of life as we have. The proper way to assess the sacrifice would be to say: in that conflict so many Australians lost their lives, so many Turks lost their lives, relationships were cut for so many years and we do not know what our way of life and their way of life would be like had those Australians and Turks not died but lived to pass on their genes. Neither do we know what our way of life and their way of life would be like now had the survivors of that conflict, who passed on their genes, not been part of that conflict. When we start to assess losses that way we have a basis from which to negotiate, avoid racially prejudiced statements and avoid conflicts that span generations.

Although there is a popular assumption among western people that colonialism is all but dead — save a French or American presence on a few little islands here or there — and that imperialism died for lack of emperors, the reality worldwide is scarcely one that supports this view. On every continent there are small nations overrun or harassed by big neighbours brandishing one ideology or another, small ethnic groups ruled by hostile majorities of a different cultural persuasion. Land ownership certainly is a crucial aspect of all these situations, as is the case in Romania where the government proposes to raze eight thousand villages to the ground — mainly in Transylvania — affecting over three million people from ethnic minorities. Excesses like this cannot just be remedied by laws and missions to the United Nations. Or the president of Libya.

What is needed now is a new theory and understanding of race. The push everywhere for people to identify themselves as this or that has completely overshadowed the fact that but for a few small, extremely isolated groups tucked away in rapidly disappearing jungles, all people in the world are now of mixed blood!

This leads me to the greater reality about Australian society. We all know we have about one hundred and forty ethnic groups in the country. But these hundred and forty odd tributaries and the Anglo-Saxon mainstream are becoming one river. A sluggish, grey river sometimes, silted up by sandbanks of diehard traditions and past prejudices. But more and more I see a quickening stream, constantly being replenished, changing its riverbed around obstructions, eager to reach the wider ocean.

Or, in more pragmatic terms, Australia has citizens from practically every country in the world. If we then can't have peace with all nations, who can? The most important contribution each migrant can make to the future of Australia is a new and better understanding of his or her culture of origin. When Australian politicians start to make full use of the information their ethnic constituents have to offer, we may see fewer foot-in-mouth performances by our leaders overseas, and this goes for politicians of all ethnic backgrounds including the Anglo-Saxon.

In Papua New Guinea, where tribal conflicts sometimes lead to war, certain tribes have built up the reputation of peacemakers and may be approached by conflicting parties to prevent war or end a conflict. Australia, rather than getting into the so-called defence programs and the armament racket, could, better than any other nation, play a positively beneficial role as mediator in regional conflicts elsewhere, on the basis of some of its citizens being somehow related to both parties.

That the multicultural society in Australia largely works is attested to by the number of Americans who have come to live here. Having seen the American melting pot fail, they flee to the last continent where the experiment is still in the early stages, where it is still all possible, where time hasn't run out as yet.

The brain drain from areas such as South-East Asia,

the Eastern European bloc and, to a lesser extent, from Britain, the US and Latin America, has brought to Australia a human potential that should begin to manifest in the last decade of this century, as the descendants of immigrants from these regions start to make their mark on all sections of society. When they do, a national consciousness with a world orientation will have to be in place.

Many have come here with a will to have peace and have instilled this in their children. They are people who will not want to offer up their hard-won prosperity for ideological conflict, and will be even less willing to offer up their children to protect it. Nor, hopefully, will they be lulled or bullied into a false sense of security by allowing Australia to be led by one self-seeking ally after another. The brainpower that is coming to maturity in Australia ought to be able to come up with better solutions than all of these, to keep Australia a continent of peace and let it spread from here.

The most powerful nations in the world today are Japan, the USA, China and the USSR. Australia makes overtures to all, mainly in the name of trade. It is still being done in the way a teenager might stand up to an ungenerous parent: by beating one's own drum loudly while overlooking one's failings, by occasional impotent protest and by bribery. The Australian media, as the main information source about the outside world, and sour about the absence of real blood and gore on local soil, is a major culprit in maintaining these futile tantrums on the world stage.

It is a question of how much time Australia will have to grow up and become responsible for itself, asking no favours and abandoning the idea that the world owes it a living. If this can come about, then Australia can assume a role of great benefit in a world of the future, which will be groping to achieve peace without the loss of liberty for all. If that is to eventuate the turning point must be marked now.

The turning point cannot be marked by just a raising of our voice against prejudices. That is the very least we can do. Words cost too little, carry too light an impact in a world choking on words, in a world without a shared culture to give depth to their meanings. Deeds must be seen to be done. Deeds of justice to Australia's Aboriginal population in the first place, to its underprivileged sections of society secondly, to underdeveloped countries thirdly, but all three proceeding simultaneously.

The selling of resources that can be used for war and repression elsewhere does not sit well with words of friendship. Friendships bought with trade agreements can never be relied on. The raping of the land for raw materials for export to buy those friendships, which are made for purposes of war and repression, will eventually have a backlash on Australia, the likes of which only its non-English speaking immigrants have known.

If the turning point is not negotiated, the tide not reversed, we migrants of the world may as well tell our grandchildren to cast their eyes on the moon and beyond. Cultural understanding, not trade, is the basis for all good relations across borders.

To be critical of other ethnic groups merely because they behave differently from oneself, really implies a lack of pride in one's own uniqueness. For if one expects the entire world to act like oneself, one's own uniqueness dies. It is a matter of recognising each group's uniqueness and exploring common ground for negotiation or cooperation. Both must be based in an understanding of each other's cultures. Cultural Studies should be taught in primary schools as a matter of fact.

They should be taught in high schools as social anthropology and not kept for specialty courses in a few universities. Cultural advisers should be employed by appropriate government departments and public institutions.

Having no specific culture myself, but having cultural baggage from east and west, north and south, I do have the profile of a typical migrant. Always ready to criticise the home situation — I did the same in Holland — and think the fields greener on the other side, I carry an image of Utopia and will not give it up.

When pouring over books on Tibet, it has often occurred to me that its people must be the descendants of tribes from the surrounding regions, who were persecuted until they fled into those incredible mountains. Harbouring a racial memory of strife, they melded into a nation that has been largely peaceful and whose best minds turned the search for peace of mind into a science.

With Tibet in conflict, where will the centre of peace shift to? There are many people in Australia now who would like it to shift to Australia. But again, Australia, although an island, is not an island. There are also moves in other countries to turn the tide of events away from destruction and towards coexistence in diversity.

Always the pessimist, I can see a danger in these people movements merely becoming other political parties, getting caught up in duality, instead of attracting people from all walks of life with one collective aim. On the other hand, always the optimist, I can see the end of duality coming in sight.

By duality I plainly mean the "us" versus "them" syndrome, usually played out by adjoining groups, but also by immigrants who have only known two cultures, the one they were born into and the one they migrated to.

My saving grace was firstly migration itself, for it brought me a German neighbour in the migrant hostel. The Germans had always been "them". Now this neighbour and I became "us" versus the Australians as "them". From there I graduated to "us migrants". Naturalisation tempered my use of these words in these contexts, but it wasn't until I left Australia that "us" meant myself and other Australians, wherever they might have come from.

Papua New Guinea saved me from cultural duality. To have lived in such diverse cultures as the Dutch, Australian and Papua New Guinean, is a privilege and one I would wish for every human being (any three countries will suffice). All three were, in different ways, multicultural, as indeed so many countries are, no matter what the majority pretends: Holland with its many tribes and centuries of migratory waves from the east; Australia with its Aboriginal culture, its world language and a population representing all the world; and Papua New Guinea with its seven hundred tribes, its racial links with the Pacific and Irian Jaya and also its usage of the world language English as one of its unifying tools.

I was fortunate to travel and see countries where things went awry because of continual dominance of one race over another, as in the USA, or because of the conflict of two races, as in Sri Lanka, Fiji and other places.

I think of these things when we go eating out at Adelaide's International Food Plaza. It is tucked away in the central market complex — itself the tower of Babel — and on Friday nights you have to patrol around to grab a table. There the food of some ten cultures unites a dining public so rich in diversity that I pay more attention to the people than to the food on my plate. Here westerners fight with their chopsticks to pick up a reluctant pea or slippery mushroom, while Chinese diners tuck into roast beef with fork and knife, sipping a Riesling, while I drink jasmine tea. All the mixed marriage partners imaginable come to have their meals here and their offspring wear the faces of future Australia. They are, moreover, *in situ!*

I could have been a member of a lot of races that would have suited me better than being a so-called European. My face in the mirror is still the wrong face. However, it is partly on account of that face that I have had my particular experiences. And although I did not produce a child with a multicultural face, there is always a hope I may be one myself in another life.

The last decade has been for me one of reworking past experiences into stories and books which one day, I hope, will help others to formulate their visions of an Australian nation in tune with the ancient Australian land. It has also been a time for making space in which things can happen. The ideal life that so many people crave, of no upheavals and endlessly pleasant routines has neither been my goal nor my lot. As long as the wheel of life keeps turning, there are times of going up and times of coming down and I hope to do a few more revolutions before I get off!

For Australia, my adopted homeland, I wish what I have found here myself. I have lived my life here largely in poverty. My houses were rented, my furniture second-hand. My clothes, too, were second-hand and so are my books. "Second-hand" was a term understood by my children as pertaining to things other people no longer wanted. So when the local bakery started to sell Friday's buns for half price on Saturday mornings, they asked me if I would bring back some "second-hand buns'' on top of the brand new weekly groceries! So we even ate second-hand buns for a few years, as part of our second-hand luxury style of living!

These comforts, combined with a climate milder than European winters, enabled me to be poor with dignity. Thus, relieved from material worries, I used the space and the quietude of non-material Australia to free my mind from much of its European conditioning and filled it with some of the best that the great cultures of the world have brought forth. That to me has been a first-hand experience for which I owe gratitude and to reciprocate where the opportunity arises will be the aim of my latter years.